AMONG FRIENDS

Volume II

A New Collection of 500 International Recipes

BY
Verneil Martin

FRONT COVER
Baked Crown Roast of Pork, page 132

AMONG FRIENDS, VOLUME II
By Verneil Martin

First Printing - June 1989 (20,000 copies)
Second Printing - November 1989 (50,000 copies)

Copyright 1989 by
Among Friends Publishing Ltd.
P.O. Box 6127, Station "A"
Calgary, Alberta
Canada T2H 2L4

Canadian Cataloguing in Publication Data
Main entry under title:

Among friends, volume II

Includes index.
ISBN 0-949845-70-3 (v. 2)

1. Cookery International. I. Martin, Verneil
TX725.AlA53   1987   641.59   C87-098042-4rev

**We wish to thank and acknowledge Birks Jewellers
who so generously donated items
for our photography sessions.**

Photography by
Patricia Holdsworth
Holdsworth Photography
Regina, Saskatchewan

Illustrations by
John Paine
Beauchesne, Storla & Paine
Regina, Saskatchewan

Designed, Printed and Produced in Canada by
Centax Books, A Division of M•C•Graphics Inc.
Publishing Director, Photo and Food Stylist: Margo Embury
1048 Fleury Street
Regina, Saskatchewan, Canada S4N 4W8
(306) 359-3737 / 359-7580

INTRODUCTION

Among Friends, Volume I was Verneil Martin's project to help Rotarians raise funds for Rotary International's PolioPlus Campaign, which is explained on page 3 in Volume I.

This book was distributed by Rotarians and Rotary clubs internationally. It was an outstanding success. Through book sales, they raised over $1,000,000.00 for this excellent project, helping to immunize children against polio in the developing countries of the world. It was a triumph for Rotary International and for the world's children.

Among Friends, Volume II is a completely new set of extraordinary international, family, ethnic, contemporary and gourmet recipes. These thoroughly tested recipes are a collection of favorites from Rotarians and Rotary Anns and include many superb, recipes from the author's extensive collection. She has collected recipes, over the years from family, friends and many famous chefs.

Indulge your family and friends with these exceptional recipes and you will truly be "Among Friends".

DEDICATION

This book is proudly dedicated to
my late grandmother, Nana,
my dear mother Beulah and
my wonderful husband Doug.

It is also dedicated to all Rotary volunteers, past
and present, around the globe.

MY PRAYER FOR A FRIEND

I said a prayer for you today and know God must have heard.
I felt the answer in my heart, although he spoke no word.
I didn't ask for wealth or fame, I knew you wouldn't mind.
I asked him to send treasures of a far more lasting kind.

I asked that he be near you at the start of each new day
To grant you health and blessings and friends to share your way.
I asked for happiness for you in all things great and small
But it was for His loving care for you my friend
I prayed the most of all.

ACKNOWLEDGEMENTS

To Margo Embury, Publishing Director, food stylist and artist, and to Patricia Holdsworth, Holdsworth Photography, I wish to give special thanks for their combined artistry, expertise and incomparable assistance.

We are truly grateful and wish to thank Jeannie Horsman and Iona Glabus for their hours of assistance in the kitchen during the photography sessions for Among Friends, Volume II.

A special acknowledgement to artist, John Paine who created the illustrations on the heading pages throughout the book.

My sincere thank you and gratitude to all Rotarians and Rotary Anns, friends, family and the professional chefs who so generously contributed the wonderful recipes for this book.

GLUTEN-FREE INFORMATION

The many gluten-free recipes featured in this book are specially listed in the index on page 247.

For information on gluten-free recipes and Celiac disease, contact:

The Canadian Celiac Association
1087 Meyerside Drive, Suite 5
Mississauga, Ontario
Canada   L5T 1M5

For a comprehensive and continually updated list of gluten-free commercial products, contact:

Dietetic Services
Ontario Hospital Association
150 Ferrand Drive
Don Mills, Ontario
Canada M3C 1H6

For information on gluten-free Ener-G products, contact:

Mr. George Waite
c/o Allergy Shop
#10 - 630 - 1 Avenue N.E.
Calgary, Alberta
Canada T2E 0B6

TABLE OF CONTENTS

Recipes have been tested in U.S. Standard measurements. Common metric measurements are given as a convenience for those who are more familiar with metric. Recipes have not been tested in metric.

MEASUREMENT ADAPTATIONS

Food measurements in this cookbook are given in both U.S. standard and metric. Recipes have been tested in standard and the rounded metric equivalents are given as a convenience for those who are more familiar with metric. Most North American cooks tend to measure food, other than meats, cheeses, etc. by volume. Cooks in other parts of the world tend to measure dry ingredients, fats, etc. by weight. The following adaptations should be helpful in converting measurements.

Equipment

				exact	rounded
1 tsp.			=	(5 mL)	5 mL
3 tsp.	=	1 tbsp.	=	(15 mL)	15 mL
4 tbsp.	=	¼ cup	=	(59.12 mL)	50-60 mL
5⅓ tbsp.	=	⅓ cup	=	(75.6 mL)	75 mL
8 tbsp.	=	½ cup	=	(118.25 mL)	125 mL
16 tbsp.	=	1 cup	=	(236 mL)	250 mL
1 fl. oz.	=	2 tbsp.	=	(29.56 mL)	30 mL
4 fl. oz.	=	½ cup (1 gill)	=	(118.25 mL)	125 mL
8 fl. oz.	=	1 cup	=	(236 mL)	250 mL
16 fl. oz.	=	2 cups (1 pint)	=	(473 mL)	500 mL
32 fl. oz.	=	4 cups (1 quart)	=	(946 mL)	1000 mL (1 L)

Weight Measure

				exact	rounded
1 oz.			=	(28.3 g)	30 g
4 oz.	=	¼ lb.	=	(113.4 g)	125 g
8 oz.	=	½ lb.	=	(226.8 g)	250 g
16 oz.	=	1 lb.	=	(453 g)	500 g
32 oz.	=	2 lbs.	=	(917.2 g)	1000 g (1 kg)

Food Equivalents

biscuit/cookie crumbs	1 cup	=	236 mL	=	4 oz.	=	114 g
bread/cracker crumbs, dry pkg.	1 cup	=	236 mL	=	5 oz.	=	144 g
bread crumbs, fresh	1 cup	=	236 mL	=	2 oz.	=	60 g
butter/margarine/lard	1 cup (2 sticks)	=	236 mL	=	½ lb.	=	227 g
cheese, grated Cheddar	1 cup	=	236 mL	=	1/4 lb.	=	114 g
eggs	1 cup	=	236 mL	=	4-5 whole large or extra large or 8 egg whites or 12 egg yolks		
flour, all-purpose	1 cup	=	236 mL	=	4 oz. (¼ lb.)	=	114 g
	4 cups	=	946 mL	=	1 lb.	=	453 g
flour, whole-wheat	3¾-4 cups	=	890-946 mL	=	1 lb.	=	453 g
fruit, dried mixed or raisins	1 cup	=	236 mL	=	6 oz	=	170 g
gelatin, 1 envelope (unflavored)	1 tbsp.	=	15 mL	=	¼ oz.	=	7 g
honey, golden syrup, treacle	1 cup	=	236 mL	=	12 oz.	=	340 g
lemon, 1 medium (juice)	3 tbsp.	=	45 mL	=	1½ fl. oz.		
nuts, chopped	1 cup	=	236 mL	=	4 oz.	=	114 g
rice, uncooked	1 cup	=	236 mL	=	8 oz. (½ lb.)	=	227 g
sugar, brown, firmly packed	2¼ cups	=	532 mL	=	1 lb.	=	920 g
sugar, granulated (castor)	1 cup	=	236 mL	=	8 oz.	=	227 g
sugar, icing (confectioner's)	3½-4 cups	=	828-946 mL	=	1 lb.	=	920 g

HIGH-ALTITUDE BAKING

Too much sugar and low humidity are the two major problems in high-altitude baking, over 3,000 feet (900 metres).

Butter Cakes or Quick Breads — use ½ the amount of sugar as flour (in chocolate cakes cocoa counts as flour), e.g. 1 cup (250 mL) sugar to 2 cups (500 mL) of flour.

Sponge/Angel Cakes — use 1½ cups (375 mL) sugar to 1½ cups (375 mL) of egg whites.

Other Tips — underbeat eggs, as compared to sea level, or keep them refrigerated until use.
— over 5000 feet (1500 m), decrease baking powder or baking soda by ⅛-¼ tsp. (0.5-1 mL) for each teaspoon (5 mL) called for in recipe.
— over 5000 feet (1500 metres), raise baking temperature by 25°F (10°C).

Low Humidity — store flour in moisture-vapor-proof containers. Seasonal variations also increase this problem.
— bread recipes may vary from 6 cups (1.5 L) of flour at sea level to 4½-5 cups (1.125-1.25 L), over 3000 feet (900 metres) in low-humidity areas.
— cakes, quick breads and pastries: try reducing flour 1-3 tbsp. (15-45 mL) from recipe amount.
— alternatively, liquid may be increased 2-4 tbsp. (30-60 mL) for each cup (250 mL) of liquid in the recipe as altitude varies from 3000-10,000 feet (900-3,000 metres).

Thickening Agents — gluten-free recipes may be adapted from flour-based recipes by substituting: 1 tbsp. (15 mL) cornstarch = 2 tbsp. (30 mL) all-purpose flour; 1 tbsp. (15 mL) waxy corn flour = 1 tbsp. (15 mL) all-purpose flour; 1 tbsp. (15 mL) waxy rice flour = 1 tbsp. (15 mL) all-purpose flour.

Brunch, Lunch & Breads

BRUNCH & LUNCH

FRESH FRUIT SALAD AND DIP

A sumptuous dip for fresh fruit.

watermelon
strawberries
cantaloupe
honeydew
pineapple
apples
oranges
bananas
grapes

1 cup	whipping cream, whipped	250 mL
4 oz.	cream cheese, softened	115 g
1 tbsp.	lemon juice OR orange juice	15 mL
⅓-½ cup	sugar	75-125 mL
½ tsp.	vanilla	2 mL
	Grand Marnier (optional)	

Use your favorites or any fruit in season. ● Hollow out ½ of the watermelon (cut lengthwise). Fill this natural salad bowl with the rest of your favorite fruit cut into bite-sized pieces. ● Whip cream, add cheese and whip together until smooth. Add lemon juice, sugar, vanilla and Grand Marnier, if used.

Putting on weight is the penalty for exceeding the feed limit!

FRUIT DIP

3½ oz.	pkg. instant vanilla pudding mix	100 g
1¾ cups	milk	425 mL
6 tbsp.	Grand Marnier (or other fruit liqueur)	90 mL
½ cup	whipping cream, whipped	125 mL
1 tsp.	shredded orange peel	5 mL

Mix pudding and milk together thoroughly and refrigerate for 3 hours. Fold in the Grand Marnier, whipped cream and orange peel. ● Use as a dip for a fresh fruit tray. This also works well as a filling for cakes.

FRUIT COMBO

9	peaches,* peeled and sliced	9
9	pears,* peeled and sliced	9
1 cup	blueberries	250 mL
	lemon juice	
⅔ cup	orange juice	150 mL
2 tbsp.	lemon juice	30 mL
⅓ cup	white sugar	75 mL
⅛ tsp.	salt	0.5 mL
2 tsp.	grated orange rind	10 mL
1 tsp.	grated lemon rind	5 mL

Combine peaches, pears and blueberries in a large bowl, sprinkle with a little lemon juice and set aside. ● In a pan, combine orange juice, lemon juice, sugar, salt, grated orange and lemon rinds. Boil for 2 minutes, simmer for 5 minutes. Cool and pour over fruit. ● Serves 15 for a brunch. ● This recipe may be halved. ● * Canned fruit may be used, if fresh is not available. Use 3 x 14 oz. (398 mL) cans, each, of peaches and pears.

Recipe for a Happy Day

1 cup of friendly words
2 heaping cups of understanding
4 heaping tsp. of time and patience
pinch of warm personality
dash of humor

Method

Measure words carefully. Add heaping cups of understanding; use generous amounts of time and patience. Cook on the front burner but keep temperature low, and do not boil. Add generous dash of humor and a pinch of warm personality. Season to taste with spice of life. Serve in individual molds.

GÂTEAU DE CRÊPES SAINT IVOR

1½ cups	milk	375 mL
1½ cups	water	375 mL
8	eggs	8
1 tsp.	salt	5 mL
2½ cups	flour	625 mL
½ cup	melted butter	125 mL

Place milk, water, eggs and salt in blender. Add flour, then the butter. Cover and blend at top speed for about 1 minute. Refrigerate mixture, covered, for at least 2 hours. • The batter should be a very light cream, just thick enough to coat a wooden spoon. • Make at least 18 crêpes, 6½" (17 cm) in diameter. Set aside.

MORNAY SAUCE

3 tbsp.	butter	45 mL
3 tbsp.	flour	45 mL
2 cups	boiling milk	500 mL
½ tsp.	salt	2 mL
	freshly ground pepper	
1 tbsp.	dry vermouth	15 mL
pinch	nutmeg	pinch
¼ cup	cream	50 mL
¼ lb.	natural Swiss cheese, grated	115 g

Melt butter in saucepan, add flour and stir. Cook slowly for about 2 minutes without changing color. • Remove from heat, stir in boiling milk and add seasonings. Simmer and stir with wire whisk for another minute. Add cream gradually. The sauce should now be smooth and fairly thick. • Remove from heat and add all but 2 tbsp. (30 mL) of the cheese.

SPINACH FILLING

1¼ tbsp.	butter	20 mL
1 tbsp	minced shallots	15 mL
12 oz.	pkg. frozen spinach, cooked, drained	340 g
pinch	salt	pinch
⅓ cup	Mornay Sauce	75 mL
2 tbsp.	sour cream	30 mL

In a skillet, melt butter and sauté shallots. Add spinach and salt and stir over medium heat for a few minutes in order to evaporate moisture. Add to this about ⅓ cup (75 mL) of the Mornay Sauce. • Cover and simmer gently for another 5 minutes. Set aside and let cool. • When cool, stir in sour cream.

A frown is a wrinkle hunting for a place to roost.

½ lb.	bulk (dry curd) cottage cheese	250 g	*CHEESE AND MUSHROOM FILLING*
	salt and pepper		
	Mornay Sauce		
1	egg	1	
1 cup	chopped mushrooms	250 mL	
1 tbsp.	minced shallots	15 mL	
2 tbsp.	butter	30 mL	
1 tbsp.	oil	15 mL	

Mash the cheese in a bowl with salt and pepper. Add about ⅓ of the Mornay Sauce and the egg. ● Sauté mushrooms and shallots in butter and oil for 3 minutes in a skillet. Add them to the cheese mixture. ● Set aside.

3	tomatoes, peeled and diced	3	*TOMATO AND CAPER FILLING*
2 tbsp.	butter	30 mL	
1 tbsp.	red vermouth	15 mL	
	salt and freshly ground pepper		
½ tsp.	basil	2 mL	
½ tsp.	oregano	2 mL	
2 tbsp.	capers	30 mL	

Sauté the tomatoes in butter until fairly soft; add vermouth, seasonings and capers, and simmer another minute.

TO ASSEMBLE GÂTEAU:

Preheat oven to 350°F (180°C). Butter a 9″ (23 cm) springform pan or round baking dish and center a crêpe on the bottom. Spread it with a layer of the spinach filling. Press a crêpe on top, and spread it with a layer of cheese and mushroom filling, and top with another crêpe, then spread with tomato filling. Continue the process of alternate crêpes and filling until you have used up the fillings and end up with a crêpe on top. ● Pour the Mornay Sauce over the top of the cake and around the sides. Sprinkle the top with 2 tbsp. (30 mL) of grated cheese. ● Bake for about 20 minutes until thoroughly hot and the top is brown. ● To serve, cut into wedges as you would a cake. ● Serve this "gourmet" main dish with garlic bread and a green leafy salad! Bon Appétit! ● This fabulous brunch dish takes time to prepare but it is inexpensive and supremely elegant. ● Serves 6.

Hint: A few drops of vinegar in the water when poaching eggs will keep the eggs from running all over the pan.

INDIVIDUAL CABBAGE PIES

Great for quick lunches.

1 cup	butter	250 mL
1 cup	flour	250 mL
2-4 tsp.	water or sour cream	10-20 mL
1	egg	1
1½ cups	chopped onion	375 mL
⅓ cup	butter	75 mL
½ tsp.	salt	2 mL
1	fresh cabbage, finely chopped	1
½ tsp.	pepper	2 mL
2	hard-boiled eggs, chopped	2
1	egg white, slightly beaten	1

Cut butter into flour. Add water and 1 egg. Mix until smooth. Put dough into refrigerator in wax paper for at least 1 hour. ● Meanwhile, fry onion in butter, add salt. ● Let cabbage simmer with onion for a few minutes until limp. Add pepper and salt to taste. ● Drain cabbage and add chopped eggs. ● Cut dough in 4″-6″ (10-15 cm) rounds. Put filling in center of rounds and pull dough over. Seal all edges. ● Brush pies with egg white. ● Bake on an ungreased baking sheet at 375°F (190°C) until nicely browned, about 30-40 minutes. ● Serve with tomato soup.

CREAMY ONION PIE

10″	unbaked pastry shell	25 cm
3	large mild onions, chopped	3
3 tbsp.	butter or margarine	45 mL
1 tsp.	salt	5 mL
3	eggs, beaten	3
¾ cup	sour cream	175 mL
1 tsp.	oregano	5 mL
¾ cup	mayonnaise or salad dressing	175 mL

Line a 10″ (25 cm) pie plate with pie pastry or biscuit dough. ● Cook onions in butter until soft but not brown. Add remaining ingredients. ● Pour onion mixture into pie plate, bake at 375°F (190°C) for 40 minutes or until filling is set. ● Serves 8.

Food-for-Thought: no cooking — no dishes!

ONION PASTA PIE

¾ cup	flour	175 mL
½ tsp.	salt	2 mL
¼ tsp.	dry mustard	1 mL
1 cup	grated Cheddar cheese	250 mL
¼ cup	melted butter OR margarine	50 mL
2 cups	thinly sliced onions	500 mL
2 tbsp.	butter OR margarine	30 mL
1 cup	cooked fine egg noodles	250 mL
1 cup	hot milk	250 mL
1 cup	grated cheese	250 mL
	grated cheese for garnish	

Mix first 5 ingredients and press into a 9″ x 9″ (2.5 L) pan or pie plate. • Sauté onions in butter. Mix with remaining ingredients and pour onto base. Sprinkle additional grated cheese on top. • Bake at 350°F (180°C) for 40 minutes or until set. • Serves 6.

QUICHE LORRAINE

9″	unbaked pie crust	23 cm
1 cup	chopped onions	250 mL
½ cup	green pepper, diced	125 mL
1 cup	sliced mushrooms	250 mL
3	eggs	3
1 cup	grated Swiss cheese	250 mL
1 cup	whipping cream	250 mL
	salt, garlic and pepper to taste	
9	slices of bacon, or more to taste, fried and crumbled*	9

Prepare pie crust. • Sauté onions, green pepper and mushrooms. • Beat eggs and add grated cheese. Then add cream (not whipped). Add spices. • Place half the onion, green pepper and mushroom mixture into the unbaked pie crust, add the egg and cheese mixture, then the rest of the vegetable mixture. Top with the crumbled bacon. • Bake at 375°F (190°C) for 25 to 30 minutes. • Serves 6.

Noise is not in the market place, nor quiet in the hills . . . but in the ever-changing hearts of men. (Daniele Vare)

BROCCOLI QUICHE

9"	unbaked pastry shell	23 cm
1 cup	cooked broccoli	250 mL
½ cup	sliced mushrooms	125 mL
2-3	green onions, chopped	2-3
6 oz.	Swiss or Gruyère cheese, sliced	170 g
2 cups	cream or rich milk	500 mL
4	eggs	4
½ tsp.	salt	2 mL
dash	EACH pepper, cayenne and nutmeg	dash

Line pie plate with pastry and make a firm double rim. • Arrange precooked vegetables in the pastry; cover with cheese slices. • Heat cream slowly. Make custard mixture by beating eggs with a whisk and adding hot cream and seasonings. Pour into pastry-lined plate. • Bake in a 450F (230°C) oven for 10 minutes; reduce heat immediately to 300F (150°C) and continue baking until custard is firm, about 30 minutes or until a knife inserted in the center comes out clean. • Serves 6.

NEVER-FAIL CHEDDAR CHEESE SOUFFLÉ

6 oz.	sharp Cheddar cheese	170 g
6 tbsp.	butter or margarine	90 mL
6 tbsp.	all-purpose flour	90 mL
1 tsp.	salt	5 mL
½ tsp.	paprika	2 mL
dash	cayenne	dash
1½ cups	milk	375 mL
6	large eggs, separated	6

Dice cheese finely and set aside. There should be about 1½ cups. • In top of double boiler melt butter, blend in flour and seasonings. Add milk all at once and cook, stirring constantly until mixture is smooth and thickened. While still over boiling water add cheese; stir until melted. • Remove cheese mixture from water. • Beat egg yolks until thick. Gradually stir into cheese mixture. • Beat egg whites in 2½-quart bowl until stiff but moist. Gradually pour cheese mixture into whites, folding in carefully. • Bake uncovered in an 8"-9" (20-23 cm) soufflé dish at 350°F (180°C) for 45 minutes. Serve at once. • Serves 4-6.

Hint: When hot cloths are needed to relieve pain, heat them in a steamer or microwave instead of wringing them out in hot water.

SPINACH OVEN OMELET

9	eggs	9
10 oz.	pkg. frozen chopped spinach, thawed and drained	283 g
2 tbsp.	finely chopped onion	30 mL
2 tbsp.	milk	30 mL
1 tsp.	salt	5 mL
½ tsp.	dried basil leaves	2 mL
¼ tsp.	garlic powder	1 mL
8	tomato slices	8
1 cup	shredded mozzarella cheese (about 4 oz. [115 g])	250 mL

Beat eggs until light and fluffy. Stir in spinach, onion, milk, salt, basil and garlic powder. Pour into greased 11″ x 7″ (2.5 L) baking dish. Arrange tomato slices on top; sprinkle with cheese. • Cook uncovered in 350°F (180°C) oven until set, 25-30 minutes. • Serves 8.

BACON BRUNCH BAKE

	butter	
12 slices	bread	12 slices
8 oz.	Monterey Jack cheese, grated	250 g
8 oz.	Cheddar cheese, grated	250 g
8	eggs	8
3 cups	milk	750 mL
½ tsp.	salt	2 mL
¼ tsp.	pepper	1 mL
1 tsp.	dry mustard	5 mL
6	slices bacon, cut in half	6

Butter bread, cube, mix with grated cheeses, spread in buttered 9″ x 13″ (4 L) pan. • Beat eggs, milk, salt, pepper and mustard. Pour over bread. Lay bacon strips on top. Cover. Refrigerate overnight. • Uncover, bake at 350°F (180°C) for 55-60 minutes. Serve immediately. • Serves 8-10. • Fruit salad and muffins go nicely with this. It also makes a nice luncheon or light supper served with tossed salad. I serve it Christmas morning, letting it bake while we open gifts. This recipe may be halved.

"Our prayers are answered not when we are given what we ask, but when we are challenged to be what we can be". (Morris Alder)

HEARTY FRITTATA CASSEROLE

Microwave Recipe

2 cups	frozen hashbrown potatoes	500 mL
½ cup	grated carrot	125 mL
¼ cup	finely chopped onion	50 mL
2 tbsp.	chopped fresh parsley	30 mL
2 tbsp.	butter	30 mL
	salt and pepper to taste	
8	eggs	8
½ cup	milk	25 mL
¼ tsp.	dry mustard	1 mL
dash	Tabasco	dash
1 cup	chopped cooked ham	250 mL
½ cup	shredded Cheddar cheese	125 mL

Mix together frozen hashbrowns, carrots, onion, parsley and butter in a 2-quart (2 L) casserole and microwave, covered, 5-7 minutes on HIGH, until hashbrowns are cooked, stirring once or twice. Season with salt and pepper if desired. • In a medium-sized bowl, combine eggs, milk and spices. Pour over the cooked potato mixture. • Sprinkle chopped ham evenly on top and cover dish. Microwave on HIGH for 3 minutes. • Draw cooked egg portion to center. Recover dish. Continue to cook on MEDIUM for 8-12 minutes or until set, rotating dish 2 or 3 times as necessary. • Sprinkle grated cheese on top, cover,and microwave on HIGH 30-60 seconds or until cheese is melted. • Let stand 5 minutes before serving.

TAKE TIME FOR "10 THINGS"

1. *Take time to work —*
   it is the price of success.
2. *Take time to think —*
   it is the source of power.
3. *Take time to play —*
   it is the secret of youth.
4. *Take time to read —*
   it is the foundation of knowledge
5. *Take time to worship —*
   it is the highway of reverence and washes
   the dust of the earth from our eyes.
6. *Take time to help and enjoy friends —*
   it is the course of happiness.
7. *Take time to love —*
   it is the one sacrament of life.
8. *Take time to dream —*
   it hitches the soul to the stars.
9. *Take time to laugh —*
   it is the singing that helps with life's loads.
10. *Take time to plan —*
    it is the secret of being able to have time
    to take time for the first nine things.

Coquilles St Jacques, page 49
Hot "Dressed" Spinach Salad, page 75

BREADS PLUS

OVEN SCONES

1 tbsp.	yeast (7 g pkg.)	15 mL
1 tbsp.	sugar	15 mL
½ cup	lukewarm water	125 mL
2 cups	scalded milk	500 mL
⅓ cup	butter	75 mL
1 tsp.	salt	5 mL
1 cup	sugar	250 mL
1	egg, beaten	1
6½ cups	flour	1.625 L
1 cup	raisins	250 mL
½ cup	peel	125 mL

This was my mother-in-law's Christmas tradition and now it is ours.

Dissolve yeast and 1 tbsp. (15 mL) sugar in water. • Scald milk and allow to cool. Add butter, salt and 1 cup (250 mL) sugar. Stir in egg. Add flour, raisins and peel. Knead. • Form into 12 round cakes, of equal size. Allow to rise 15 minutes. • Roll down to ¼" (1 cm) and cut cakes across, each way, ¾ through. Let rise 1 hour. • Bake at 375-400°F (190-200°C) for 15 minutes.

CORN MIX SCONES

½ cup	vegetable shortening	125 mL
2 cups	Ener-G corn mix	500 mL
3 tbsp.	sugar	45 mL
1 tsp.	grated lemon OR orange rind	5 mL
½ cup	raisins OR currants	125 mL
1	egg, beaten	1
⅔ cup	milk	150 mL
1 tbsp.	lemon juice	15 mL

Gluten-Free

In mixing bowl, cut shortening into corn mix with 2 knives. Add sugar, lemon rind and raisins. • In separate bowl, combine beaten egg, milk and lemon juice. Slowly stir egg mixture into corn mix until thoroughly mixed. • Turn out onto a corn mix coated board. Divide dough into 2 equal parts. Pat each into a circle ½" (1.3 cm) thick. With sharp knife, cut each circle into 6 triangles. Place on greased baking sheet. Brush tops with milk or slightly beaten egg whites; sprinkle with sugar. • Bake at 450°F (230°C) for 12-15 minutes. • Makes 12 scones.

SMALL BANNOCK

Chef Zimmerman
Westin Hotel, Calgary

3 cups	flour	750 mL
dash	salt	dash
6 tsp.	baking powder	30 mL
2 tbsp.	lard	30 mL
	water	

Combine dry ingredients in a bowl. Make a little well and pour in the water. Mix into a dough and knead it. • Flatten dough out and put in a frying pan. • Cook on hot ashes over an open fire or in the oven. Especially good fresh, eaten with lard. • **Variation:** Can also be made with boiled potatoes added.

BANNOCK - ENRICHED

Chef Zimmerman
Westin Hotel, Calgary

2½ cups	flour	625 mL
¼ cup	skim milk powder	50 mL
2 tbsp.	egg powder	30 mL
½ tsp.	salt	2 mL
4 tsp.	baking powder	20 mL
¾ cup	water	175 mL
1 tbsp.	melted fat	15 mL

Sift the dry ingredients. Mix them well in a bowl. Add water and melted fat. Stir until the flour is wet. Knead slightly, if desired. • Shape into mounds. Place into a greased frying pan. Cook until golden brown on 1 side and then turn over to cook other side. **Note:** Raisins may be added to bannock. • If the bannock is not stiff enough, more flour may be added.

POTATO FLOUR BISCUITS

Gluten-Free

½ cup	Ener-G pure rice flour	125 mL
1 tbsp.	Ener-G pure potato flour	15 mL
2 tsp.	sugar	10 mL
¼ tsp.	salt	1 mL
1 tsp.	baking powder	5 mL
½ tsp.	baking soda	5 mL
5 tbsp.	milk	75 mL
1 tbsp.	margarine, melted	15 mL

Preheat oven to 400°F (200°C). • Mix all dry ingredients together. Add milk and margarine and mix until well blended. • Partially flatten pieces of dough with hand and place on cookie sheet. • Bake for 10-12 minutes. • Makes 4 large or 5 medium-sized biscuits.

Hint: Dry biscuits are caused from baking in too slow an oven and from handling too much.

2 cups	sifted flour	500 mL		
1 tbsp.	sugar	15 mL		
4 tsp.	baking powder	20 mL		
½ tsp.	salt	2 mL		
½ tsp.	cream of tartar (optional)	2 mL		
½ cup	shortening, butter or margarine	125 mL		
1	egg, beaten	1		
⅔ cup	milk	150 mL		

CLOUD BISCUITS

Mix dry ingredients together. Cut in shortening. Add beaten egg and milk; mix lightly. • Roll dough out to ¾" (2 cm) thick and cut with a round cookie cutter. • (Dough may be chilled at this stage. You can make dough a couple of days ahead and bake when needed.) • Bake on an ungreased baking sheet at 450°F (230°C) for 10-12 minutes. • **Note:** For drop biscuits put in ¾ cup (175 mL) of milk.

---

6 cups	flour	1.5 L	
½ cup	instant dry milk powder	125 mL	
¼ cup	baking powder	50 mL	
¼ cup	sugar	50 mL	
2 tsp.	salt	10 mL	
2 tsp.	cream of tartar	10 mL	
2 cups	shortening	500 mL	

HOT BISCUIT MIX

Combine dry ingredients, mixing well. Cut in shortening until mixture looks like coarse cornmeal. Store in a dry place. • To make up, use the desired amount of mix and add enough water to make up dough. Use approximately ¾ cup (175 mL) water to 2 cups (500 mL) of mix for rolled biscuits and 1 cup (250 mL) of water for drop biscuits. • For rolled biscuits, knead dough quickly and turn out onto a lightly floured surface. Roll out to desired thickness and cut with a biscuit cutter. • Tops of biscuits may be brushed with milk or melted butter. • Bake biscuits on an ungreased baking sheet for 20-25 minutes in a 400°F (200°C) oven.

⅓ cup	butter or margarine	75 mL	
2¼ cups	biscuit mix (see below)	550 mL	
⅔ cup	milk	150 mL	
1 tbsp.	sesame seeds	15 mL	

SESAME BUTTER STIX

Heat oven to 450°F (230°C). • Melt margarine in a 9" x 13" (4 L) pan. • Make dough using Bisquick and milk and mix well or use Cloud Biscuit dough, above. • Pat dough and roll into a rectangle. Cut into strips about ¾" (2 cm) wide. • Dip strips in melted margarine to coat all sides; arrange in single layer in pan. Sprinkle sesame seeds over strips. • Bake 12-15 minutes.

FRENCH TOAST

Gluten-Free *

2	eggs, beaten	2
2 tsp.	sugar OR artificial sweeteners	10 mL
½ tsp.	cinnamon	2 mL
⅛ tsp.	nutmeg	0.5 mL
½ cup	whole OR skim milk	125 mL
4	slices bread, thickly sliced *	4
	icing (confectioners') sugar	
	syrup	
	preserves	

Blend eggs, sugar, spices and milk. Dip bread and let soak until saturated. Place bread on rack for broiling. Broil until light to golden brown, turn over and broil until golden brown. Dust with icing sugar. • You may also pan fry, in your frying pan, until golden brown, turn over and fry other side of bread. Dust with icing sugar. • Remove and serve with syrup or your favorite preserve. We like it with preserves and back bacon. • For gluten-free diets, use one of our many gluten-free bread recipes, see gluten-free index. • Serves 2.

CORN CAKE CRISPS

Gluten-Free

1 cup	yellow cornmeal	250 mL
½ tsp.	salt	2 mL
1 tsp.	freshly ground pepper, or to taste	5 mL
1 tsp.	brown sugar	5 mL
⅔ cup	water	150 mL
3 tbsp.	butter	45 mL

Place cornmeal, salt and pepper in medium-sized bowl and stir. • Place sugar, water and butter in small saucepan. Heat until butter has melted and then bring liquid to a rolling boil. Remove from heat. • Pour boiling liquid into cornmeal and stir well. • Lightly butter a baking sheet. Place cornmeal batter in 8 separate mounds on baking sheet. Press each mound with the bottom of a tumbler, flour tumbler bottom between each, until each is flattened to ¼" (1 cm) thick wafer. Bake at 375°F (190°C) for 20 minutes, until golden brown. • Serve hot with butter and honey or apple butter on the side.

Hint: *For interesting biscuits add minced onion to the milk you use in mixing dough.*

½ cup	flour	125 mL
1 tsp.	salt	5 mL
1 tsp.	baking powder	5 mL
⅛ tsp.	pepper	0.5 mL
½ cup	milk	125 mL
1	egg	1
2 tbsp.	melted butter	30 mL
2 cups	grated raw potato	500 mL
1	medium onion, grated	1

POTATO PANCAKES

Sift dry ingredients together. • Add milk, egg, melted butter, grated potatoes, and onion. • Put in blender for 2 minutes. Liquify. • Drop by spoonfuls onto a greased hot griddle. Fry until golden brown on each side. • Serve with applesauce and bacon or ham.

1	egg, beaten	1
1 cup	buttermilk	250 mL
1 tbsp.	vegetable oil	15 mL
1 tbsp.	brown sugar (optional)	15 mL
½ cup	Ener-G potato mix	125 mL
¼ cup	Ener-G rice mix	50 mL
1 tsp.	baking soda	5 mL
½ tsp.	baking powder	2 mL

POTATO AND RICE MIX PANCAKES

Gluten-Free

Beat the egg; mix in the buttermilk, oil and brown sugar. Mix the other dry ingredients together. Mix into liquid ingredients. • Fry pancakes on medium-hot griddle, 365°F (185°C).

⅓ cup	Ener-G pure rice polish	75 mL
⅔ cup	Ener-G pure rice flour	150 mL
1 tsp.	baking soda	5 mL
½ tsp.	baking powder	2 mL
½ tsp.	salt	2 mL
1 cup	buttermilk	250 mL
2 tbsp.	oil	30 mL
1	egg, beaten	1

RICE POLISH BUTTERMILK PANCAKE

Gluten-Free

Sift dry ingredients together. • Add remaining ingredients and stir just until blended. • Drop by spoonfuls onto a lightly oiled griddle.

If you are making flap jacks, don't leave out anything or your result will be flop jacks!

GIANT PUFF

This is great served with soup and a salad.

3 tbsp.	butter or margarine	45 mL
2	eggs	2
½ cup	flour	125 mL
½ cup	milk	125 mL
¼ cup	shredded cheese	50 mL

Melt butter in a large ovenproof skillet. • Combine butter and all other ingredients in blender and whirl until smooth. Pour mixture into skillet used for melting butter. • Bake in preheated 475°F (245°C) oven for 12 minutes or until puffed and brown. Puff should be dark on outside and soft on inside. • Serve immediately.

STAY-CRISP BATTER

1 cup	flour	250 mL
1 tsp.	salt	5 mL
1 tsp.	baking powder	5 mL
1	egg (optional)	1
1 cup	ice water, ginger ale OR beer, ice cold *	250 mL

Combine all ingredients, mix well but do not overmix. • Use batter for vegetables, fish, fowl, etc. Always dip vegetables, etc. in beaten egg and then in flour, before dipping in batter and deep-frying. • * You can use the ginger ale or beer, instead of water, for French-fried onion rings.

CHOCOLATE BANANA MUFFINS

Indulge yourself!

1½ cups	whole-wheat flour	375 mL
2 tsp.	baking powder	10 mL
½ tsp.	baking soda	2 mL
¼ tsp.	cinnamon	1 mL
¼ tsp.	nutmeg	1 mL
½ cup	brown sugar	125 mL
3	large ripe bananas	3
⅓ cup	vegetable oil	75 mL
2 tbsp.	crunchy peanut butter	30 mL
1	egg	1
½ cup	semisweet chocolate chips	125 mL

In a large bowl, stir dry ingredients with a fork. • In a small bowl, mash or purée bananas. Whisk or blend in oil, peanut butter and egg. Stir banana mixture into the dry ingredients and add the chocolate chips. • Fill greased muffin cups ¾ full and bake at 400°F (200°C) for 15 minutes. • Makes 12 large muffins or 24 mini-muffins.

½ cup	butter or margarine	125 mL	**BANANA-**
¾ cup	white sugar	175 mL	**PINEAPPLE**
1	egg	1	
1 tsp.	vanilla	5 mL	**MUFFINS**
1 cup	mashed bananas	250 mL	
½ cup	drained crushed pineapple	125 mL	
1½ cups	flour	375 mL	*Be careful - they are habit forming!*
1 tsp.	baking soda	5 mL	
1 tsp.	baking powder	5 mL	
½ tsp.	salt	2 mL	
1 tsp.	nutmeg (optional)	5 mL	

Cream together butter, sugar and egg. Add vanilla. ● Mix together bananas and pineapple and add to the creamed mixture. ● Mix together flour, baking soda, baking powder, salt and nutmeg. Then add to the banana mixture. ● Grease and flour muffin tins and fill about half full. ● Bake in a 375°F (190°C) oven for 20 minutes or until brown. ● Makes 18 medium muffins.

1	whole orange	1	**DATE AND**
½ cup	orange juice	125 mL	**ORANGE**
½ cup	chopped dates	125 mL	
1	egg	1	**MUFFINS**
½ cup	butter or margarine	125 mL	
1½ cups	all-purpose flour	375 mL	
1 tsp.	baking soda	5 mL	
1 tsp.	baking powder	5 mL	*Delicious!*
¾ cup	sugar	175 mL	

Cut orange into pieces, remove seeds and drop pieces into blender. Blend until the rind is finely ground. Add juice, dates, egg and butter and whirl briefly in blender. ● Sift dry ingredients into bowl. Pour orange mixture over dry ingredients and blend only until dry ingredients are moist. ● Spoon into 18 medium or 12 large buttered muffin tins. ● Bake at 400°F (200°C) for 15 minutes.

12 oz.	cottage cheese	340 g	**SOUR CREAM**
3 tbsp.	sugar	45 mL	**MUFFINS**
½ cup	melted butter	125 mL	
2 tsp.	baking powder	10 mL	
2	eggs	2	
dash	salt	dash	*A delightful Sunday brunch!*
1 cup	flour	250 mL	
	sour cream / strawberries		

Combine all ingredients, except sour cream and strawberries, in a bowl and mix lightly. ● Fill well-greased muffin tins ¾ full with muffin mixture. ● Bake at 400°F (200°C) for 20 minutes. ● Serve with a tablespoon (15 mL) of sour cream spread on each muffin and top with fresh or thawed strawberries.

COFFEE CAKE MUFFINS

Very Tasty!

1½ cups	flour	375 mL
½ cup	sugar	125 mL
2 tsp.	baking powder	10 mL
½ tsp.	salt	2 mL
¼ cup	shortening	50 mL
1	egg, slightly beaten	1
½ cup	milk	125 mL
½ cup	brown sugar	125 mL
½ cup	chopped nuts	125 mL
2 tbsp.	flour	30 mL
2 tbsp.	cinnamon	30 mL
2 tbsp.	butter, melted	30 mL

Sift dry ingredients into a large bowl and cut in shortening. • Blend egg and milk and add to the flour mixture all at once. Stir just until moistened. • Combine brown sugar, nuts, flour, cinnamon and melted butter. • Alternate layers of batter and brown sugar mixture in greased muffin pan. • Fill muffin cups ¾ full. • Bake at 375°F (190°C) for 20 minutes. • Yields 12 muffins.

SPICY CARROT MUFFINS

4 cups	flour	1 L
2 cups	sugar	500 mL
4 tsp.	baking soda	20 mL
4 tsp.	cinnamon	20 mL
1 tsp.	salt	5 mL
4 cups	grated carrots	1 L
1 cup	raisins	250 mL
1 cup	chopped nuts	250 mL
1 cup	coconut	250 mL
2	apples, peeled and grated	2
6	eggs	6
1½ cups	salad oil	375 mL
4 tsp.	vanilla	20 mL

In a large bowl, blend all dry ingredients. Stir in carrots, raisins, nuts, coconut and apples. • In a second bowl, mix eggs, salad oil and vanilla. • Combine with the dry ingredients and mix until just combined. • Spoon into greased muffin tins, filling ¾ full. • Bake for 35 minutes at 350°F (180°C). • Makes 48 large muffins.

Hint: When cutting quilt blocks, make a pattern out of an ink blotter or felt. When placed on the material, it will not slide as paper does.

1¼ cups	all-purpose flour	300 mL	
1½ tsp.	baking powder	7 mL	
¼ tsp.	baking soda	1 mL	
½ tsp.	salt	2 mL	
1½ tsp.	cinnamon	7 mL	
⅛ tsp.	nutmeg	0.5 mL	
½ cup	golden raisins	125 mL	
2	large eggs	2	
⅓ cup	vegetable oil	75 mL	
¾ cup	packed brown sugar	175 mL	
¼ cup	buttermilk	50 mL	
1 tsp.	vanilla extract	5 mL	
½ cup	shredded zucchini	125 mL	
½ cup	shredded carrots	125 mL	

CARROT AND ZUCCHINI MUFFINS

Preheat oven to 350°F (180°C) and prepare (grease or line muffin cups) tins. ● Combine first 6 ingredients in a large bowl. ● In a medium bowl, combine eggs and all the remaining ingredients. ● Add egg mixture to dry mixture all at once and stir just until dry ingredients are moistened. ● Fill greased muffin cups completely full. ● Bake for 30 minutes. ● Makes 12 large muffins.

⅓ cup	oil	75 mL
1	egg	1
⅔ cup	brown sugar	150 mL
½ tsp.	vanilla	2 mL
1 cup	buttermilk *	250 mL
½ cup	raisins OR dates	125 mL
1½ cups	bran	375 mL
½ cup	zucchini	125 mL
¾ cup	white flour	175 mL
1 tsp.	baking soda	5 mL
1 tsp.	baking powder	5 mL
½ tsp.	salt	2 mL
1 tsp.	cinnamon	5 mL

ZUCCHINI BRAN MUFFINS

Beat oil, egg, sugar and vanilla together. Add buttermilk, raisins, bran, and zucchini. ● Sift dry ingredients together. ● Add quickly to liquid mixture. Stir just to moisten. ● Bake in greased muffin tins at 350°F (180°C) for 15-20 minutes. ● Makes 24 muffins. ● * To substitute for buttermilk, make your own sour milk by putting 1 tbsp. (15 mL) lemon juice in a cup and filling the cup with milk.

We don't stop playing because we grow old; we grow old because we stop playing.

YOGURT BRAN MUFFINS

1 cup	plain yogurt	250 mL
1 tsp.	baking soda	5 mL
½ cup	brown sugar	125 mL
¼ cup	white sugar	50 mL
1	egg	1
½ cup	oil	125 mL
1 cup	bran	250 mL
1 tsp.	vanilla	5 mL
1 cup	flour	250 mL
2 tsp.	baking powder	10 mL
¼ tsp.	salt	1 mL
½ tsp.	cinnamon (optional)	2 mL
½ cup	finely chopped walnuts *	125 mL

Measure yogurt into a large bowl and mix in the baking soda. • In another large bowl beat together sugars, egg and oil. Stir in the bran and vanilla. • Sift flour, baking powder, salt and cinnamon, if used. • Add flour mixture to sugar mixture alternately with yogurt. Fold in nuts. • Pour into greased muffin tins. • Bake at 350°F (180°C) for 35 minutes. • Makes 12 large muffins. •
* Raisins, dates or blueberries may be substituted for the nuts.

MINCEMEAT BRAN MUFFINS

Moist and flavorful!

2	eggs	2
¾ cup	vegetable oil	175 mL
1 cup	white sugar	250 mL
1 cup	All-Bran cereal	250 mL
2 cups	milk	500 mL
2 cups	flour	500 mL
1 tsp.	baking soda	5 mL
1½ tsp.	baking powder	7 mL
1 tsp.	salt	5 mL
1 cup	mincemeat	250 mL

In a large bowl beat eggs well, then stir in oil and sugar. Stir in All-Bran and milk. • Sift together flour, baking soda, baking powder and salt and add to liquid mixture, stirring just enough to blend well. Fold in mincemeat. • Grease muffin tins or line with muffin cups and bake for 15-25 minutes in 375°F (190°C) oven. • Batter may be stored in the refrigerator for up to 3 weeks, and baked as required. • Makes 24 muffins.

Hint: Coarse-textured muffins are caused by insufficient stirring and cooking at too low a heat.

1½ cups	natural bran (not bran cereal)	375 mL
1 cup	whole-wheat flour	250 mL
½ cup	raisins OR dates	125 mL
1 tsp.	baking soda	5 mL
1 tsp.	baking powder	5 mL
2	eggs	2
¾ cup	milk	175 mL
2 tbsp.	oil	30 mL
½ cup	molasses	125 mL

DATE BRAN MUFFINS

Preheat oven to 400°F (200°C). • In a medium bowl, stir together bran, flour, raisins or dates, baking soda and baking powder and then set aside. • In a small bowl, beat eggs then add milk, oil and molasses, combining thoroughly. Add this to dry ingredients. Stir until just moistened. • Spoon batter into greased muffin cups. • Bake 15 minutes, or until muffins begin to pull away from the sides. • Makes 12 muffins. • Extra muffins may be frozen; wrap in foil or place in a covered container. Place frozen muffins in a 350°F (180°C) oven for 15-20 minutes to reheat. • 1 muffin contains 4 grams of protein.

2 cups	flour	500 mL
¾ cup	sugar	175 mL
1 tbsp.	baking powder	15 mL
1 tsp.	salt	5 mL
½ tsp.	baking soda	2 mL
½ tsp.	nutmeg	2 mL
1 cup	coarsely chopped walnuts	250 mL
1	egg, well-beaten	1
1 cup	medium-thick applesauce	250 mL
¼ cup	cooking oil	50 mL

APPLESAUCE BREAD

Sift dry ingredients together and stir in the nuts. • Combine egg, applesauce, and cooking oil. Stir into dry ingredients until just blended. • Pour into a 9″ x 5″ (2 L) greased loaf pan. • Bake at 350°F (180°C) for 50 minutes.

Hint: Keep a wet sponge handy when ironing. Works well to dampen dried hot spots.

BANANA LOAF SUPREME

2 cups	sifted flour	500 mL
2 tsps.	baking powder	10 mL
½ tsp.	baking soda	2 mL
1 tsp.	salt	5 mL
2	ripe bananas, mashed (1 cup [250 mL])	2
¼ cup	butter, shortening OR margarine	50 mL
½ cup	white sugar	125 mL
2	eggs	2
½ cup	sour cream	125 mL
1 tsp.	almond flavoring	5 mL
½ cup	chopped walnuts (optional)	125 mL

Sift dry ingredients together and then cream remaining ingredients together. Lightly combine both mixtures and mix evenly. • Pour into greased loaf pan. • Bake at 350°F (180°C) for 45-60 minutes or until a toothpick inserted in the loaf comes out clean. • Cool loaf for a few minutes before removing from pan. • Allow to cool completely on a cake rack.

PUMPKIN NUT BREAD

2 cups	sifted flour	500 mL
2 tsp.	baking powder	10 mL
½ tsp.	baking soda	2 mL
1 tsp.	salt	5 mL
1 tsp.	cinnamon	5 mL
½ tsp.	nutmeg	2 mL
¼ tsp.	allspice	1 mL
1 cup	pumpkin	250 mL
1 cup	sugar	250 mL
½ cup	milk	125 mL
2	eggs	2
¼ cup	softened butter	50 mL
1 cup	chopped pecans	250 mL

Sift together the first 7 ingredients. • Combine pumpkin, sugar, milk and eggs in a bowl. • Blend in dry ingredients and butter. Stir in pecans. • Bake in a 9″ x 5″ (2 L) pan at 350°F (180°C) for 45-55 minutes.

Hint: Toast the nut meats and while hot add a little butter. Your nut bread will take on a new aristocracy.

3 cups	grated OR shredded cooked carrots	750 mL	**CARROT LOAF**
2 cups	sugar	500 mL	
1½ cups	oil	375 mL	
4	eggs	4	
1 tsp.	baking soda	5 mL	
1 tbsp.	warm water	15 mL	
½ tsp.	salt	2 mL	
1 tsp.	vanilla	5 mL	
3 cups	unsifted flour	750 mL	
1 cup	currants OR raisins	250 mL	
½ cup	chopped walnuts	125 mL	
½ cup	quartered maraschino cherries	125 mL	
¼ cup	grated orange rind	50 mL	
¼ cup	grated lemon rind	50 mL	

Scrub carrots and cut each into 3″-4″ (7-10 cm) lengths. Cook in covered saucepan in unsalted water until barely tender. Drain and cool. Grate and measure to equal 3 cups (750 mL). • Combine sugar, oil and eggs. • Dissolve soda in warm water; add dry ingredients and beat for 2 minutes. • Add the remaining ingredients, including the prepared carrots. Stir to blend. • Pour mixture into 2 greased 9″ x 5″ (2 L) loaf pans and bake at 325°F (160°C) for approximately 90 minutes. Let cool in pans. • Makes 2 loaves.

¾ cup	salad oil	175 mL	**BEET AND CARROT LOAF CAKE**
1½ cups	sugar	375 mL	
3	egg yolks	3	
1 tsp.	vanilla	5 mL	
3 tbsp.	hot water	50 mL	
2 cups	flour	500 mL	
3 tsp.	baking powder	15 mL	
¼ tsp.	salt	1 mL	
1 tsp.	cinnamon	5 mL	
1 cup	grated raw beets	250 mL	
1 cup	grated raw carrots	250 mL	
½ cup	shredded coconut OR walnuts OR raisins	125 mL	
3	egg whites,	3	

Beat together the first 5 ingredients. • Then add the flour, baking powder, salt and cinnamon. Stir in the beets, carrots and coconut, walnuts or raisins. • Beat egg whites until stiff and fold into the batter. • Pour into 2 greased loaf pans or a greased angel food cake pan. • Bake at 350°F (180°C) for 30-40 minutes if using the loaf pans, and 50-60 minutes for the angel food cake pan.

ZUCCHINI LOAF

3	eggs, beaten		3
2 cups	sugar *		500 mL
¾ cup	oil		175 mL
2 cups	grated raw zucchini		500 mL
2 cups	flour		500 mL
1 tsp.	salt		5 mL
2 tsp.	baking soda		10 mL
1 tbsp.	vanilla *		15 mL
1 tbsp.	cinnamon		15 mL
1 cup	chopped walnuts		250 mL
½ cup	raisins		125 mL
½ cup	cherries (optional)		125 mL
½ cup	coconut (optional)		125 mL

Mix all ingredients by hand in the order given. • Pour into greased loaf pans and bake at 350°F (180°C) for 1 hour. • Makes 2 large loaves or 4 small. • * You may use 1 cup (250 mL) white sugar and 1 cup (250 mL) brown sugar and also substitute 2 tsp. (10 mL) maple flavoring for the vanilla for an interesting variation.

ORANGE ZUCCHINI BREAD

1½ cups	all-purpose flour	375 mL
1 cup	sugar	250 mL
2 tsp.	baking powder	10 mL
½ tsp.	baking soda	2 mL
¼ tsp.	salt	1 mL
¼ tsp.	ground ginger	1 mL
2	eggs	2
½ cup	oil	125 mL
1½ cups	grated zucchini	375 mL
1 tsp.	chopped orange peel	5 mL
½ cup	chopped nuts (optional)	125 mL

Combine dry ingredients. • In a medium-sized bowl beat the eggs, then add the oil and the grated zucchini. Stir in the dry ingredients, the nuts and the orange peel. (Strip the peel from the orange and chop it, don't grate it - it has more crunch this way.) • Pour the batter into a buttered 9" x 5" (2 L) loaf pan and bake at 375°F (190°C) for 50 minutes. • Then cool on a rack. • Makes 1 loaf. • **Note:** Use unpeeled zucchini; it gives color to your loaf.

Hint: A little vanilla poured on a piece of cotton and placed in the refrigerator will eliminate odors.

3 oz.	lemon gelatin powder	85 g
1 cup	hot water	250 mL
19 oz.	lemon cake mix	520 g
¾ cup	oil	175 mL
4	eggs	4
3 tbsp.	lemon juice	45 mL
¼ cup	white sugar	50 mL

LEMON BREAD

Add hot water to gelatin, let cool but do not let set. • Mix cake mix and oil together; add 1 egg at a time, beating well after each addition. • Add cooled gelatin. Beat until very foamy. • Bake in 2, 4″ x 8″ (1.5 L) loaf pans at 350°F (180°C) for 1 hour. • Mix lemon juice and sugar together and spread over warm loaves. Allow loaves to cool in pans, to soak up lemon glaze. • Makes 2 loaves.

3 oz.	butter (5½ tbsp. [82 mL])	85 g
1 tbsp.	grated orange rind	15 mL
¾ cup	sugar	175 mL
2	eggs	2
1½ cups	flour	375 mL
½ tsp.	baking soda	2 mL
½ cup	sour cream	125 mL
	icing sugar	

ORANGE SOUR CREAM LOAF

Line a 9″ x 5″ (2 L) loaf pan with 1 layer of buttered waxed paper. Bring paper 1″ (2.5 cm) above edge of the pan. • Beat butter and orange rind until soft and creamy. Add sugar and beat until light and fluffy. Add eggs, 1 at a time, and beat well after each addition. • Stir in sifted flour and soda, alternately with sour cream. Beat lightly until smooth. • Pour into prepared pan. • Bake at 300°F (150°C) for 1¼ hours, or until a straw inserted into the center comes out clean. • Cool on a wire rack. • Before slicing, dust the top with icing sugar.

3	eggs, separated	3
1 cup	butter	250 mL
2 cups	white sugar	500 mL
1 cup	milk*	250 mL
1 tsp.	vanilla	5 mL
1 tsp.	almond extract	5 mL
4 cups	sifted flour	1L
1 tbsp.	baking powder	15 mL
1 tsp.	salt	5 mL
½ lb.	maraschino OR glacé cherries, halved *	250 g

CHERRY LOAF

Beat egg yolks, butter, sugar, milk, vanilla and almond extract together. Add flour, baking powder and salt. Stir in cherries, then fold in the stiffly-beaten egg whites. • Bake in 2 greased and floured 9″ x 5″ (2 L) loaf pans at 350°F (180°C) for 1 hour. • * For a lovely pink-colored bread, use bottled maraschino cherries and replace part of the milk with the cherry liquid.

POPPY SEED LOAF

6	eggs	6
2 cups	sugar	500 mL
1¼ cups	oil	300 mL
1 cup	poppy seeds	250 mL
½ cup	milk	125 mL
2 tsp.	almond extract	10 mL
2 cups	flour	500 mL
2 tsp.	baking powder	10 mL
½ tsp.	salt	2 mL
1 cup	walnuts OR sunflower seeds	250 mL
1 tsp.	vanilla	5 mL

Beat eggs; add sugar and oil. • Blend in poppy seeds, milk and almond extract. Add flour, baking powder and salt. Stir in nuts and vanilla; mix well. • Pour into 2 greased and floured 9″ x 5″ (2 L) loaf pans. • Bake 1 hour at 325°F (160°C).

PINEAPPLE-CHEESE LOAF

2¼ cups	flour	550 mL
½ cup	sugar	125 mL
2½ tsp.	baking powder	12 mL
½ tsp.	baking soda	2 mL
½ tsp.	salt	2 mL
1 cup	grated cheese*	250 mL
1	egg	1
¼ cup	milk	50 mL
¼ cup	oil	50 mL
1 cup	undrained, crushed pineapple	250 mL

Combine the first 5 ingredients. Stir in the grated cheese. • Beat egg, milk, oil and pineapple together. Add to dry ingredients and beat well. • Bake in a 9″ x 5″ (2 L) loaf pan at 350°F (180°C) for approximately 1 hour. • * Use your favorite cheese, sharp Cheddar if you want a tangy flavor, mild if you prefer.

CHEESE QUICK BREAD

2 cups	flour	500 mL
4 tsp.	baking powder	20 mL
½ tsp.	salt	2 mL
¼ cup	butter	50 mL
1 cup	grated old Cheddar	250 mL
2	eggs	2
¼ cup	sugar	50 mL
1 cup	milk	250 mL

In a large bowl, sift together flour, baking powder and salt. Cut in butter as for pastry, then stir in the cheese. • In a small bowl, beat eggs until foamy, add sugar and milk, beating well. • Pour egg mixture into flour mixture, stirring only until moistened. • Transfer batter to a buttered 9″ x 5″ (2 L) pan. • Bake in 350°F (180°C) oven, for 50 minutes or until done. • Serve hot or cold.

⅓ cup	margarine OR butter	75 mL
½ cup	white sugar	125 mL
1 tsp.	almond extract	5 mL
2	eggs	2
⅓ cup	milk	75 mL
1⅔ cups	flour	400 mL
2 tsp.	baking powder	10 mL

MANDELKAGE

This is a traditional Norwegian Coffee Cake.

TOPPING

⅓ cup	margarine OR butter	75 mL
½ cup	white sugar	125 mL
1 cup	finely chopped almonds OR walnuts	250 mL
2 tbsp.	cinnamon	30 mL

Cream butter, sugar and almond extract. Add eggs. • Stir in the milk alternately with the flour and baking powder. This batter will be thick. • Spread batter in a 8″ x 8″ (2 L) pan. • Combine margarine, sugar and nuts. Spread topping on batter before baking. Sprinkle cinnamon on top. • Bake at 375°F (190°C) for 30 minutes. • Serves 8-10.

½ cup	butter or margarine	125 mL
1 cup	sugar	250 mL
2	eggs	2
1 tsp.	vanilla	5 mL
2 cups	cake flour	500 mL
2 tsp.	baking powder	10 mL
½ tsp.	salt	2 mL
1 cup	milk	250 mL
4	MacIntosh apples	4
½ cup	brown sugar	125 mL
3 tbsp.	flour	45 mL
2 tsp.	cinnamon	10 mL
3 tbsp.	butter	45 mL

APPLE CINNAMON COFFEE CAKE

Delicious served warm with ice cream or whipped cream.

Cream butter and sugar well. Beat in eggs 1 at a time, then add vanilla. • Sift flour, baking powder and salt together. • Fold the dry ingredients, alternately with the milk, into the butter mixture • Spread the batter in a 9″ x 13″ (4 L) cake pan. • Peel and core the apples. Slice and arrange on top of uncooked batter. • Combine remaining ingredients with a fork to make crumb topping. Sprinkle topping over the apples. • Bake at 350°F (180°C) for 40-45 minutes or until a toothpick comes out clean. • **Variation:** Quartered prune plums may be used instead of apples.

QUICK APPLE KUCHEN

1½ cups	butter OR margarine, softened	375 mL
19 oz.	pkg. yellow cake mix	520 g
½ cup	flaked coconut	125 mL
19 oz.	can sliced apples, well drained	540 mL
½ cup	sugar	125 mL
1 tsp.	cinnamon	5 mL
1 cup	sour cream	250 mL
2	egg yolks (or 1 egg)	2

Heat oven to 350°F (180°C). • Cut butter into dry cake mix until crumbly. Mix in coconut. • Pat mixture lightly into an ungreased 9″ x 13″ (4 L) pan, building up slight edges. Bake 10 minutes. • Arrange apple slices on warm crust. Mix together sugar and cinnamon, sprinkle on apples. Blend sour cream and egg yolks then drizzle over apples. Topping will not completely cover apples. • Bake 25 minutes or until edges are light brown. Do not overbake. • Serve warm. • Serves 12-15.

ORANGE COFFEE CAKE

½ cup	sugar	125 mL
½ cup	butter OR margarine	125 mL
1	egg, slightly beaten	1
½ cup	milk	125 mL
2 tsp.	finely grated orange rind	10 mL
2 cups	flour	500 mL
1 tbsp.	baking powder	15 mL
½ tsp.	salt	2 mL
½ cup	orange juice	125 mL
½ cup	brown sugar	125 mL
2 tbsp.	butter	25 mL
1 tsp.	cinnamon	5 mL
½ cup	coconut OR walnuts	125 mL

Cream together sugar and butter; beat in egg. Stir in milk and orange rind. Combine flour, baking powder and salt. Add flour to butter mixture, alternately with the orange juice. • Pour batter into greased 9″ x 9″ (2.5 L) cake pan. • Mix the remaining ingredients together in a small bowl. Spread on top of the cake. • Bake 30 minutes at 350°F (180°C). • Serves 12-14.

Hint: Before turning out cake onto the serving plate, dust it with icing sugar and the cake won't stick to the plate when serving.

3 cups	flour	750 mL	
3 tbsp.	sugar	45 mL	
½ tsp.	salt	2 mL	
1 cup	butter	250 mL	
1 tbsp.	yeast (7 g pkg.)	15 mL	
½ cup	lukewarm milk	125 mL	
2	eggs, beaten	2	
	soft butter		
	sugar		
	blueberries, fresh OR frozen OR raisins and nuts		
	melted butter		

BLUEBERRY KUFFLES

Combine dry ingredients and cut in butter as for pastry. • Dissolve the yeast in the warm milk. Add the beaten eggs and then mix in the dry ingredients. • Place dough in bowl, cover it with wax paper and leave overnight in the refrigerator. • Next day, divide dough into 5 parts and shape each into balls and roll out as for round pie crust. • Spread each round with soft butter and sprinkle with sugar. Cut into 8 pie-shaped wedges. Fill each wedge with fresh or frozen blueberries (or raisins and nuts) and roll each piece from wide end to centre. Dip top of each Kuffle in melted butter, then sugar. • Butter cookie sheets and arrange Kuffles in well-spaced manner. Allow to rise 1 hour. Bake at 375°F (190°C) for 15 minutes or until brown. Cool on rack. • Makes 40.

¼ cup	shortening	50 mL	
1 cup	sugar	250 mL	
2	eggs, lightly beaten	2	
1 cup	sour milk	250 mL	
1 tsp.	vanilla	5 mL	
2 cups	flour	500 mL	
½ tsp.	baking soda	2 mL	
1 tsp.	baking powder	5 mL	
2 tbsp.	brown sugar	30 mL	
1 tsp.	cinnamon	5 mL	

CINNAMON SWIRL BREAD

Cream shortening and sugar together. Add eggs, sour milk and vanilla. • Combine flour, baking soda and baking powder and mix into egg mixture. • Spread ½ of the batter in the bottom of a 9″ x 5″ (2 L) loaf pan. • Combine brown sugar and cinnamon. Sprinkle ½ of the brown sugar mixture on top of batter in pan. • Spread remaining ½ of batter over this, and sprinkle remainder of brown sugar on top. • Bake at 350°F (180°C) for 1 hour.

We are not put on this earth to see through one another, but to see one another through.

POTATO MIX MILK-FREE QUICK BREAD

Gluten-Free

3	eggs, separated		3
½ cup	unsweetened orange juice concentrate undiluted OR ½ cup (125 mL) water and 1 tbsp. (15 mL) vinegar		125 mL
1 tbsp.	oil		15 mL
1¼ tsp.	baking soda		6 mL
1½ cups	Ener-G potato mix		375 mL

Preheat the oven to 350°F (180°C). • Separate the eggs. Beat the egg whites to dry peaks and set aside. • Beat the egg yolks, orange juice, oil and baking soda together until foamy, about 5 seconds. Mix in the potato mix. Fold in the egg whites. • Bake in a greased 8½" x 4½" (1.8 L) breadpan for 40 minutes or until done.

RICE FLOUR QUICK BREAD

Gluten-Free

8 tsp.	Ener-G egg replacer	40 mL
2 cups	milk	500 mL
2 tsp.	baking powder	10 mL
2 tsp.	baking soda	10 mL
4 tbsp.	granulated sugar	60 mL
4 cups	Ener-G pure rice flour	60 mL

Preheat oven to 350°F (180°C). • Whip the first 5 ingredients together. • Mix in the rice flour. Bake in a greased 8" x 4" (1.5 L) pan for 45 minutes until brown. • Tap out of pan onto wire rack to cool.

HONEY WHOLE-WHEAT BREAD

½ cup	warm water	125 mL
2 tbsp.	yeast (2 x 7 g. pkg.)	30 mL
½ cup	melted honey	125 mL
1 tbsp.	salt	15 mL
¼ cup	margarine, melted	50 mL
2½ cups	warm water	625 mL
6-7 cups	flour (½ white, ½ whole-wheat) *	1.5-1.75 L

Measure warm water into a large bowl. Sprinkle yeast over water, and stir until dissolved. • Stir in honey, salt, margarine, 2¼ cups (550 mL) warm water and 3½ cups (875 mL) flour. Beat with mixer until smooth. Mix in enough remaining flour to make an easy-to-handle dough. Knead until smooth. • Place in a greased bowl. Cover and let rise until double in bulk. • Punch down and shape into loaves or buns. • Let rise until light. • Bake at 375°F (190°C) for 40-45 minutes for loaves, 15-20 minutes for buns. • * For darker bread use more whole-wheat flour and less white flour. Makes 2 large or 3 small loaves.

WHOLE-WHEAT BREAD PLUS

2 tsp.	sugar	10 mL
2 tbsp.	yeast (2 x 7 g pkgs.)	30 mL
1 cup	lukewarm water	250 mL
½ cup	sunflower seeds	125 mL
2 cups	cracked wheat OR Sunny Boy Cereal	500 mL
½ cup	rolled oats	125 mL
¼ cup	cornmeal OR Cream of Wheat	50 mL
2 tsp.	wheat germ	10 mL
1⅛ cups	bran	280 mL
4 cups	whole-wheat flour	1 L
15-20 cups	white flour	3.5-4.75 L
8 cups	water	2 L
4 tsp.	salt	20 mL
½ cup	honey	125 mL
2 tbsp.	vinegar	30 mL
2 tbsp.	molasses	30 mL
1 cup	oil	250 mL

Measure sugar and warm water into a large bowl. Sprinkle yeast over water, let stand until dissolved. • Combine the next 8 ingredients. Mix well. • Stir remaining ingredients into yeast mixture. Add flour mixture and knead into a ball. • Place dough into a large greased bowl and cover. • Let rise until double in bulk. • Punch down. Cut into 8 sections, form into loaves and let rest for 5 minutes. Put in pans and let rise until doubled. • Bake for 30 minutes at 400°F (200°C) and 30 minutes more at 350°F (180°C). • Makes 8 loaves.

POTATO FLOUR BROWN RICE BREAD

Gluten-Free

3 cups	Ener-G pure brown rice flour	750 mL
¼ cup	sugar	50 mL
1½ tsp.	salt	7 mL
⅓ cup	Ener-G pure potato flour	75 mL
⅔ cup	dry nonfat milk	150 mL
1 tbsp.	dry yeast (7 g pkg.)	15 mL
2	large eggs	2
¼ cup	shortening, melted	50 mL
1¾ cups	warm water	425 mL

Preheat oven to 400°F (200°C). • Mix dry ingredients together. • In separate bowl, whip eggs until fluffy. Add shortening and warm water to eggs. • Thoroughly mix in dry ingredients, scraping sides of bowl to ensure a well-mixed dough. • Place dough in 2, 7¾" x 3⅜" x 2½" (1.5 L) loaf pans. • Let rise in a warm oven or area until bread reaches top. • Bake for 50 minutes.

CORN BRAN AND BROWN RICE BREAD

Gluten-Free

1 cake	refrigerated yeast OR 1 pkg. dry yeast	1 cake
1⅛ cups	warm water	275 mL
⅓ cup	Ener-G corn bran	75 mL
2⅔ cups	Ener-G brown OR white rice baking mix	650 mL

Preheat oven to 425°F (220°C). • Oil a 9″ x 5″ x 3″ (2 L) or 2, 8″ x 4″ x 3″ (1.5 L) bread pans. • Dissolve yeast in water. • Add dry ingredients and mix using a table top mixer with paddle attachment. Beat for 5 minutes at high speed. Using rubber spatula, drop dough into bread pan. Dip the spatula in some oil and evenly press out dough in pan. • Place warm wet towel over pan and let dough rise in warm draftless place to top of pan (a good method is to drape warm wet towel over a 10″ (25 cm) square bread rack and to rest the rack between 2 large coffee cans. This provides a warm and humid place to proof the bread). • Bake for 25-35 minutes until done. • Tap bread out onto wire rack and let cool.

CHEESE PAN-BREAD

½ cup	milk	125 mL
2 tsp.	white sugar	10 mL
1¼ tsp.	salt	6 mL
½ cup	butter	125 mL
½ cup	lukewarm water	125 mL
1 tsp.	granulated sugar	5 mL
1 tbsp.	yeast (7 g pkg.)	15 mL
3	eggs, well beaten	3
2¾ cups	all-purpose flour	675 mL
½ cup	Parmesan OR Romano cheese	125 mL
	few grains pepper	
¼ tsp.	dry mustard cheese	1 mL

Scald milk, and stir in 2 tsp. (10 mL) sugar, salt and butter. Cool to luke-warm. • Measure lukewarm water into a large bowl, stir in 1 tsp. (5 mL) sugar and sprinkle with yeast. Let stand 10 minutes, then stir well. • Add lukewarm milk mixture, eggs and 1¾ cups (425 mL) of flour. Beat until smooth and elastic. • Combine cheese, pepper and mustard and stir into batter. Gradually add flour to make a thick batter (may have to use approximately 1 cup [250 mL] more flour than originally used). • Cover with damp tea towel and let rise in a warm place, until double in bulk, about 1¼ hours. • Stir down the batter and divide between 2 greased 8″ (20 cm) round layer cake pans. • Sprinkle with additional cheese; cover loosely with waxed paper. Let rise until double, approximately 45 minutes. • Bake at 375°F (190°C) for 25-30 minutes. • Serve warm or freeze and reheat. • Makes 2 round loaves.

¼ cup	sugar	50 mL
2 tsp.	salt	10 mL
2 tbsp.	shortening	30 mL
2 cups	hot water	500 mL
1 tsp.	sugar	5 mL
½ cup	warm water	125 mL
2 tbsp.	yeast (2 x 7 g pkgs.)	30 mL
6½ cups	flour	1.6 L

EASY, EASY FRENCH BREAD

Mix together the sugar, salt, shortening and hot water. Cool.   •   In a small bowl, stir 1 tsp. (5 mL) sugar into the warm water and sprinkle on the yeast.   •   When the first mixture is cool, combine both mixtures and gradually add the flour.   •   Knead the dough into a ball and place in a greased bowl. Push this mixture down with a spoon every 10 minutes. Do this 5 times.   •   Divide into 2 balls, and let rest for 10 minutes. Roll out each ball ½" (1.3 cm) thick then roll up like a jelly roll, seal ends and seam.   •   Place on greased cookie sheet and slash diagonally across the top of each roll with a knife.   •   Let rise until double in size and then bake at 400°F (200°C) for 30 minutes.   •   Makes 2 loaves.

1 tbsp.	yeast (7 g pkg.)	15 mL
½ cup	warm water (105-115°F [40.5-46°C])	125 mL
1½ cups	lukewarm milk (scalded, cooled)	375 mL
1 cup	cornmeal	250 mL
½ cup	sugar	125 mL
½ cup	softened butter OR margarine	125 mL
2	eggs, lightly beaten	2
2 tsp.	salt	10 mL
6 cups	all-purpose flour butter OR margarine cornmeal	1.5 L

CORNMEAL CRESCENTS

In a large bowl, dissolve yeast in warm water . Stir in milk, cornmeal, sugar, margarine, eggs, salt and 2 cups (500 mL) of flour. Beat until smooth.   •   Stir in enough remaining flour to make dough easy to handle. Turn dough onto lightly floured surface; knead until smooth and elastic, about 5 minutes.   •   Place in greased bowl, turn greased side up. Cover and let rise in a warm place until double, approximately 1½ hours (dough is ready if indentation remains when touched).   •   Grease 2 cookie sheets, and sprinkle with cornmeal.   •   Punch down dough and divide in half. Roll 1 portion into a 12" (30 cm) circle. Spread with butter and cut into 16 wedges. Roll up wedges, beginning at rounded end. Place crescents, with points underneath, on cookie sheets. Repeat with remaining dough.   •   Cover, let rise until double, approximately 40 minutes.   •   Heat oven to 400°F (200°C).   •   Brush crescents lightly with butter and sprinkle with cornmeal.   •   Bake until golden brown, 15-20 minutes.   •   Makes 32 crescents.   •   **Note:** High altitude (3500-6500 feet) rising times may be slightly shorter.

OVERNIGHT BUNS

1 tbsp.	yeast (7 g pkg.)	15 mL
1½ tsp.	sugar	7 mL
½ cup	warm water	125 mL
11-12 cups	flour	2.75-3 L
4 cups	cold water	1 L
¾ cup	vegetable oil	175 mL
1 cup	sugar	250 mL
1½ tsp.	salt	7 mL

Dissolve yeast and sugar in warm water. Let stand for 10 minutes. • In a large bowl combine flour, cold water, vegetable oil, sugar and salt. Blend well. Add yeast mixture. Mix until thoroughly moistened. Turn out on board and knead well. • Place in a greased bowl (can prepare around 4:00 P.M.). Set dough in a cool place. • When dough is doubled (at approximately 10:00 P.M.) shape into buns. Place on a greased cookie sheet. • Cover with a cloth and put in a cool place overnight. • Bake at 375°F (190°C) for approximately 15 minutes. • Makes about 6 dozen buns.

CINNAMON BUNS

½ cup	warm water	125 mL
2 tsp.	sugar	10 mL
1 tbsp.	yeast (7 g pkg.) *	15 mL
1	egg	1
½ cup	sugar	125 mL
½ cup	oil	125 mL
1 tbsp.	salt	15 mL
1 cup	warm milk	250 mL
1 cup	boiling water	250 mL
2 cups	white flour	500 mL
3½ cups	flour * use more or less as required to make a soft dough.	
	butter	
	brown sugar	
	cinnamon	

Combine warm water, 2 tsp. (10 mL) sugar and yeast and let stand for about 10 minutes. • Combine egg, ½ cup (125 mL) sugar, oil and salt. Beat and then add warm milk, 1 cup (250 mL) boiling water, yeast and 2 cups (500 mL) white flour. Beat 400 strokes. Then add enough flour to make a soft dough. * • Oil hands to shape dough into a ball, cover and set in a warm place. Let rise until double in size. • Roll out dough into a rectangle, 10″ x 14″ (25-36 cm) approximately, and spread with butter, brown sugar and cinnamon. Roll up and cut into 12 pieces. • Set buns in a 9″ x 13″ (4 L) baking pan.. Cover and let rise until double. • Bake about 20 minutes at 375°F (190°C). • * You can use a combination of whole-wheat and white flour. I use ⅓ whole-wheat to ⅔ white. If you want to use more whole-wheat then white flour, use 2 tbsp. (30 mL) yeast.

Appetizers
&
Beverages

QUAIL À MA FAÇON

Chef Zimmerman
Westin Hotel, Calgary

6	quail	6
3	large apples	3
½ cup	seedless raisins	125 mL
2 oz.	Curaçao	60 mL
1 cup	white wine	250 mL
6 slices	fatback OR salt pork	6
2 oz.	butter (4 tbsp. [60 mL])	60 g
1 cup	brown stock	250 mL
½	small onion, chopped	½
2 oz.	brown sugar (⅓ cup [75 mL])	60 g

Marinate raisins for 5-6 hours in Curaçao. • Bone quail, except for wing bones and drumsticks. Save bones. Stuff quail with marinated raisins, shape, and put bacon on breasts. • Peel apples, cut in half, take out core and place in buttered baking dish. Put brown sugar, butter and white wine on apples. Place in oven at 350-375°F (180-190°C) for 20-30 minutes, until just tender. • Place quail in skillet with bones and roast for 15-20 minutes. Take out quail and keep hot. Add chopped onions and roast with bones until golden brown. Deglaze pan with white wine, add stock and simmer, reduce, strain and reduce until there are 5-6 tbsp. (75-90 mL) left. • When serving, place each quail on center of baked apple and pour sauce over it. Garnish with wild rice and vegetables. • Serves 6.

JAPANESE CHICKEN WINGS

3 lbs.	chicken wings	1.5 kg
1	egg, beaten	1
1 cup	flour	250 mL
1 cup	butter	250 mL
¼ cup	Worcestershire sauce	50 mL
3 tbsp.	soy sauce	45 mL
3 tbsp.	water	45 mL
1 cup	white sugar	250 mL
½ cup	vinegar	125 mL
1 tsp.	Ac'cent	5 mL
½ tsp.	salt	2 mL

Remove wing tips and save for stock. Cut wings in half. • Dip in slightly beaten egg and then in flour. Fry wings in butter until deep brown and crisp. • Put wings in shallow roasting pan. • Combine remaining ingredients and pour over wings. • Bake, uncovered, at 350°F (180°C) for 30-40 minutes. • Spoon sauce over wings during cooking.

5-6	wings per person	5-6
1 cup	butter	250 mL
½ cup	honey	125 mL
4-5 tbsp.	prepared mustard	60-75 mL
2-4 tsp.	curry powder, depending on your own taste	10-20 mL

DEVILLED CHICKEN WINGS

Remove tips of wings with kitchen shears. Place wings on a baking sheet with 1" (2.5 cm) sides. This can also be achieved by using foil and extending it higher than the edge of a cookie sheet by at least 1" (2.5 cm) on all sides. • Combine remaining ingredients and heat to make a sauce. This will coat at least 30 wings. • Pour the sauce over the wings, making sure all are coated. Bake wings at 325°F (160°C) until done, 1 hour or less. • This recipe may be doubled and the flavor does not change. Also great for a cold snack. • These are very tasty and different. If you wish, place on a platter garnished with parsley. Serve with a dish of your favorite chutney for dipping.

2 lbs.	ground pork *	1 kg
2 lbs.	ground beef	1 kg
2 cups	bread crumbs **	500 mL
2	eggs, slightly beaten	2
2	garlic cloves, minced	2
½ tsp.	ground sage	2 mL
½ tsp.	onion salt	2 mL
15 oz.	water chestnuts, drained and chopped	450 mL
1 cup	water	250 mL
1 cup	ketchup	250 mL
1 cup	brown sugar	250 mL
¼ cup	soy sauce	50 mL
¼ cup	vinegar	50 mL

SEASON'S DELIGHT COCKTAIL BITS

*Gluten-Free ***

Combine first 8 ingredients. Shape into 1" (2.5 cm) balls. • Brown in frying pan on medium heat until cooked through. Pour off excess fat. • Combine remaining ingredients and pour over meatballs. • Cover and simmer at 200°F (100°C) for about 15 minutes. • Insert cocktail picks in meatballs and serve in a chafing dish. • **Variations:** * Use all ground pork if you prefer. • ** For an interesting, gluten-free variation substitute 2 cups (500 mL) of Rice Krispies for the bread crumbs to add real snap, crackle and pop!

Conditions are never just right. People who delay action until all factors are favorable do nothing.

ORIENTAL MEATBALLS

½ cup	cooking oil	125 mL
1½ lbs.	ground beef	750 g
1	garlic clove, crushed	1
1	onion, finely chopped	1
1 tsp.	salt	5 mL
¼ tsp.	pepper	1 mL
2	eggs	2
¼ cup	flour	50 mL
1 tsp.	salt	5 mL
¼ tsp.	pepper	1 mL
	water	
½ cup	chicken stock OR bouillon	125 mL
2	large green peppers, in 1" (2.5 cm) squares (optional)	2
14 oz.	can pineapple chunks, drained, reserve juice	398 mL
3 tbsp.	cornstarch	45 mL
½ cup	brown sugar	125 mL
¼ tsp.	ginger	1 mL
½ cup	pineapple juice	125 mL
½ cup	vinegar	125 mL
3 tbsp.	soy sauce	45 mL
½ cup	ketchup (optional)	125 mL
1	large tomato, peeled and chopped (optional)	1

Heat oil in frying pan. • Combine beef, garlic, onion, salt and pepper. Shape into meatballs of size desired. • Beat eggs, flour, salt and pepper together, adding water, if necessary, to make thin batter. • Dip meatballs in batter with tongs, shaking off excess and drop into hot oil. Cook slowly to brown on all sides. • Remove meatballs as they brown and, when all are cooked, discard all but 1 tbsp. (15 mL) of oil, as well as any pieces of batter. Add chicken stock, green peppers, if used, and pineapple chunks to pan. Cover and simmer for 5 minutes. • Return meat to pan and simmer 3 minutes more. • Mix cornstarch, sugar, ginger, pineapple juice, vinegar, soy sauce and ketchup, if used, together until smooth. • Add to pan, stirring constantly until thickened. • If adding tomato pieces, add just before serving. • These may be made as appetizers and kept warm in a chafing dish, or served as an entrée over rice. • This will freeze well and may be made well in advance. • Serves 6-8.

Insanity is hereditary — you get it from your children. (Sam Levenson)

1 cup	fine bread crumbs *	250 mL
1 lb.	ground round steak	500 g
½ lb.	ground pork	250 g
½ cup	mashed potatoes	125 mL
1	egg, beaten	1
1 tsp.	salt	5 mL
1 tsp.	brown sugar	5 mL
¼ tsp.	pepper	1 mL
¼ tsp.	allspice	1 mL
¼ tsp.	nutmeg	1 mL
¼ tsp.	cloves	1 mL
¼ tsp.	ginger	1 mL
½ cup	finely chopped onion (optional)	125 mL
3 tbsp.	butter	50 mL
1 cup	beef broth	250 mL
2 tbsp.	flour *	30 mL
¼ tsp.	salt	1 mL
1 cup	cream	250 mL

SWEDISH MEATBALLS

*Gluten-Free **

Lightly mix together ½ cup (125 mL) of the bread crumbs and the beef, pork, mashed potatoes, egg, salt, brown sugar, the 5 spices and onion, if used. Shape mixture into balls about 1" (2.5 cm) in diameter. Roll balls in remaining crumbs. Brown meatballs in the butter. • Make a gravy using the pan drippings and add beef broth, flour and salt. Heat until mixture comes to a boil, stirring constantly. Gradually add the cream. • Return meatballs to gravy and simmer about 30 minutes. • **Note:** These meatballs are also a Danish favorite. They call them Frikadeller. • * For a gluten-free variation, substitute crushed cornflakes or rice cereal for bread crumbs and use cornstarch, not flour, to thicken gravy.

5 oz.	can water chestnuts, drained	140 g
¼ cup	soy sauce	50 mL
¼ cup	sugar	50 mL
4 slices	bacon, each cut in ½ crosswise and lengthwise	4 slices
	toothpicks	

WATER CHESTNUT APPETIZERS

Marinate water chestnuts in soy sauce for 30 minutes. • Roll each chestnut in sugar, then wrap with a strip of bacon and secure with a cocktail pick. • Arrange on a cake rack in a shallow pan or on broiler. Bake in hot oven 400°F (200°C) for 20 minutes. • Drain on paper towel. • Before serving, return to a moderate oven 350°F (180°C) for 5 minutes, to reheat and crisp the chestnuts. • These are best when made in the morning and reheated. • Makes about 16.

SAUSAGE ROLLS WITH CHEESE PASTRY

CHEESE PASTRY

1 lb.	sausage meat	500 g
1 tsp.	poultry seasoning	5 mL
½ tsp.	sage	2 mL
¼ tsp.	seasoned pepper	1 mL
1	small onion, minced	1
¾ cup	flour	175 mL
½ tsp.	seasoned salt	2 mL
½ tsp.	baking powder	2 mL
½ tsp.	paprika	2 mL
4 oz.	Cheddar cheese, grated	115 g
¼ cup	shortening	50 mL
3 tbsp.	ice water	15 mL
1	egg	1
1 tbsp.	cold water	5 mL

To make sausages, combine all ingredients in a bowl, using your hands to mix well. Shape into 24 sausage-shaped rolls about 2" (5 cm) long. • Fry until well-browned, draining on paper towels. • Refrigerate while you prepare pastry wrappings. • To make cheese pastry, stir together flour, seasoned salt, baking powder, paprika and cheese. Cut in the shortening. Sprinkle with ice water and cut through with a knife. • To asssemble sausage rolls, on a lightly floured board, roll pastry into a rectangle, ⅛" (0.5 cm) thick. Cut strips of pastry slightly narrower than sausage rolls, then cut these strips into squares to wrap each sausage. Pinch closed and place seam-side-down on ungreased baking sheet. • Beat an egg with a little cold water, by hand with a fork, and brush each roll. • Bake at 400°F (200°C) about 15 minutes, until golden.

BACON AND MUSHROOM ROLL-UPS

4	bacon slices, diced	4
2½ cups	mushrooms, finely chopped	625 mL
1	medium onion, minced	1
4 oz.	cream cheese	115 g
15 slices	sandwich bread	15 slices
⅓ cup	melted butter	75 mL

Cook the bacon until tender but not crisp. • Cook mushrooms and onion until the onion is clear, stir in cheese until melted and set aside. • Trim crusts from bread and flatten slices slightly with rolling pin. Spread each slice with about 2 tbsp. (30 mL) of the mushroom mixture and roll up. Fasten with a toothpick. • Place seam-side-down on a cookie sheet. • Cover and chill 1 hour or overnight. • These may be frozen in an airtight container. If frozen, let stand 30 minutes at room temperature before baking. • Brush rolls with melted butter and bake in 375-400°F (190-200°C) oven until lightly browned. • Remove picks and cut each roll in 2 or 3 pieces. • Makes 30-45 rolls. • **Variation:** For a deluxe version, combine a 5 oz. (142 g) can of lobster with 8 oz. (250 g) of cream cheese melted with ¼ cup (50 mL) of butter and substitute for bacon-mushroom filling.

2 x 10 oz.	pkgs. frozen spinach	2 x 283 g	# SPINACH POM POMS
2 cups	crushed herb seasoned stuffing mix	500 mL	
1 cup	grated Parmesan cheese	250 mL	
dash	nutmeg	dash	
6	eggs, beaten	6	
¾ cup	softened butter	175 mL	
⅓ -½ cup	dry mustard	75-125 mL	*MUSTARD SAUCE*
½ cup	vinegar	125 mL	
½ cup	sugar	125 mL	
1	egg yolk	1	

Thaw spinach, drain and squeeze out all excess moisture. Place in a medium bowl and blend in stuffing mix, cheese, nutmeg, eggs and butter. Shape into balls the size of walnuts and refrigerate, or freeze on cookie sheet and put in plastic bags. Put frozen balls on lightly greased cookie sheet and cook at 400°F (200°C) for 10-15 minutes or until hot (or microwave about 20 balls for 5 minutes on MEDIUM-HIGH (80%) power. • To make mustard sauce, combine mustard and vinegar. Cover and let stand for 1 hour at room temperature. • In saucepan, combine mustard and vinegar mixture, sugar and egg yolk. Simmer over low heat until slightly thickened. Cover and store in refrigerator for up to 1 month. • Serve hot Pom Poms with Mustard Sauce for dipping. Sauce should be at room temperature.

4 tbsp.	butter	60 mL	# MUSHROOM CANAPES
3	finely chopped green onions	3	
1 cup	chopped mushrooms	250 mL	
2 tbsp.	flour	30 mL	
1 cup	whipping cream	250 mL	
1 tsp.	salt	5 mL	
1½ tbsp.	finely chopped parsley	22 mL	
1½ tbsp.	chopped olives	22 mL	
⅛ tsp.	cayenne	0.5 mL	
½ tsp.	lemon juice	2 mL	
2 tbsp.	grated Parmesan cheese	30 mL	

Melt butter and sauté onions and mushrooms. Cook for 10 minutes, until moisture is gone. • Sprinkle in flour and stir well. Stir in cream and bring to a boil; cook until mixture thickens, about 2 minutes. • Remove from heat and add remaining ingredients, except for cheese. • Fill crustadoes or small, baked puff pastry shells. Sprinkle with cheese and serve.

HOT MUSHROOM TURNOVERS

3 x 3 oz.	pkg. cream cheese, softened	3 x 85 g
½ cup	softened butter	125 mL
1½ cups	sifted all-purpose flour	375 mL
½ lb.	mushrooms, minced OR 2 x 10 oz. (284 mL) cans drained, chopped	250 g
1 large	onion, minced	1
3 tbsp.	butter	45 mL
1 tsp.	salt	5 mL
¼ tsp.	thyme	1 mL
2 tbsp.	all-purpose flour	30 mL
¼ cup	sour cream	50 mL
1	egg, beaten	1

Early in the day beat, at medium speed, the cream cheese, butter and flour. • Wrap soft dough in wax paper and refrigerate at least 1 hour. • About 1 hour before serving, preheat oven to 450°F (230°C). • In a 10" (25 cm) skillet over medium heat, sauté mushrooms and onion in butter until tender, about 5 minutes. Stir in salt, thyme and flour until blended; stir in sour cream. Remove from heat. • On a floured board, roll out dough to ¼" (1 cm) thickness. Cut into 3" (7 cm) circles. • Refrigerate scraps. • On ½ of each circle, place a teaspoonful (5 mL) of mushroom mixture. • Brush edges with egg; fold edge over filling to meet bottom edge. Press edges together with fork and prick tops in 3 places. • Place on ungreased cookie sheets. Brush with egg. • Bake 12-15 minutes until golden. • These freeze beautifully and can be re-heated. • Makes 3-4 dozen.

ESCARGOT BUTTER

½ cup	butter, softened	125 mL
2	green onions, chopped	2
1	garlic clove	1
1 tsp.	mustard	5 mL
1 tsp.	Worcestershire sauce	5 mL
	pepper and salt	
	chopped parsley	

Melt butter, stir in remaining ingredients. • To bake escargot, place a dab of butter in each clean shell. Place washed snail in each shell and pack with escargot butter. • Bake at 425°F (220°C) for a few minutes, just until hot.

There's one reason the war between the sexes will never be won.
There's too much fraternizing with the enemy.

Tiger Prawns Duxelle, page 53

2 lbs.	scallops	1 kg
2 cups	white wine	500 mL
1	bay leaf	1
¼ tsp.	thyme	1 mL
1	celery leaf	1
3	sprigs of parsley	3
1 tsp.	salt	5 mL
6 tbsp.	butter, divided	90 mL
½ cup	chopped mushrooms	125 mL
6	green onions, chopped	6
1 tbsp.	chopped parsley	15 mL
1 tsp.	lemon juice	5 mL
¼ cup	water	50 mL
3	egg yolks	3
½ cup	cream	125 mL
4 tbsp.	flour	60 mL
½ cup	bread crumbs	125 mL
4 tbsp.	grated Parmesan cheese	60 mL

COQUILLES ST JACQUES

A fabulous appetizer and a great brunch idea.

If frozen, thaw scallops enough to separate. • Combine next 6 ingredients, add scallops, and simmer 8 minutes. Drain, reserving broth, and chop scallops coarsely. • Melt 2 tbsp. (30 mL) of the butter in a saucepan, add mushrooms, onions, parsley, lemon juice and water. Mix well, cover and simmer for 10 minutes. Strain, reserving vegetables, and add liquid to the wine broth. • Beat egg yolks with the cream. • Melt remaining 4 tbsp. (60 mL) butter in a saucepan, add flour, and mix well. Add combined liquids and cook over medium heat, stirring constantly, 3-4 minutes. Remove from heat and stir in egg yolk mixture with a whisk or wooden spoon. Stir in scallops and vegetables. • Spoon into scallop shells and sprinkle with bread crumbs mixed with cheese. • Bake at 450°F (230°C) for 5-8 minutes or until the top is brown. • Serves 4-6. • See photograph, page 16A.

6.5 oz.	can crab meat	184 g
2 tbsp.	minced onion	25 mL
1 tbsp.	butter	15 mL
8 oz.	pkg. cream cheese	250 g
2 tbsp.	milk	25 mL
1 tbsp.	lemon juice	15 mL
¼ cup	sliced green olives	50 mL
2 tsp.	Worcestershire sauce	10 mL
2	drops Tabasco sauce	2

HOT CRAB DIP

Drain crab meat and pick out any shell. • Sauté minced onion in butter. Add cream cheese and stir over low heat until smooth and heated through. Blend in milk, lemon juice, crab, olives, Worcestershire and Tabasco sauces. • Put in a small chafing dish to keep warm. • Serve with crackers. • This is a little thick for a "true dip". • It can be made ahead and reheated slowly just before serving.

COASTAL CRUSTACEAN ROUNDS

3 oz.	softened cream cheese	85 g
5	dashes Tabasco sauce	5
5 tbsp.	softened butter OR margarine	75 mL
1 cup	grated Cheddar cheese	250 mL
4 oz.	can green chilies, chopped and drained	115 mL
4 oz.	can tiny shrimp, drained	115 g
6.5 oz.	can crab meat, drained and flaked	184 g
⅔ cup	sour cream	150 mL
½ cup	grated Cheddar cheese	125 mL
¼ tsp.	salt	1 mL
	party rye bread OR round melba toast	
	paprika	

Preheat oven to 350°F (180°C). • Place softened cream cheese, Tabasco, butter, and 1 cup (250 mL) Cheddar cheese in a mixing bowl. Blend well and add chilies, shrimp and crab. Stir and set aside. • In a small bowl, combine sour cream, ½ cup (125 mL) Cheddar cheese and salt. • Spread a spoonful of the seafood mixture on a bread or cracker round. Top each with a spoonful of the sour cream mixture. Sprinkle with paprika. • Place on a cookie sheet and bake for about 15 minutes. • Serve hot. • Makes approximately 3 dozen.

HOT DIP

2 x 8 oz.	pkg. cream cheese	2 x 250 g
1 cup	mayonnaise	250 mL
2 cups	grated medium Cheddar cheese	500 mL
2 tsp.	dillweed	10 mL
½ cup	dried onion flakes	125 mL
1 cup	shrimp OR crab OR chopped ham OR 1 large package of fresh spinach, chopped	250 mL
1	round French loaf	1
	Parmesan cheese	

Combine all ingredients except the French loaf and Parmesan cheese. Use a food processor, if you have one, to mix ingredients. • Hollow out the French loaf (use insides to make croutons for salads, soups, etc.) and stuff with filling. • Wrap in foil, leaving the top open. • Bake at 325°F (160°C) for 1½ hours, uncovered. • For added flavor, sprinkle with Parmesan cheese. • Serve with crackers or bread rounds, then devour the bread container!

12	slices white bread	12
¼ cup	butter OR margarine	50 mL
1 cup	grated sharp cheese	250 mL
2	eggs, slightly beaten	2
1 cup	milk OR beer	250 mL
1 tsp.	salt	5 mL
¼ tsp.	paprika	1 mL
½ tsp.	dry mustard	2 mL

BAKED CHEESE FONDUE

Cut 2 of the slices of bread across in an X, making 8 small triangles. Butter lightly. Butter the remaining bread, then cut into neat cubes (you should have about 4 cups [1 L]). • Place a layer of bread cubes in buttered 1¼-quart (1.5 L) casserole dish, sprinkle with cheese, repeat with cubes and cheese again. • You should have plenty for 2 or 3 layers. • Combine the remaining ingredients, beating until the eggs are well broken up, then pour over the bread. Let stand 20 minutes until the bread soaks up the mixture (this is important). • Now, place the triangles of bread upright around the edges to form a crown. Bake at 350°F (180°C) for about 30 minutes. • Serve at once. • Serves 4. • **Variation:** The sauce may be used separately as a hot dip for crudités or for cooked vegetables or fish.

---

1 cup	cold water	250 mL
½ cup	sugar	125 mL
½ cup	lemon juice	125 mL
2	juniper berries, crushed	2
½ tbsp.	grated lemon rind	7 mL
⅓ cup	vodka (store in freezer until ready to use)	75 mL
8 tsp.	black caviar OR more crystallized lemon rind	40 mL
8	sprigs dill	8

VODKA SORBET WITH CAVIAR

First course for a special dinner.

In a heavy saucepan, combine water, sugar, lemon juice and juniper berries. Bring to a boil for 5 minutes, then add lemon rind. Remove from heat and let cool. • When cool, strain through cheesecloth and pour into sorbet machine (or pour into champagne or martini glasses and place in freezer.) • To assemble, chill 8 martini glasses or champagne coupes in freezer. • With a teaspoon (5 mL), place 2 scoops of the sorbet into each glass. Splash about 1 tsp. (5 mL) vodka over sorbet and add 1 tsp. (5 mL), or as much as you can afford, of caviar in the center or on the side of sorbet. Sprinkle with crystallized lemon rind and top with a sprig of dill. Serve immediately. • Serves 8.

To a friend's house, a road is never long.

MARINATED SALMON AND BLINIS

Chef Williams
Palliser Hotel, Calgary

1	side of salmon (approx. 4 lbs. [2 kg] skin on, no bones)	1
1 oz.	fresh dill (2 tbsp. [30 mL])	30 g
1 oz.	fresh parsley (2 tbsp. [30 mL])	30 g
6 oz.	salt, preferably rock salt, (¾ cup [175 mL])	170 g
8 oz.	Demerara sugar (1 cup [250 mL])	250 g
2 oz.	dark rum (4 tbsp.)	60 mL
1 oz.	lemon juice (2 tbsp.)	30 mL
1	bay leaf	1
6	crushed peppercorns	6

Place salmon in an acid-proof pan. • Combine remaining ingredients in a blender. Blend well. • Pour over the salmon. Marinate 48 hours, turning every 12 hours. • Remove from the marinade. Remove excess seasoning and residue. Slice as thinly as possible. • Serve cold with Blinis, recipe follows.

BLINIS

5 oz.	buckwheat flour (1¼ cups [300 mL])	140 g
2½ oz.	all-purpose flour (⅔ cup [150 mL])	70 g
2 tsp.	sugar	10 mL
½ tsp.	baking powder	2 mL
1 cup	milk	250 mL
2	eggs	2
¼ cup	sour cream	50 mL
2 oz.	butter, melted (4 tbsp. [60 mL])	60 g

Combine flour, sugar, baking soda and salt. • Combine milk and eggs. Add alternately with the sour cream to dry ingredients. Mix until smooth. • Add the melted butter and blend. • Pour batter onto a greased cookie sheet and bake at 325°F (160°C) for 25 minutes. • Cut to the shape required.

Hint: To prevent lemons or limes from drying out, place them in cold water and then put into the refrigerator. Change the water at least once a week.

1 oz.	butter	30 g
1 oz.	shallots (2 tbsp. [30 mL]), minced	30 g
3 oz.	button mushrooms, (6 tbsp. [90 mL]), finely chopped	85 g
	salt and pepper	
¼ tsp.	chopped fresh thyme	1 mL
½ tbsp.	brandy	7 mL
4	tiger prawns, peeled and deveined	4
4	slices smoked salmon	4

TIGER PRAWNS DUXELLE

Chef Williams
Palliser Hotel, Calgary

To make Mushroom Duxelle, melt butter, add shallots and cook until transparent. Add mushrooms and cook for 4-6 minutes, stirring occasionally. Add seasonings. Add brandy to mushrooms and flambé. Cool. • Draw a knife down the back of the prawns to make a butterfly incision. Add 1 slice of smoked salmon to each prawn. Place ¼ of the Mushroom Duxelle over each salmon slice. • Bake in a 350°F (180°C) oven for 5 minutes. Serve hot. • Serve with a lemon butter sauce. • Serves 2-4. • See photograph, page 48A.

	shrimp (use 15 per lb. [500 g] size)	
	flour	
	shredded fresh coconut (not toasted)	
1 cup	all-purpose flour	250 mL
½ cup	whole-wheat flour	125 mL
¼ cup	cornstarch	50 mL
1 oz.	sesame oil (2 tbsp.)	30 mL
5 dashes	Tabasco	5 dashes
¾ tsp.	paprika	3 mL
1 cup	beer	250 mL

COCONUT SHRIMP

Chef W. David Jones
Penn Tower Hotel,
Philadelphia

TEMPURA BEER BATTER

Peel and devein shrimp. Leave tails on. Combine all batter ingredients, except beer. Mix and incorporate with beer until mixture reaches light batter texture. • Add a little water if texture is too tight. • Dip shrimp in flour, then into batter and then into shredded coconut. • Deep-fry at 375°F (190°C) until golden brown. Serve with Orange Horseradish Sauce, recipe follows.

2 tbsp.	horseradish	30 mL
2 cups	orange marmalade	500 mL
dash	lemon juice	dash
dash	Tabasco	dash
1 tbsp.	brown sugar	15 mL

ORANGE HORSERADISH SAUCE

Combine all ingredients. Mix well and serve with Coconut Shrimp, above.

MARINATED SHRIMP

1 lb.	large, deveined shrimp	500 g
6 tbsp.	olive or vegetable oil	90 mL
6 tbsp.	lemon juice	90 mL
⅓ cup	tarragon vinegar	75 mL
1	garlic clove, crushed	1
1 tsp.	salt	5 mL
1	bay leaf	1
2 tsp.	sugar (optional)	10 mL
2 tbsp.	chopped parsley	30 mL
¼ tsp.	pepper	1 mL
	sliced, stuffed, green olives (optional)	

Cook and devein shrimp. • In a small saucepan, combine next 7 ingredients. Bring to a boil. • Pour over the shrimp, and add the parsley, pepper and green olives. Toss lightly. • Marinate in refrigerator. May be marinated 2-3 days for extra flavor. • Serve with brown bread and butter or crackers. • Serves 4.

SALMON MOUSSE

1 tbsp.	gelatin (7 g pkg.)	15 mL
¼ cup	cold water	50 mL
2 tbsp.	lemon juice	30 mL
1	small onion, sliced	1
½ cup	boiling water	125 mL
½ cup	mayonnaise	125 mL
½ tsp.	paprika	2 mL
1 tsp.	dried dillweed	5 mL
7.5 oz.	can salmon, drained	225 g
1 cup	heavy cream	250 mL

Soften gelatin in cold water, then stir in lemon juice, onion and boiling water, until gelatin is dissolved. Mix in mayonnaise, paprika, dillweed and salmon. Add cream ⅓ at a time. Mix well. • Pour into a 4-cup (1 L) mold. • Chill until firm. • Serve with crackers.

LUXURY CRABMEAT SPREAD

3	hard-boiled eggs, chopped	3
6.5 oz.	can snow crabmeat	184 g
⅓ cup	mayonnaise	75 mL
¼ tsp.	mustard	1 mL
¼ cup	finely diced onion OR green onion	50 mL
2	sprigs parsley, chopped	2

Combine all ingredients. • Refrigerate for 2 hours. • To serve spread on melba toast rounds or rye bread rounds. • Garnish with parsley.

8 oz.	pkg. cream cheese, softened	250 g	
3-4 tbsp.	milk	45-60 mL	
2 tbsp.	dry sherry	30 mL	
¼ tsp.	prepared horseradish	1 mL	
1	garlic clove, minced	1	
4 oz.	can shrimp, drained and finely chopped	113 g	
2 tbsp.	sliced green onions	30 mL	
2 tbsp.	chopped pimiento raw vegetables	30 mL	

CHEESE SHRIMP DIP

In a mixing bowl, beat together cream cheese, milk, sherry, horseradish and garlic. Fold in shrimp, green onion and pimiento. ● Turn mixture into a serving bowl, cover and chill. ● Serve with raw vegetables. ● Makes 1¾ cups (425 mL). **Variation:** Cheese Crab Dip: Prepare as above except substitute 6.5 oz.(184 g) can crab meat, drained, flaked and cartilage removed, for the shrimp.

6 oz.	Swiss Cheese, shredded (1½ cups [375 mL])	170 g	
½ cup	softened butter OR margarine	125 mL	
⅓ cup	milk	75 mL	
20 oz.	cream cheese, softened	625 g	
½ cup	finely chopped pitted ripe olives	125 mL	
2-3 tbsp.	tomato paste	30-45 mL	

SWISS CHEESE TORTE

Swiss Cheese Mixture; in a small mixing bowl, beat the shredded Swiss cheese and ¼ cup of butter until nearly smooth. Add milk, 8 oz. [250 g] and 4 oz. [125 g] cream cheese and continue beating until smooth. ● Line a 4-cup (2 L) mold or dish with clear plastic wrap. ● Spread ⅔ of the cheese mixture on the bottom and sides of the mold. ● Chill until firm. ● Reserve the remaining Swiss cheese mixture, unchilled. ● Cream Cheese Mixture; for the inside layer use 8 oz. (250 g) of cream cheese and ¼ cup (50 mL) of butter. Cream until smooth. ● Take ⅓ of this cheese mixture and add the olives, blending until smooth. To the remaining ⅔ of the Cream Cheese Mixture, blend in the tomato paste until smooth. ● To assemble; use ½ of the tomato paste mixture and spread evenly over the center and on the sides of the Swiss Cheese Mixture in the mold. ● Spread all of the olive-cheese mixture over the tomato layer. ● Spread the remaining tomato paste mixture over the olive layer. ● Use the reserved Swiss Cheese Mixture to cover the last tomato layer. ● Cover with clear plastic wrap and chill several hours or overnight. ● To serve, invert the chilled torte and carefully peel off the plastic wrap. ● Smooth top and edges with a narrow spatula if necessary. ● Serve with crackers or cocktail bread. ● Serves 12-14.

ANTIPASTO

1 cup	olive oil	250 mL
1	cauliflower, cut into tiniest florets	1
2 x 15 oz.	cans ripe pitted olives, sliced	2 x 425 g
2 x 14 oz.	jars stuffed olives, sliced	2 x 400 mL
24 oz.	jar whole pickled onions	720 mL
2 x 10 oz.	cans mushrooms (either small, whole OR pieces)	2 x 284 mL
48 oz.	jar sweet mixed pickles, chopped	1.35 mL
2 x 4 oz.	cans pimiento, cut up	2 x 113 mL
75 oz.	ketchup OR ½ ketchup, ½ chili sauce	2.25 L
2 x 2 oz.	cans anchovies, cut up, and add the oil	2 x 50 g
3 x 6.5 oz.	cans tuna, broken up	3 x 184 g
1 cup	vinegar	250 mL

Combine first 5 ingredients and boil for 10 minutes. • Add remaining ingredients. Put in sterilized jars and process for 15 minutes. • Serve with a variety of your favorite crackers.

CHICKEN-LIVER PÂTÉ

2 tbsp.	butter OR margarine	30 mL
½ lb.	chicken livers	250 g
2	hard-boiled eggs	2
4 oz.	pkg. cream cheese, softened	115 g
1 tbsp.	finely chopped parsley	15 mL
¾ tsp.	salt	3 mL
⅛ tsp.	pepper	0.5 mL
1 tbsp.	cognac	15 mL
	aspic	
	parsley for garnish	
	thinly sliced radish for garnish	

Melt butter in frying pan. Cook chicken livers, stirring occasionally, over medium heat, 3-5 minutes or until tender. Drain. • Chop liver and eggs in food processor or food grinder. • With wooden spoon, stir cream cheese until light and fluffy. Mix cheese into liver mixture along with the remaining ingredients. • Refrigerate for several hours. • Glaze with aspic and decorate with parsley and radish. • Serve pâté with hot toast or crackers. • Makes 1¼ cups (300 mL).

2 lbs.	baby beef OR chicken liver, ground	1 kg	
2 lbs.	sausage meat	1 kg	
1	garlic clove, crushed	1	
3	eggs, slightly beaten	3	
½ cup	apple juice	125 mL	
2 tsp.	thyme	10 mL	
2	bay leaves OR 2 strips of bacon	2	

PÂTÉ DE CAMPAGNE

Excellent.

Combine all ingredients, except bay leaves. Mix well; pack in loaf tin. Place 2 bay leaves or 2 strips of bacon on top of pâté. ● Bake at 375°F (190°C) for 2 hours. Place weight on top when cooling. ● Store in refrigerator when cool.

---

4 lb.	pheasant	2 kg
½ oz.	olive oil (2 tbsp.)	30 mL
3 oz.	grainy mustard (5½ tbsp.)	85 g
3 oz.	gooseliver (paste) (5½ tbsp. [85 mL])	85 g
	salt and pepper to taste	
6 oz.	whipping cream (32%), (¾ cup) whipped	170 mL

PHEASANT PÂTÉ

Chef Williams
Palliser Hotel, Calgary

Remove all bones from pheasant. ● In a heavy-bottomed pan, heat olive oil and add pheasant meat. Brown meat on both sides and put in a 350°F (180°C) oven for 8 minutes. ● Remove from pan and cool. ● In a blender, combine the cold pheasant, mustard, and gooseliver. Season with salt and pepper and blend to a fine consistency. Slowly add the whipping cream. Blend thoroughly. Pour into a mold or serving dish. Refrigerate. Serve cold. Garnish with butter lettuce, Cumberland sauce, chopped toasted hazelnuts or almonds. Serves 8.

---

6 oz.	jar pineapple preserves	170 g
6 oz.	jar orange marmalade	170 g
4 oz.	white horseradish	115 g
½ tsp.	curry powder	2 mL
16 oz.	cream cheese	500 g
	plain crackers	

JEZEBEL

Combine first 4 ingredients. Chill. ● Spread pineapple mixture on top of cream cheese. ● Serve as a spread with plain crackers.

CHEESE CANDLE

8 oz.	pkg. cream cheese, softened	250 g
3 cups	grated Cheddar cheese	750 mL
¼ cup	sour cream	50 mL
¼ cup	finely chopped green onions	50 mL
¼ cup	finely chopped green pepper (optional)	50 mL
dash	Worcestershire sauce	dash
dash	Tabasco sauce	dash
	caraway seeds	
	chopped nuts (optional)	

Blend all inredients together, except for the seeds and nuts. • Shape mixture into a ball. Roll in nuts if desired. • Wrap loosely in foil and chill until firm. • Sprinkle caraway seeds on top and sides to represent dripped candle wax. • Top with a carrot "flame". • Serve as a spread for crackers. • **Variation:** Add 8 oz. (250 mL) drained crushed pineapple and ½ cup (125 mL) chopped pecans.

VEGETABLE AND CHIP DIP

2 cups	sour cream	500 mL
2 cups	mayonnaise	500 mL
1 tbsp.	Beau Monde seasoning	15 mL
1 tbsp.	dillweed	15 mL
1 tbsp.	chopped green onion	15 mL

Combine all ingredients and let stand for 2 hours to allow dillweed and onions to release their flavors. • Serve with chips and/or fresh vegetables. • **Variation:** Try 1 part sour cream to 2 parts mayonnaise. For each 1 cup (250 mL) of base add 1 tsp. (5 mL) EACH onion flakes, parsley, seasoned salt and dillweed, a splash of Worcestershire sauce and a few drops of Tabasco.

STUFFED DILLS

5 oz.	deviled ham	140 g
1 tbsp.	minced celery	15 mL
1 tsp.	mayonnaise	5 mL
	large dill pickles	

Combine ham, celery and mayonnaise. • Cut ends off pickles and hollow out centers. Pack solid with ham mixture. • Place in the refrigerator for several hours. • Cut into thin slices and serve on buttered crackers.

4 oz.	can chopped ripe olives	115 g
¾ cup	mayonnaise	175 mL
¼ cup	chopped green onions	50 mL
1 cup	Parmesan cheese	250 mL

OLIVE HORS D'OEUVRES

Combine all ingredients and spread on thinly sliced sourdough bread or biscuits. Place on broiler rack and broil until bubbly.

1 cup	chopped black olives	250 mL
½ cup	chopped green onions	125 mL
1½ cups	shredded Cheddar cheese	375 mL
½ cup	mayonnaise	125 mL
	salt	
1 tsp.	mild curry powder	5 mL
1 pkg.	English muffins, split	1 pkg.

HAWAIIAN PUPUS

Combine olives, onions, cheese, mayonnaise, salt to taste and curry powder. ● Spoon olive mixture onto muffin halves. Broil until cheese melts. Cut muffins into quarters and serve hot.

6-12	hard-boiled eggs	6-12
1-2	green onions, chopped	1-2
1-2	dill pickles, chopped	1-2
4-6	stuffed green olives, chopped	4-6
1 tbsp.	dill pickle juice (or more)	15 mL
1 tsp.	Dijon OR prepared mustard (optional)	5 mL
¼ cup	mayonnaise	50 mL
¼ cup	sour cream	50 mL
dash	garlic salt (optional)	dash
	salt and pepper	
	paprika	

DEVILLED EGGS

Cut the cooled eggs in ½ lengthwise and carefully remove the yolks without breaking the whites. Mash the yolks and add the remaining ingredients except the paprika. ● Refill egg whites with yolk mixture and sprinkle with a dash of paprika. ● Use as canapés or as decorations for cold ham or roast dishes.

Friends are never far apart in heart.

BLUE CHEESE APPETIZERS

2 tbsp.	butter OR margarine	30 mL
2 tbsp.	crumbled blue cheese	30 mL
8 oz.	pkg. refrigerator biscuits	235 g

Preheat oven to 450°F (230°C). Melt butter and stir in cheese until smooth. • Cut uncooked biscuits into quarters and place on pan, touching. • Pour cheese mixture over biscuits and bake for approximately 10 minutes or until browned. • Serve while hot.

CHEESE SHORTBREAD

Great with drinks!

8 oz.	sharp cold-packed Cheddar cheese, grated	250 g
8 oz.	butter	250 g
2 cups	flour	500 mL
2 tbsp.	corn syrup	25 mL

Mix all ingredients together and knead. Form into a roll. • Chill in waxed paper for 4 hours. • Slice thinly and bake for 1 hour at 250°F (120°C).

CHEESE CRISPS

A great nibbler.

¼ lb.	butter	125 g
¼ tsp.	salt	1 mL
8 drops	Tabasco sauce	8 drops
1 cup	flour	250 mL
½ tsp.	baking powder	2 mL
1½ cups	grated sharp Cheddar cheese	375 mL

Combine ingredients as for pastry. • Roll out and cut into desired shapes, preferably quite small. • Bake at 400°F (200°C) for 10 minutes.

IMPERIAL CHEESE SQUARES

4 oz.	Imperial cheese	125 g
½ cup	butter	125 mL
1½ cups	flour	375 mL
1 tbsp.	brown sugar	15 mL
1 tsp.	baking powder	5 mL
	pinch of salt	
	crab apple jelly	

Combine all ingredients, except jelly. • Pat half of mixture in the bottom of an 8" x 8" (2 L) pan. • Spread crab apple jelly over mixture. • Pat rest of cheese mixture over the jelly. • Bake at 350°F (180°C) for 30 minutes. • Cut into small squares to serve.

CHEESE PUFF STRAWS

puff pastry sheets
eggs, beaten
Parmesan cheese
garlic
salt
pepper

Chef W. David Jones
Penn Tower Hotel,
Philadelphia

Lay out puff pastry sheets, brush with beaten eggs. • Sprinkle with Parmesan cheese, garlic, salt, pepper. Pat down cheese mixture. • Cut sheets in finger-size strips and twist into straws. • Bake at 350°F (180°C) until golden

---

CHEESE STRAWS

1 cup	all-purpose flour	250 mL
½ tsp.	baking powder	2 mL
1 tsp.	paprika	5 mL
dash	cayenne	dash
½ cup	butter	125 mL
1 cup	grated sharp Cheddar cheese	250 mL
3 tbsp.	cold water	45 mL

In a medium bowl, stir together the flour, baking powder, paprika and cayenne. Cut in butter and cheese. Add water and mix well. • Fill a cookie press and, using a star plate or any desired shape, form into straws on an ungreased cookie sheet. Cut into desired lengths. • Bake at 375°F (190°C) for 8 minutes, or until lightly browned. • Makes 3-4 dozen. • Serve with drinks or soup.

GLAZED ALMONDS

2 cups	whole blanched almonds	500 mL
1 cup	white sugar	250 mL
4 tbsp.	butter OR margarine	60 mL
½ tsp.	vanilla	2 mL
¼ tsp.	salt (optional)	1 mL

Heat almonds, sugar and butter in electric frying pan over high heat, stirring constantly until almonds are toasted and sugar is syrupy and golden brown (15-20 minutes). • Stir in vanilla. • Spread nuts on a sheet of foil. • Sprinkle lightly with salt. Using 2 forks, separate nuts into clusters, and cool. **Note:** Wear oven mitts while stirring, mixture can spit.

Wouldn't it be great if the person who writes the bank ads was also the one who made the loans?

PEACH HUMMER *

A summer fantasy!

2 oz.	Peach Cordial	60 mL
2 oz.	Vodka OR 7-Up	60 mL
1 oz.	Triple Sec	30 mL
2	peaches, canned OR fresh	2
2	scoops, vanilla ice cream	2
1 cup	chopped ice	250 mL

Put above ingredients into blender and blend well. • Pour into your favorite stemmed glasses. Garnish with a small mint sprig. • * For children, replace liquors with 7-Up. • See photograph, page 62A.

STRAWBERRY DELIGHT *

The name says it all!

1 cup	sliced fresh strawberries	250 mL
2 oz.	Triple Sec OR 1 oz. (30 mL) Triple Sec and 1 oz. (30 mL) strawberry liqueur	60 mL
2 oz.	vodka	60 mL
2	scoops vanilla OR strawberry ice cream	2
1 cup	chopped ice	250 mL

Put above ingredients into blender and blend well. Pour into your favorite stemmed glasses. Garnish with a small mint sprig. • * For children, replace liquors with 7-Up. • See photograph on back cover.

HOLIDAY EGGNOG

1 cup	orange juice	250 mL
2 qts.	commercial eggnog	2 L
1 cup	vodka (optional)	250 mL
1 cup	whipping cream	250 mL
	nutmeg (optional)	

Stir the orange juice into the eggnog. If you want to add the vodka, add it now. • Whip the cream until stiff and fold gently into eggnog mixture. Sprinkle with nutmeg. • Serve chilled in a large glass bowl or punch bowl. • Serves 10.

Hint: If whipped cream becomes buttery, add 2 tablespoons (30 mL) of cold milk and whip again — very carefully.

Soups Plus

SOUPS

GAZPACHO SOUP

Quick and easy!

14 oz.	can stewed tomatoes	398 mL
10 oz.	can condensed beef broth	284 mL
1 cup	peeled and chopped cucumber	250 mL
1 cup	chopped green peppers	250 mL
1 cup	chopped onion	250 mL
1 cup	chopped celery	250 mL
2 tbsp.	lemon juice	30 mL
dash	pepper	dash
	finely chopped onions, cucumber, celery, green pepper and croûtons for garnish	

Combine first 8 ingredients. Simmer gently until onions and celery are tender, approximately 10 minutes. • Chill for several hours in the refrigerator, the longer the better. Serve cold. • Garnish with chopped onions, cucumbers, celery, green peppers and croûtons to taste. • Serves 6-8. • **Note:** If you like a little spice in your life, add 1 garlic clove, finely minced and a dash each of Worcestershire and Tabasco sauces. Add these just before refrigerating soup.

ZUCCHINI SOUP

2 lbs.	small zucchini, thinly sliced	1 kg
⅓ cup	chopped onion	75 mL
4 cups	chicken broth	1 L
1½ tsp.	curry powder	7 mL
⅛ tsp.	salt	0.5 mL
⅛ tsp.	pepper	0.5 mL
	croûtons (to garnish)	

Cook zucchini and onion in chicken broth until tender. Add the remaining ingredients and simmer for a few minutes. • Serve hot, garnished with croûtons. • Serves 6.

Running people down is a bad habit, whether you are a motorist or a gossip.

Cream of Crab Broccoli Soup, page 69
Lobster Bisque, page 70

5 cups	chicken broth	1.25 L	
14 oz.	can cream corn	398 mL	
½ tsp.	salt	2 mL	
dash	white pepper	dash	
1 tbsp.	sherry	15 mL	
2 tbsp.	cornstarch	30 mL	
2 tbsp.	water	30 mL	
2	eggs, beaten	2	
	finely chopped green onion for garnish		

VELVET CORN SOUP

Bring broth to a boil, add corn, salt, pepper and sherry. • Mix cornstarch with the water until smooth. • Bring broth mixture back to a boil, then add the cornstarch and continue to boil, stirring occasionally, until some thickening takes place, approximately 10-15 minutes. • Reduce the heat, and when the soup has stopped boiling, add the eggs in a thin stream, stirring continuously. • Sprinkle with green onions and serve immediately. • **Variations:** Add cooked chicken or ham or both when adding the cornstarch, for a more full-bodied soup.

1½ cups	thinly sliced onions	375 mL
½ cup	chopped garlic	125 mL
¼ cup	butter	50 mL
½ cup	flour	125 mL
6⅓ cups	brown stock OR beef broth	1.5 L
1 cup	dry white wine	250 mL
½ tsp.	salt	2 mL
½ cup	sour cream	125 mL
	freshly grated nutmeg	
	salt and pepper	
	croûtons and minced fresh parsley for garnish	

AL'S SPECIAL GARLIC SOUP

In a stainless steel or enameled kettle, cook the onions, garlic and butter over moderate heat until the vegetables are golden. • Add flour and cook mixture, stirring, for 3 minutes. Add brown stock or beef broth, wine and salt. Bring the mixture to a boil and simmer for 20 minutes. • Strain the mixture, through a sieve lined with rinsed and squeezed cheesecloth, into another stainless steel kettle. (Soup can be made ahead of time to this point and left to finish until just before serving.) • Stir in sour cream, nutmeg, salt and pepper to taste. • Ladle soup into heated bowls and garnish with croûtons and minced fresh parsley.

CABBAGE SOUP

1 lb.	hamburger	500 g
1	medium onion, chopped	1
½ cup	diced celery	125 mL
½	green pepper, chopped (optional)	½
2 tsp.	oil	10 mL
2 tsp.	salt	10 mL
2 tbsp.	sugar	30 mL
¼ tsp.	pepper	1 mL
28 oz.	can tomatoes	796 mL
1 cup	tomato soup	250 mL
4 cups	water	1 L
2	bouillon cubes	2
1 tbsp.	parsley	15 mL
2 cups	raw, chopped potatoes	500 mL
1 cup	diced carrots	250 mL
6-7 cups	diced cabbage	1.5-1.75 L

Sauté first 4 ingredients in oil. Add the rest of the ingredients except the cabbage. Simmer, uncovered, for 1 hour. ● Add cabbage and simmer, covered, for 1 hour longer.

LUSCIOUS LENTIL SOUP

This soup has a high vitamin B and iron content.

1 lb.	dry lentils	500 g
2	fresh carrots, cut in circles or cubes	2
1	medium onion, cut in rings or diced	1
1	celery stalk, diced	1
1	garlic clove, minced (optional)	1
2-3 tbsp.	oil (olive oil is best)	30-45 mL
	salt and pepper	

Wash lentils, and cover with water. Soak for 1½-2 hours. ● To soaked lentils add carrots, onion, celery, and garlic (if used). Simmer until tender, or pressure cook in a stainless steel pot for 10 minutes. Add the oil, salt and pepper to taste. ● Soup is very thick and may be thinned if you prefer. ● **Variation:** For additional color make a small cavity in the center of each soup bowl and fill with steamed spinach.

Hint: Save cooking water from vegetables and potatoes. Store in jars in the refrigerator. Use when preparing soups requiring water, the soup will be more flavorful and nutritious.

1	large onion, sliced into rings	1
½ cup	diced celery, with leaves	125 mL
1-2 cups	diced raw carrots	250-500 mL
1	garlic clove, crushed	1
3 tbsp.	butter OR margarine	45 mL
4 cups	diced raw potatoes (5 medium)	1 L
2 cups	chicken broth	500 mL
1½ tsp.	salt	7 mL
¼ tsp.	pepper	1 mL
¼ tsp.	tarragon	1 mL
2 cups	milk	500 mL
½ cup	grated Cheddar cheese	125 mL

POTATO CHOWDER

In a large pot, sauté onion, celery, carrot and garlic briefly, in butter or margarine. Stir in potatoes, broth and seasonings. Cover and simmer until potatoes are tender (approximately 20 minutes). ● Add milk and reheat without boiling. ● Top each serving with grated cheese. ● Serves 6 generously, and keeps well in the refrigerator for several days.

3	broccoli stalks, peeled and chopped	3
1	medium onion, chopped	1
1	garlic clove, crushed (optional)	1
2½ cups	chicken stock	625 mL
3 tbsp.	butter	45 mL
3 tbsp.	flour	45 mL
1 cup	milk	250 mL
	salt and pepper to taste	
1 tsp.	curry powder	5 mL

CREAM OF BROCCOLI SOUP

Combine first 4 ingredients, and cook until softened. Purée cooked vegetables in blender with some of the liquid. Reserve the rest of the liquid. ● Make a roux by melting the butter and stirring in the flour. Gradually stir in milk and reserved liquid. Add salt, pepper and curry powder. Cook until thickened. Add broccoli purée. ● Serves 6.

Friendship is a rainbow between two people.

SPECTACULAR PUMPKIN SOUP

Wonderful flavor and a fantastic presentation!

1	whole pumpkin	1
	peanut oil	
	bread cubes	
4 cups	half and half cream OR more if needed	1 L
1 tsp.	salt	5 mL
½ tsp.	black OR ¼ tsp. (1 mL) red pepper	2 mL
¼-½ tsp.	grated nutmeg	1-2 mL
1 cup	grated Swiss cheese	250 mL

A whole pumpkin is required, with stem intact. Make the pumpkin into a saucepan by cutting a lid in the top of the pumpkin, using the stem as the handle. Make the hole large enough to serve the contents after cooking and it is suggested that a "V" be used in the cutting procedure to mark the proper location of the "lid" when replacing it. • Wash the pumpkin and remove the fibers and seeds. Oil all of the outside of the pumpkin with peanut oil and place on a sturdy baking sheet to be used as a tray to take to the table after cooking. A heavy round pizza pan does the job. • Toast, in the oven, sufficient firm white bread (Italian not French type) cubes to fill ¾ of pumpkin, until cubes are golden brown. • Mix together sufficient half and half cream with salt, black or red pepper (if you like it hot) and grated nutmeg or alter these measurements to suit your taste, to just cover the bread when placed in the pumpkin. • Place in alternate layers in the pumpkin a layer of bread cubes and a layer of freshly grated Swiss cheese (approximately a cup [250 mL]), until the pumpkin is ¾ full. Cover with cream mixture. • Put the lid on the pumpkin and place in preheated oven, 350-375°F (180-190°C) for approximately 2 hours. Stir occasionally. • When the pumpkin is orange rust and the pulp is tender, remove and serve immediately. Ladle out the thickened soup, including some of the pulp, and wait for the compliments.

BEEF/LAMB/PORK/CHICKEN & CUCUMBER SOUP

¼-½ lb.	beef OR lamb OR pork OR chicken	125-250 g
1 tbsp.	light soy sauce	15 mL
⅛ tsp.	sesame oil	0.5 mL
dash	sherry	dash
5 cups	chicken stock	1.25 L
pinch	ground white pepper	pinch
1	thinly sliced cucumber	1
1 tbsp.	white OR wine vinegar	15 mL
	chopped green onions for garnish	

Cut meat or chicken into small pieces and marinate with soy sauce, sesame oil and sherry for approximately 15 minutes. • Bring chicken stock to a boil with white pepper and add meat or chicken, until just cooked, 1-2 minutes, then remove meat. Add cucumber and bring stock to a boil again. Simmer for 2 - 3 minutes. • Return meat or chicken to the stock, add vinegar and return to a boil. • Serve immediately. • Soup may be garnished with chopped green onions.

3-4 lb.	chicken *	1.5-2 kg
3-4 qts.	cold water (1 quart [1 L] water for each 1 lb. [500 g] chicken)	3-4 L
2	carrots, ovals or sticks	2
2	celery stalk with leaves	2
2	medium whole onions	2
1	whole parsnip	1
6	sprigs fresh parsley OR some fresh dill	6
4	peppercorns	4
1 tbsp.	salt, or to taste	15 mL
	boiled egg noodles OR rice OR matzo balls	

KOSHER CHICKEN SOUP

Place prepared chicken pieces in stockpot and cover with cold water. Bring to a boil slowly and start skimming carefully, and as often as necessary, for about 1 hour. • Transfer chicken to a clean pot, then strain broth into it. Cover and continue simmering for another half hour. • Add vegetables and seasoning and cook until chicken is tender. • When done, remove chicken, * vegetables may be sieved through strainer and carrot ovals reserved to be returned to the soup. Chill broth, preferably overnight, so fat will solidify for easy removal. • Serve broth with boiled egg noodles or rice or matzo balls ** • * Save boiled chicken for chicken salad. • ** Matzo Ball Mix is available at most supermarkets.

---

2 cups	chopped broccoli (use frozen if fresh is unavailable)	500 mL
½ cup	chopped onion	125 mL
3 tbsp.	butter	45 mL
2 tbsp.	flour	30 mL
2 cups	milk	500 mL
2 cups	half and half cream	500 mL
2 cups	chicken broth	500 mL
½ tsp.	salt	2 mL
⅛ tsp.	black pepper	0.5 mL
⅛ tsp.	cayenne pepper	0.5 mL
¼ tsp.	thyme	1 mL
1 cup	crab meat, drained	250 mL

CREAM OF CRAB BROCCOLI SOUP

Cook broccoli until tender. • In a soup pot, sauté onion in butter. Blend in flour. Gradually add the milk and half and half; stir and cook until thickened and smooth. Add broth, seasonings, crab and broccoli to soup mixture. • Heat through. • Makes 6 cups (1.5 L). • See photograph, page 64A.

LOBSTER BISQUE

Chef Williams
Palliser Hotel, Calgary

2 oz.	olive oil (4 tbsp.)	60 mL
2 lbs.	lobster shells	1 kg
2 oz.	onions, chopped (4 tbsp. [60 mL])	115 g
4 oz.	leeks, chopped (½ cup [125 mL])	115 g
1	garlic clove	1
2 oz.	carrots, chopped (4 tbsp. [60 mL])	60 g
8 oz.	tomato, chopped (1 cup [250 mL])	250 g
1 oz.	tomato paste (2 tbsp. [30 mL])	30 g
3 oz.	Cognac	80 mL
6 oz.	flour (1½ cups [375 mL])	170 g
½ oz.	paprika (1 tbsp. [15 mL])	15 g
4 oz.	white wine (½ cup)	115 mL
1 qt.	fish stock	1 L
2	bay leaves	2
8	black peppercorns	8
1	sprig fresh thyme	1
½ oz.	salt (1 tbsp. [15 mL])	15 g
	salt and pepper	

Heat oil in a heavy-bottomed pan, add lobster shells, stir constantly for 3-4 minutes. • Add chopped onions, leeks, garlic and carrots. Stir again for 3-4 minutes. • Add tomato and tomato paste and flambé with cognac. • Sprinkle with flour, paprika and stir in very well. • Add white wine and hot fish stock. Stir vigorously until smooth. • Bring to a slow boil, add bay leaf, peppercorns, thyme, and salt and simmer for 1 hour, skimming occasionally. • Strain, through a sieve, and correct seasoning; add salt and pepper to taste. Serve hot. • Garnish with a dollop of whipped cream, small pieces of chopped lobster, chopped parsley. • Makes 1 quart (1 L). • See photograph, page 64A.

EMERGENCY GOURMET CRAB BISQUE

10 oz.	can green pea soup	284 mL
1½ cups	milk	375 mL
28 oz.	can tomatoes	796 mL
6.5 oz.	can crab meat	184 g
5	drops Tabasco	5
¼ cup	sherry OR apple juice	50 mL

Combine all ingredients, simmer and hide the cans. • Serve. • When the guests ask what is in the soup, just smile. • **Variation:** See page 152 for a delicious Lobster Casserole variation.

10 oz.	can mushroom soup	284 mL
10 oz.	can asparagus soup	284 mL
1 cup	water	250 mL
1 cup	milk	250 mL
½ cup	heavy cream	125 mL
½ cup	shredded crab meat	125 mL
¼ cup	sherry	50 mL

CREAM OF CRAB MEAT SOUP

Another great timesaver.

Mix soups, water, milk and cream. Heat but do not boil. Add crab meat and heat through. Just before serving stir in the sherry. ● Serves 6.

1	large onion, chopped	1
3	celery stalks, chopped	3
1 tbsp.	soy sauce	15 mL
1 tbsp.	butter OR margarine	15 mL
dash	Tabasco	dash
2 x 10 oz.	cans beef broth, undiluted	2 x 284 mL
10 oz.	can tomato soup	284 mL
4 oz.	can shrimp	113 mL
6.5 oz.	can crab meat	184 mL
1 cup	water	250 mL
¼ cup	wine or sherry	50 mL

SHRIMP AND CRAB SOUP

Delicious and extremely quick and easy.

Sauté the onion and celery in butter. Stir in remaining ingredients and simmer mixture for ½ hour. ● Serves 8.

---

4 oz.	salt fat pork, finely diced	115 g
2	large onions, chopped	2
2 cups	chopped clams, fresh or canned	500 mL
½ cup	clam juice	125 mL
1 tbsp.	salt	15 mL
½ tsp.	black pepper	2 mL
3 cups	boiling water	750 mL
1	large potato, diced	1
2 cups	light cream	500 mL
2 cups	milk	500 mL
	paprika	

NEW ENGLAND CLAM CHOWDER

In a large frying pan, fry pork fat until crisp. Add onions and fry until transparent, then add clams and simmer for 5 minutes. Transfer mixture to a sauce-pan. ● Add clam juice, salt, pepper, boiling water and potato and cook for ½ hour. Stir in cream and milk and heat but do not boil. ● Pour into soup bowls and sprinkle lightly with paprika. ● Serves 6.

HEALTHY FISH CHOWDER

3	large potatoes (4 cups [1 L])	3
1 cup	chopped onions	250 mL
2 tbsp.	butter OR margarine	30 mL
2 cups	water	500 mL
1 tsp.	salt	5 mL
1 tsp.	basil	5 mL
¼ tsp.	freshly ground pepper	1 mL
1 lb.	cod fillets	500 g
2 cups	frozen corn kernels	500 mL
12 oz.	can evaporated skim milk	342 mL

Scrub potatoes, cut into bite-sized pieces and steam until just tender. • Sauté onion in butter. Add potatoes, water, salt, basil, pepper and fish and bring to a boil. Reduce heat, cover and simmer until fish flakes easily, about 10 minutes. • Stir in corn and milk. Heat until corn and milk are hot (but do NOT allow soup to boil) and serve. • Makes 9, 1 cup (250 mL) servings.

TUNA CHEESE CHOWDER

Delicious, and children love this also.

1 cup	shredded carrots	250 mL
½ cup	chopped onion	125 mL
¼ cup	butter OR margarine	50 mL
¼ cup	flour	50 mL
2 cups	milk	500 mL
2 cups	chicken broth	500 mL
6.5 oz.	can flaked tuna, drained	184 g
1 cup	shredded Cheddar cheese	250 mL

In a saucepan, cook carrots and onion in margarine until onion is tender but not brown. Blend in flour. Gently stir in milk and chicken broth and simmer until mixture is thick and bubbly. Add tuna and heat through. Stir in cheese until melted. • Serve with croûtons, hot muffins and a green salad. • Makes 4 servings.

Hint: *When soup is too salty add slices of raw potatoes and boil for a few minutes or add a couple of pinches of brown sugar. This will overcome the salty taste but will not sweeten it.*

SALAD

2 oz.	anchovies, drained	55 g
2-3	garlic cloves	2-3
1-2	eggs, coddled*	1-2
4 tbsp.	lemon juice	60 mL
1 tsp.	dry mustard (scant)	5 mL
1 tsp.	Worcestershire sauce	5 mL
dash	Tabasco sauce	dash
1 cup	oil	250 mL
½-¾ cup	grated Parmesan	125-175 mL
2	heads Romaine lettuce	2
6	slices bacon, cooked crisp and crumbled	6
1 cup	croûtons**	250 mL

CAESAR SALAD

In a food processor, with the steel knife, combine anchovies, garlic, egg, lemon juice, mustard, Worcestershire and Tabasco sauces. Process until smooth. With machine running, add oil very slowly. Parmesan cheese may be added to dressing in processor or sprinkled on salad. • Tear lettuce into bite-sized pieces in salad bowl. • Pour dressing over and toss well. • Add bacon, croûtons and Parmesan cheese and toss lightly. • Serve immediately. • Serves 8. • * To coddle eggs, pour boiling water over them and let stand 1 minute. • ** Homemade croûtons are best. Try oil, garlic and Parmesan cheese, see page 86.

1	garlic clove	1
½ tsp.	seasoned salt	2 mL
½ tsp.	black pepper	2 mL
3 drops	Worcestershire sauce	3 drops
1 drop	Tabasco	1 drop
1	lemon, juice of	1
1	egg yolk	1
1 tbsp.	wine vinegar	15 mL
2 tsp.	olive oil	10 mL
1-2 tsp.	anchovies (optional)	5-10 mL

CREAMY CAESAR SALAD DRESSING

2 tbsp.	roka cheese	30 mL
1 tbsp.	milk	15 mL
2 tbsp.	sour cream	30 mL

ROKA DRESSING

Crush garlic and seasoned salt together. Add pepper, Worcestershire and Tabasco. Mix well. Blend in lemon juice. Add egg yolk. Blend well. Blend in vinegar. Add oil and blend well. Blend in anchovies, if using. • To make a Creamy Caesar, add Roka Dressing. Blend all Roka ingredients in blender and add to basic Caesar Dressing.

ROMAINE SALAD

1	large head romaine lettuce	1
3 tbsp.	Parmesan cheese	45 mL
1 cup	cherry tomatoes, halved	250 mL
3	green onions, sliced	3
1	avocado	1
	seasoned croûtons, page 86	

CREAMY GARLIC DRESSING

1-2	garlic cloves, minced OR 1 tsp. (5 mL) garlic powder	1-2
1 tbsp.	lemon juice	15 mL
1	egg	1
½ tsp.	Worcestershire sauce	2 mL
⅓ cup	mayonnaise	75 mL

Combine all salad ingredients in a large salad bowl and toss gently. • Shake all ingredients for the dressing in a jar with a lid. • Pour dressing over salad just before serving and toss. • Serves 8.

STRAWBERRY SPINACH SALAD

WORCHESTERSHIRE DRESSING

Superb!

2	bunches fresh spinach, washed, torn	2
2 cups	strawberries, halved	500 mL
½ cup	sugar	125 mL
2 tbsp.	sesame seeds	30 mL
1 tbsp.	poppy seeds	15 mL
1½ tbsp.	minced onion	22 mL
¼ cup	Worcestershire sauce*	50 mL
¼ tsp.	paprika	1 mL
½ cup	vegetable oil	125 mL
¼ cup	cider vinegar	50 mL

Toss spinach and strawberries. • Prepare dressing by combining all ingredients. Mix well. Pour over salad and serve. • Serves 10-12. • * No, this amount is not a mistake. • See photograph on back cover.

Hint: Garlic cloves stored in a little olive oil will last forever.

10 oz.	pkg. fresh spinach, in bite-sized pieces (about 8 cups [2 L])	285 g	*HOT*
½ cup	julienne-cut or shredded carrots	125 mL	*"DRESSED"*
4	slices bacon	4	*SPINACH*
1½ cups	shelled medium shrimp, OR 12 oz. (340 g) frozen shrimp, thawed, drained	375 g	*SALAD*
1 cup	sliced mushrooms	250 mL	*BACON*
¼ cup	sugar	50 mL	*DRESSING*
⅓ cup	cider vinegar	75 mL	
2 tsp.	cornstarch	10 mL	*This can be a meal*
½ cup	water	125 mL	*in itself.*
¼-½ tsp.	freshly ground black pepper	1-2 mL	*Delicious!*

In a large bowl, combine spinach and carrots; refrigerate. • In a large skillet, fry bacon until crisp. Drain on paper towel, reserving 2 tbsp. (30 mL) drippings in skillet. Crumble bacon and set aside. • Sauté shrimp and mushrooms in drippings for about 1 minute or until shrimp becomes pink in color, stirring constantly. Add sugar, vinegar and bacon; blend well. Bring mixture to a boil. • Dissolve cornstarch in water; add to hot mixture, stirring constantly until slightly thickened. Add pepper and blend well. • Pour over spinach mixture; toss. • Serve immediately. • Serves 4-6. • See photograph page 16A.

1-2 tbsp.	fresh lime juice	15-30 mL	*CITRUS*
2 tbsp.	oil	30 mL	
1 tsp.	sesame seeds	5 mL	*SPINACH*
½ tsp.	finely grated lime peel	2 mL	
¼ tsp.	ground ginger salt and pepper	1 mL	*SALAD*
3 cups	torn, fresh spinach	750 mL	
1 cup	sliced fresh mushrooms	250 mL	
1	orange, peeled and sectioned	1	
½	small red onion, thinly sliced, in rings	½	

In a jar with a tight-fitting lid, combine lime juice, oil, sesame seeds, lime peel ginger, salt and pepper; shake well. Refrigerate until serving. • In a large serving bowl, combine spinach, mushrooms, orange sections and onion. • Toss with the dressing. • Serves 4.

APPLE MANDARIN SALAD

1	small apple, unpeeled, and thinly sliced	1
1 cup	fresh seedless green grapes	250 mL
10 oz.	can mandarin orange segments, drained OR 2 large oranges, peeled, sliced	284 mL
2 tbsp.	honey	30 mL
¼ tsp.	cinnamon	1 mL
2 tbsp.	lemon juice	30 mL
	lettuce	

Place apple slices in a bowl and add grapes and orange segments. ● Blend honey, cinnamon and lemon juice and pour over fruit. Cover and chill. ● At serving time, toss fruit until well coated and serve on lettuce. ● Serves 4-5.

MANDARIN ORANGE SALAD

½ cup	oil	125 mL
3 tbsp.	red wine vinegar	50 mL
1 tbsp.	lemon juice	15 mL
2 tsp.	sugar	10 mL
½ tsp.	salt	2 mL
½ tsp.	dry mustard	2 mL
1	garlic clove, crushed (optional)	1
½ cup	shelled sunflower seeds	125 mL
½ cup	slivered almonds	125 mL
1	head leaf lettuce	1
2	green onions, finely chopped	2
10 oz.	can mandarin oranges OR 2 large oranges, peeled, sliced	284 mL
1	ripe avocado, peeled, sliced (optional)	1

Combine first 7 ingredients in a jar. Shake to blend. ● Prepare remaining ingredients. ● Toss with dressing just before serving. ● Serves 4-6.

It isn't so hard to live on a small salary if you don't spend too much money trying to keep it a secret.

1-2 lbs.	fresh spinach, Romaine OR leaf lettuce	500 g- 1 kg	*KOREAN*
1 cup	bean sprouts OR fresh sprouts	250 mL	*SALAD*
2	hard-boiled eggs	2	
8	slices bacon, cooked crisp and crumbled mushroom slices	8	

2 tbsp.	Worcestershire sauce	30 mL	*KOREAN*
1 cup	oil	250 mL	*DRESSING*
1	medium onion, grated	1	
½ tsp.	salt	2 mL	
¾ cup	sugar	175 mL	
¼ cup	vinegar	50 mL	
⅓ cup	ketchup	75 mL	

Toss salad ingredients together. • Dressing ingredients may be mixed together in advance and refrigerated. • Add dressing to salad when ready to serve. • Serves 8-10.

2 tbsp.	sesame seeds	30 mL	*JAPANESE*
½ cup	slivered almonds	125 mL	*CHICKEN*
2 cups	cubed,cooked chicken	500 mL	*SALAD*
1	small head cabbage, shredded	1	
3 oz.	pkg. instant chicken noodles	85 g	
2	green onions, chopped	2	

1	pkg. noodle seasoning	1	*JAPANESE*
½ cup	salad oil	125 mL	*DRESSING*
3 tbsp.	vinegar	50 mL	
1 tsp.	sugar	5 mL	
½ tsp.	salt	2 mL	
½ tsp.	pepper	2 mL	

Put sesame seeds and almonds on a cookie sheet and toast for 5 minutes. • Put chicken in a large bowl and stir in shredded cabbage, noodles and onions. • In a small bowl, combine noodle seasoning, oil, vinegar, sugar, salt and pepper. Stir together and pour over cabbage and chicken mixture, stir well. • Marinate, covered, overnight in the refrigerator. • Before serving, sprinkle with sesame seeds and almonds and toss lightly.

CHICKEN RICE SALAD

1 tbsp.	lemon juice	15 mL
¾ cup	mayonnaise OR salad dressing	175 mL
2 cups	cooked long-grain rice	500 mL
2 cups	diced cooked chicken OR turkey	500 mL
1 cup	diced celery	250 mL
½ cup	sliced pimiento-stuffed green olives	125 mL
¼ cup	sliced almonds, toasted	50 mL
2 tbsp.	thinly sliced green onions and tops	30 mL
dash	pepper	dash
6	lettuce cups	6

Add lemon juice to mayonnaise and blend well. Combine with remaining ingredients, except lettuce cups; mix lightly and chill. • Serve in individual lettuce cups. • Garnish with additional sliced olives. • Serves 6.

ORIENTAL RICE SALAD

1 cups	raw, long-grain rice, cooked	250 mL
1 cup	sliced fresh mushrooms OR 10 oz. (284 mL) can sliced mushrooms	250 mL
½ cup	corn oil	125 mL
¼ cup	cider vinegar	50 mL
3 tbsp.	soy sauce	45 mL
½ tsp.	salt	2 mL
1 cup	thinly sliced celery	250 mL
4	green onions, thinly sliced	4
3 tbsp.	chopped green pepper	50 mL
½ cup	slivered almonds	125 mL
	lettuce	
	mandarin orange OR pineapple sections (optional)	
	pimiento (optional)	

Mix the cooked rice and mushrooms together in a bowl and set aside. • Combine oil, vinegar, soy sauce and salt in a jar; shake well to blend. • Pour oil mixture over the rice and mushrooms and toss lightly with a fork to mix well. Cover and chill at least 1 hour to season. • Just before serving, fold in celery, onions and green pepper. Sprinkle slivered almonds on top. • To serve, line salad bowl with lettuce and spoon salad mixture on top. Garnish with mandarin or pineapple sections and pimiento.

2 cups	thinly sliced cauliflower	500 mL
½ cup	chopped pitted ripe olives	125 mL
½ cup	finely chopped green pepper	125 mL
¼ cup	chopped pimiento	50 mL
3 tbsp.	chopped onion	45 mL

CAULIFLOWER SALAD

4½ tbsp.	salad oil	70 mL
1½ tbsp.	lemon juice	22 mL
1½ tbsp.	wine vinegar	22 mL
1 tsp.	salt	5 mL
¼ tsp.	sugar	1 mL
dash	pepper	dash

MARINADE DRESSING

In a medium-sized bowl, combine cauliflower, olives, green pepper, pimiento and onions. • Combine dresssing ingredients in a small bowl. Beat until well-blended. • Pour dressing over vegetable mixture. • Refrigerate until well-chilled.

1	large head iceberg lettuce	1
2	bunches broccoli	2
1	large green pepper, diced	1
1	small onion, chopped	1
1	bunch, parsley, chopped	1
2 cups	cooked shrimp	500 mL

BROCCOLI SEAFOOD SALAD

½ cup	lemon juice	125 mL
1½ cups	mayonnaise	375 mL
2 tbsp.	creamy horseradish	30 mL
1 tsp.	dillweed	5 mL
	salt and pepper to taste	

HORSERADISH DRESSING

Tear lettuce into bite-sized pieces and place in a large salad bowl. • Break broccoli into florets, and place, still wet, in a microwave dish. Cover and cook in microwave, on HIGH for 3 minutes. Drain and cool. • Add broccoli and the remaining salad ingredients to the lettuce. • Mix together all dressing ingredients. Chill for approximately 1 hour. Pour over salad ingredients and toss gently. • Refrigerate salad before serving.

MARINATED CARROT SALAD

4 qts.	water	4 L
2 tbsp.	sugar	30 mL
1 tbsp.	salt	15 mL
2 lbs.	carrots, thinly sliced	1 kg
1½ cups	tomato juice	375 mL
¾ cup	tarragon-flavored white wine vinegar OR white vinegar	175 mL
¾ cup	sugar	175 mL
1 tbsp.	prepared mustard	15 mL
1 tsp.	salt	5 mL
1 tsp.	freshly ground pepper	5 mL
2 tsp.	dried tarragon OR 2 tbsp. (30 mL) chopped fresh tarragon	10 mL
¾ cup	vegetable oil	175 mL
2	medium green bell peppers, sliced into thin strips	2
2	medium red onions, halved lengthwise, thinly sliced	2

In heavy 8-quart (8 L) stockpot, combine water, 2 tbsp. (30 mL) sugar and 1 tbsp. (15 mL) salt. Bring to a rolling boil; add carrots. Cook until crisp-tender, about 10 minutes. • Partially fill a large bowl with ice cubes and water. Drain carrots; place in iced water, stir until cooled. Drain; set aside. • In a 2-quart (2 L) bowl, whisk tomato juice, vinegar, ¾ cup (175 mL) sugar, mustard, 1 tsp. (5 mL) salt, pepper and tarragon until combined. Add oil in a slow, steady stream, whisking until combined. • Toss drained carrots, bell peppers and onions in a 9″ x 13″ (4 L) baking dish. Pour dressing over vegetables. Toss gently to coat with dressing. • Cover and refrigerate 24 hours or up to 3 days before serving. • Serves 8-10.

CARROT AND RAISIN SALAD

4	large carrots, shredded	4
½ cup	pitted dates, halved	125 mL
½ cup	raisins	125 mL
½ cup	chopped walnuts	125 mL
1 cup	plain yogurt	250 mL
¼ tsp.	dried mint	1 mL
1	lime, juice and grated rind of	1
	salt and pepper to taste	

In a serving bowl, combine carrots, dates, raisins and yogurt . • In a small mixing bowl, blend the remaining ingredients. Fold into the carrot mixture. • Refrigerate, covered, until serving. • Serves 4. • **Variation:** Peeled, seeded, sliced oranges are a wonderful addition.

½ cup	sour cream	125 mL
2 tbsp.	sugar	30 mL
2 tbsp.	white vinegar	30 mL
½ tsp.	salt	2 mL
¼ tsp.	pepper	1 mL
2 cups	thinly sliced unpeeled cucumbers	500 mL
1	small onion, thinly sliced and in rings	1

CUCUMBER SALAD

Stir together sour cream, sugar, vinegar, salt and pepper. ● Place cucumber and onion slices in a serving bowl. ● Pour sour cream mixture over vegetables. Toss to coat. ● If desired, cover and chill. ● Serves 6.

1½ cups	sliced mushrooms	375 mL
3 tbsp.	chopped green onions	45 mL
5	large tomatoes, sliced	5
1 tsp.	curry powder OR ½ tsp. (2 mL) dry mustard	5 mL
1 tsp.	sugar	5 mL
½ cup	salad oil	125 mL
¼ cup	vinegar	50 mL
1	garlic clove, crushed	1
1 tbsp.	chopped parsley OR chives	15 mL
	salt and pepper	
	lettuce	

MARINATED TOMATOES

Prepare mushrooms, onions, and tomatoes. ● Combine all remaining ingredients, except lettuce, in a jar, shake well. ● Pour dressing over vegetables and marinate several hours. ● Before serving, arrange vegetables on a bed of lettuce. ● **Variation:** Slice a Spanish onion into rings. Sprinkle with salt and cover with half vinegar and half water. ● Drain after 1 hour and add to tomatoes.

2¼ cups	white sugar	550 mL
1½ cups	vinegar	375 mL
1½ cups	water	375 mL
2 tbsp.	salt	30 mL
6	large onions, sliced thinly	6
1½ cups	mayonnaise	375 mL
1 tbsp.	celery seed	15 mL
	salt and pepper	

MARINATED ONION SLICES

Great for barbecues and picnics.

Combine sugar, vinegar, water and salt and bring to a boil. Pour this solution over sliced onions. Cover and let stand for 3 hours. ● Drain off liquid. ● To drained onions add mayonnaise and celery seed. Leave, covered, in the refrigerator for 2 hours. ● More mayonnaise may be added before serving. ● **Variation:** Add slivered green pepper, pimiento or carrots for a touch of color.

SAUERKRAUT SALAD SUPREME

1 cup	white sugar	250 mL
1 cup	white vinegar	250 mL
1 cup	diced celery	250 mL
1 cup	sliced onions (rings)	250 mL
1 cup	diced green peppers	250 mL
½ cup	diced red peppers	125 mL
1 cup	grated carrots	250 mL
2 cups	sauerkraut, regular or red wine, drained, packed	500 mL
½ tsp.	celery seed (optional)	2 mL
½ cup	sliced pimiento (optional)	125 mL

Boil sugar and vinegar for 5 minutes in a large pot. Remove from heat. ● Add all the other ingredients and mix thoroughly. ● Let stand, covered, in refrigerator for 24 hours. ● Drain off all liquids before serving. ● You may add more sauerkraut. ● This salad is absolutely delicious and will keep in a covered container for at least 3 weeks.

HOT COLESLAW

5 cups	chopped cabbage	1.25 L
1 tbsp.	butter	15 mL
¾ tsp.	sugar	3 mL
1½ tsp.	vinegar	7 mL
	salt and pepper to taste	
⅓ cup	sour cream	75 mL

Cabbage should look chopped more than shredded. ● Place butter in frying pan, and add cabbage, cover and let it cook on low heat, stirring occasionally, until cabbage is soft but not thoroughly cooked. ● In a small dish, mix remaining ingredients. ● Pour over cabbage and mix well. ● Makes 2-4 servings.

Hint: To prevent cooking utensils from sliding around in a drawer; place a tea towel on the bottom of the drawer and fasten down with thumb tacks. Place cooking utensils face down on towel.

6	medium potatoes	6	
6	slices bacon	6	
⅓ cup	bacon fat	75 mL	
2 tbsp.	flour	30 mL	
2 tsp.	sugar	10 mL	
	salt and pepper		
½ tsp.	celery seed	2 mL	
¾ cup	water	175 mL	
½ cup	vinegar	125 mL	
	parsley for garnish		

AUNT LOUISE'S HOT POTATO SALAD

Boil the potatoes in skins, until tender. Peel and slice thinly into a bowl. • Fry bacon until crisp. • Heat bacon fat in skillet until yellow. • Combine flour, sugar and seasonings. • Stir into hot fat and gradually add water and vinegar. Bring to a boil for 1 minute and pour over the potatoes. Add crisp bacon, broken into pieces. • Save some for garnish. Let stand until ready to serve. • Heat salad over hot water before serving. Garnish with bacon bits and parsley.

---

3 oz.	pkg. lemon gelatin	85 g
1 cup	boiling water	250 mL
¼ tsp.	salt	1 mL
1 tsp.	vinegar	5 mL
1 cup	Clamato juice	250 mL
1 tsp.	horseradish	5 mL
½ cup	chopped celery	125 mL
3	green onions, chopped	3
1 cup	cooked salad shrimp	250 mL

TOMATO ASPIC

Mix gelatin and water, stirring until gelatin dissolves. Add salt, vinegar and Clamato juice. • Refrigerate and, when mixture is beginning to set, add all other ingredients. • Refrigerate until salad is set and serve. • **Variation:** Add ½ cup (125 mL) of stuffed green olives, whole or chopped.

---

1 tbsp.	gelatin (7 g pkg.)	15 mL
¼ cup	cold water	50 mL
½ tsp.	salt	2 mL
¼ cup	sugar	50 mL
¼ cup	vinegar	50 mL
14 oz.	can diced beets	398 mL
¾ cup	finely chopped celery	175 mL
1 tbsp.	minced onion	15 mL
1 tbsp.	horseradish	15 mL

BEET RELISH JELLIED SALAD

Sprinkle gelatin over cold water in a saucepan. Place over very low heat and stir constantly until gelatin is dissolved. Remove from heat. • Stir in salt, sugar and vinegar. • Drain beets, reserving liquid. Pour liquid into seasoned gelatin and chill to consistency of unbeaten egg white. Stir in beets, celery, onion and horseradish. • Turn into a 3-cup (750 mL) mold. • Chill. • Serves 6-8. • This is excellent with roast beef.

COTTAGE CHEESE CUCUMBER MOLD

3 oz.	pkg. lemon gelatin	85 g
1 cup	hot water	250 mL
1 tbsp.	vinegar	15 mL
1 tsp.	salt	5 mL
1 cup	mayonnaise	250 mL
2 cups	cottage cheese	500 mL
½ cup	finely chopped celery	125 mL
1	onion, finely chopped drained	1
1	cucumber, coarsely chopped and drained OR ¾ English cucumber, unpeeled	1
½ cup	chopped almonds	125 mL

Dissolve gelatin in hot water with vinegar and salt. Chill until mixture is consistency of raw egg whites. • Mix in mayonnaise and cottage cheese. Stir in vegetables and nuts. • Pour into a mold and chill until set. • This goes well with salmon or any fish dish.

CARROT AND PINEAPPLE MOLD

3 oz.	pkg. orange, lemon OR pineapple gelatin	85 g
1 cup	boiling water	250 mL
1 cup	mixed orange and pineapple juice	250 mL
1 cup	drained crushed pineapple	250 mL
1 cup	grated raw carrot	250 mL
1 tbsp.	minced green pepper	15 mL
¼ cup	finely chopped almonds	50 mL
½ cup	whipping cream, whipped	125 mL
¼ cup	mayonnaise	50 mL

Dissolve gelatin in boiling water. Add fruit juice and chill until slightly thickened. • Fold in remaining ingredients and pour into individual molds or a 1½ quart (1.5 L) mold. • Serves 6. • **Variation:** 1 cup (250 mL) each chopped apples and celery may also be added to this salad, in which case, you will need a 2-quart (2 L) mold.

3 oz.	orange-flavored gelatin	85 g
1 cup	boiling water	250 mL
¾ cup	frozen orange juice (undiluted)	175 mL
10 oz.	can orange sections, drained	284 mL
14 oz.	can pineapple bits, drained	398 mL
	mayonnaise for garnish	

TRIPLE ORANGE MOLD

Dissolve gelatin in boiling water and stir in orange juice. Chill until syrupy. • Add orange sections and pineapple bits to the thickened gelatin. Pour into a 1½-quart (1.5 L) mold. • Chill. • Garnish with a spoonful of mayonnaise to serve. • Serves 6-8.

---

4 oz.	lime-flavored gelatin	115 g
1¼ cups	boiling water	300 mL
1½ tbsp.	vinegar	22 mL
½ cup	miniature marshmallows	125 mL
2½ tbsp.	smooth mayonnaise	37 mL
2½ cups	grated green cabbage	625 mL
19 oz.	can crushed pineapple, drained (discard juice)	540 mL
	red maraschino cherries for garnish	

GRANDMA TUPPER'S GREEN JELLIED SALAD

Dissolve gelatin in hot water and stir thoroughly. • Add the rest of ingredients and stir until marshmallows are dissolved. Let cool. • When beginning to set add mayonnaise, cabbage and pineapple. Pour into a 4-cup (1 L) mold and put in refrigerator until completely set. • Unmold on lettuce leaves to serve. • At Christmas garnish with red maraschino cherries.

---

8 oz.	cream cheese, softened	250 g
2 tbsp.	mayonnaise	30 mL
14 oz.	can pineapple chunks, drained	398 mL
2 cups	whole cranberry sauce	500 mL
1 tbsp.	lemon juice	15 mL
2 tbsp.	sugar	30 mL
½ cup	chopped walnuts OR pecans	125 mL
1 cup	whipping cream, whipped	250 mL

PINK FROSTY SALAD

Good Christmas Salad.

Combine cream cheese and mayonnaise. Combine with remaining ingredients and place in a greased mold. • Set in freezer. • Remove 2 hours before serving and unmold. • Freeze until serving time. • Delicious with turkey.

MAYONNAISE

1	egg	1
½ tsp.	prepared mustard	2 mL
¾ tsp.	salt	3 mL
½ tsp.	sugar	2 mL
dash	pepper	dash
3 tbsp.	lemon juice OR vinegar OR half of each	50 mL
dash	cayenne	dash
⅓ cup	oil	75 mL
⅔ cup	oil	150 mL

Put first 8 ingredients in a blender and whirl briefly. • Add remaining oil in a slow, steady stream, blending until all oil is added and mixture is thick and smooth. • This may be used as a dip for raw vegetables or in anything that calls for mayonnaise. • **Variation:** To make Aioli, the garlic sauce of Provence, omit sugar, add 3-4 garlic cloves to blender and substitute Dijon for prepared mustard. Serve with cooked fish or a vegetable platter.

SOUR CREAM DRESSING

1 cup	sour cream	250 mL
1 tbsp.	lemon juice	15 mL
1 tbsp.	apple cider vinegar	15 mL
1 tbsp.	sugar	15 mL
½ tsp.	prepared mustard	2 mL
½ tsp.	salt	2 mL

Whip sour cream until fluffy. Add remaining ingredients and chill. • Makes 2 cups (500 mL).

SEASONED CROÛTONS

1	large loaf French bread	1
¼ tsp.	dried thyme leaves	1 mL
¼ tsp.	oregano	1 mL
1 tbsp.	dried parsley	15 mL
½ cup	vegetable oil	125 mL
¼ tsp.	salt	1 mL
⅛ tsp.	garlic powder	0.5 mL
⅛ tsp.	pepper	0.5 mL
¼ cup	grated Parmesan	50 mL

Remove crust from bread and cut bread into cubes. • Grind thyme, oregano, and parsley in mortar and pestle. • Heat the oil in a small pot, add all the seasonings except the Parmesan cheese. • Place bread cubes in a large bowl and pour the seasoned oil evenly over the bread cubes. Toss quickly, to coat evenly. Sprinkle Parmesan cheese over bread cubes and toss lightly. • Place cubes on a cookie sheet and bake at 400°F (200°C) for 12-15 minutes. Stir once or twice so cubes brown evenly. • These can be stored in the refrigerator for 1-2 weeks or can also be frozen. Just reheat in oven at 250°F (120°C) when needed.

VEGETABLES

6	medium carrots	6
3	medium zucchini, cut diagonally in ¼" (1 cm) slices	3
1 cup	cherry tomatoes	250 mL
1 cup	herb-seasoned croûtons * (see page 86)	250 mL
2 tbsp.	cornstarch	30 mL
1½ cups	milk	375 mL
¼ cup	butter	50 mL
1 tsp.	dried leaf basil	5 mL
1 tsp.	salt	5 mL
¼ tsp.	pepper	1 mL

HERBED FRESH-VEGETABLE BAKE

Gluten-Free

Preheat oven to 375°F (190°C). ● Butter a shallow 1½-2-quart (1.5-2 L) casserole or 8 " (2 L) square baking dish. ● Cut carrots into julienne strips by cutting first into 2" (5 cm) lengths, then slicing lengthwise. Stack slices and cut into ¼" (1 cm) strips. ● Drop carrots into boiling salted water; cook 10 minutes or until crisp-tender. Drain well. ● Place carrots, zucchini and cherry tomatoes in buttered casserole. Sprinkle with croûtons.* ● In a small saucepan, blend cornstarch and milk; bring to a boil. Cook, stirring constantly, until thickened and smooth. Whisk in butter until melted. Add basil, salt and pepper. Pour over vegetables in casserole. ● Bake, covered, for 20-30 minutes or until bubbly and heated through. ● Serves 6. ● **Variation:** Substitute other vegetables in season in this colorful casserole. ● * For gluten-free diets, substitute cornflake crumbs for croûtons.

Hint: When your summer gardens produce more tomatoes than you can use, simply wash them, put them in plastic bags and put them in the freezer. During the winter the tomatoes can be added to soups, stews and sauces or can be cooked as a side dish for dinners.

STIR-FRIED VEGETABLES

Gluten-Free

Lily and Nicky Chan
Lily Restaurant, Calgary

6 oz.	broccoli	170 g
3 oz.	mushrooms	85 g
½	carrot	½
3	water chestnuts	3
1	small zucchini	1
1 tbsp.	oil	15 mL
2 oz.	baby corn	60 g
2	slices ginger	2
3-4	slices of garlic	3-4

SAUCE

⅔ cup	chicken broth	150 mL
1 tsp.	oyster sauce *	5 mL
¼ tsp.	sugar	1 mL
2 tsp.	cornstarch	10 mL
1 tbsp.	water	15 mL

Cut broccoli into small pieces, slice mushrooms, carrots, water chestnuts and zucchini. Fill a large saucepan with water and bring to a boil. • Add all vegetables and boil for 1 minute. Drain well. • Place a wok or frying pan over high heat. Add oil. Add ginger and garlic; stir until golden brown. Add all of the vegetables and stir-fry. • Mix in chicken broth, oyster sauce, and sugar. Cook for 3 minutes. Mix cornstarch with water, add to stir-fry and cook until thick.
• Serve. • **Variations:** Other vegetables may be added or substituted, try cauliflower, green beans and onion. • * Use 1 tsp. (5 mL) of soy sauce and/or sherry if oyster sauce is not available.

CAULIFLOWER TOMATO MEDLEY

*Gluten-Free **

1	medium cauliflower	1
6	slices side bacon, cut in ½" (1.3 cm) pieces	6
1½ cups	soft bread crumbs *	375 mL
3 tbsp.	bacon drippings	45 mL
3	tomatoes, sliced	3
2 tbsp.	chopped green onion	30 mL
¼ tsp.	salt	1 mL
⅛ tsp.	pepper	0.5 mL
¼ tsp.	dill seed	1 mL
¾ cup	grated Cheddar cheese slivered red and green pepper, (optional)	175 mL

Separate cauliflower into florets, boil until just tender and drain. • Cook bacon until crisp. Toss crumbs with bacon and drippings. • Arrange tomatoes in a greased 6-cup (1.5 L) baking dish. Sprinkle with onion, salt, pepper and dill and add cauliflower. Top with crumb mixture. • Cover and bake for 10 minutes at 400°F (200°C). Uncover and continue baking for 10 minutes more. Sprinkle cheese over; bake until cheese melts and is slightly browned. Goes nicely with roasted meat or fish. • Serves 6. • * For gluten-free diets, substitute crushed cornflakes for bread crumbs.

1	medium cauliflower	1
½ cup	mayonnaise	125 mL
⅔ cup	shredded mozzarella cheese	150 mL
½ tsp.	dry mustard	2 mL

EASIEST CAULIFLOWER CASSEROLE

Do not core cauliflower. Just cut off bottom of core. Put in a dish to fit the cauliflower. Cover loosely with plastic wrap. Microwave on HIGH for 10 minutes, until cauliflower is tender-crisp. • Mix together remaining ingredients and spoon over cauliflower. • Microwave, uncovered for 4 or 5 minutes. Rotate occasionally until cheese is melted down into the cauliflower. • Serves 6-8. • **Variation:** Substitute sharp Cheddar cheese for the mozzarella.

1½ lbs.	fresh broccoli OR 2 x 10 oz. (283 g) frozen	75 g
¼ tsp.	dried leaf tarragon	1 mL
¼ cup	water	50 mL
¼ cup	butter	50 mL
¼ cup	dry white wine	50 mL
1 tsp.	Dijon mustard	5 mL
2	green onions, minced	2
¼ cup	sliced almonds	50 mL

BROCCOLI BAKED WITH MUSTARD BUTTER

Butter a shallow 1-quart (1 L) casserole or 8″ x 8″ (2 L) baking dish. If using fresh broccoli, cut off and discard tough stalk ends. Peel remaining stalks. Cook broccoli in boiling water 5 minutes; drain. Arrange thawed or cooked broccoli in the buttered casserole. Sprinkle with tarragon and add water. • In a small skillet or saucepan, bring butter, wine, mustard and green onions to a boil. Cook, stirring constantly, until liquid is reduced to about 2 tbsp. (30 mL). • Drizzle butter mixture over broccoli. • Bake, covered, 30 minutes at 325°F (160°C) or until broccoli is tender. • Garnish with almonds. • Serves 4-5.

2 lbs.	fresh broccoli, cut into spears	1 kg
2 tbsp.	salad oil	30 mL
2 tbsp.	vinegar	30 mL
2 tbsp.	soy sauce	30 mL
8 tsp.	sugar	40 mL
2 tbsp.	toasted sesame seeds	30 mL

SESAME BROCCOLI

Pour boiling water over broccoli and let stand 7 minutes. Drain. • Place broccoli in a 1-quart (1 L) casserole dish. Mix together remaining ingredients and heat on medium until heated through. Pour over broccoli. • Bake at 325°F (160°C) for 20-30 minutes. • Serves 4-5.

CABBAGE WITH GREEN PEPPER SAUCE

1	large green cabbage	1
1 cup	water	250 mL
½ tsp.	salt	2 mL
½ cup	chopped green pepper	125 mL
3 tbsp.	butter	45 mL
2 tbsp.	flour	30 mL
½ tsp.	onion salt	2 mL
⅛ tsp.	pepper	0.5 mL
1 cup	milk	250 mL
¼ cup	grated Parmesan cheese	50 mL

Cut cabbage into 12 wedges. • Heat water and salt to boiling in 10″ (2.5 cm) skillet (NOT cast iron) and add cabbage wedges. Heat to boiling and then reduce heat. Cover and simmer until cabbage is tender-crisp, 10-15 minutes. • In another skillet, cook and stir green pepper in butter over medium heat until pepper is tender-crisp, about 1 minute. • Blend in flour, onion, salt and pepper. Cook and stir over low heat until mixture is smooth and bubbly. Remove from heat, stir in milk. Heat to boiling, stirring constantly for 1 minute. • Place hot cabbage in serving dish. Pour sauce over; sprinkle with cheese. • Serves 8-10.

RED CABBAGE

1	medium red cabbage	1
1 cup	water	250 mL
1 cup	vinegar	250 mL
½ tsp.	salt	2 mL
1 cup	grape jelly	250 mL
½ cup	sugar	125 mL

Slice red cabbage and cook 1 hour in water, vinegar and salt mixture. • Add jelly and sugar and simmer for 1 hour. • Serve with roast goose, pork or turkey.

SPINACH PATTIES

Ukranian.

3 cups	cooked, fresh spinach (2 lbs. [1 kg])	750 mL
2 tbsp.	grated onion	30 mL
2 tbsp.	butter	30 mL
1 cup	soft bread crumbs	250 mL
1	egg, beaten	1
1 tbsp.	cream	15 mL
	salt and pepper	
	beaten egg	
	fine bread crumbs	
	butter	

Drain cooked spinach and chop finely. Cook onion in butter until transparent. Combine spinach, onion, soft bread crumbs, egg, cream, salt and pepper to taste. Mix well. • Let stand for 10 minutes to allow crumbs to swell. • Make into patties, roll in beaten egg then crumbs and fry in butter until lightly browned.

2 tbsp.	butter	30 mL
2 tbsp.	flour	30 mL
dash	EACH salt, pepper, and paprika	dash
1 cup	milk	250 mL
19 oz.	can cream corn	540 mL
1 tbsp.	minced green pepper	15 mL
1 tsp.	finely chopped onion	5 mL
½ tsp.	dry mustard	5 mL
dash	Tabasco	dash
½ tsp.	Worcestershire sauce	2 mL
3 oz.	uncooked extra fine noodles, cooked	85 g

BAKED CORN

To make a cream sauce, melt butter in a saucepan. Stir in flour, salt, pepper and paprika. Gradually stir in milk. Cook until smooth and thickened. • Combine corn, green peppers, onion, mustard, Tabasco and Worcestershire, and add to cream sauce. Mix well, then add drained noodles and mix again. • Pour into a 2-quart (2 L) casserole, and bake at 325-350°F (160-180°C) for about 40 minutes. • Do not stir after you take casserole out of the oven as it gets too runny. • Serves 4-5. • Great with roast beef or ham.

6 oz.	pkg. corn chips	170 g
1 cup	grated Cheddar cheese	250 mL
¼ cup	sliced green onion	50 mL
¾ cup	chopped celery	175 mL
2	eggs, lightly beaten	2
½ cup	milk	125 mL
½ tsp.	crumbled oregano	2 mL
¼ tsp.	salt	1 mL
12 oz.	can creamed corn	341 mL
12 oz.	can niblet corn	341 mL

CORN CHIP CASSEROLE

Gluten-Free

Mix the corn chips with the grated Cheddar cheese, and set aside. • Sauté green onion and celery in a frying pan. • Mix together the eggs, milk, oregano, salt and corn. Stir in the onion and celery. • In a 1½-quart (1.5 L) casserole, layer corn and corn chip mixtures. • Alternate layers, ending with corn chips on top. • Bake for 40 minutes at 325°F (160°C).

Hint: Place a heel of bread on top of cabbage before putting the lid on the pot and cooking it, there will be no odor. The bread has no effect on the cabbage and should be removed after cooking. Also good for broccoli and Brussels sprouts.

CORN CUSTARD

Gluten-Free

10 oz.	pkg. frozen corn	283 g
2 cups	milk	500 mL
3	eggs	3
¼ cup	melted butter	50 mL
2 tbsp.	cornstarch	30 mL
1½ tsp.	sugar	7 mL
½ tsp.	salt	2 mL

Put all ingredients, except for ½ cup (125 mL) corn, in a blender. Cover and process until smooth. • Place the remaining corn on the bottom of a greased 2-quart (2 L) dish. • Pour blended mixture over corn and place the pan in a larger pan with hot water to reach halfway up side of baking dish. • Bake for 1 hour at 350°F (180°C) or until knife inserted in center comes out clean.

ZUCCHINI CHEESE BAKE

2	medium zucchini, cut in ¼" (1 cm) slices	2
4	slices bacon, chopped	4
2	large onions, cut into ¼" (1 cm) slices	2
¼ cup	crushed herb-seasoned stuffing mix	50 mL
1 tbsp.	grated Parmsean cheese	15 mL
¼ tsp.	oregano	1 mL
½ cup	shredded Cheddar cheese	125 mL
1 tbsp.	butter OR margarine	15 mL

In a large saucepan, heat enough water to just cover zucchini. Bring to a boil and add the zucchini. Cook for only 2 minutes and drain. • In a large skillet over medium heat, cook bacon until crisp. Set bacon aside and add the onion to the bacon drippings in the skillet. Cook for 5 minutes and set aside. • In a small bowl, combine stuffing mix, Parmesan cheese and oregano. • To assemble casserole, sprinkle 1 tbsp. (15 mL) stuffing mixture on the bottom of a greased 8" x 8" (2 L) pan. • Arrange half of the zucchini slices on top of the stuffing mixture. • Sprinkle with another tablespoon of the stuffing. and top with half of the onion. • Repeat layers, ending with the stuffing mixture. • Sprinkle with Cheddar cheese, then the bacon. • Dot with butter. • Cover and bake at 350°F (180°C) for 30 minutes or until the zucchini is tender. • Serves 4.

Hint: For mashed potatoes, cook the potatoes with their skins on, then peel them and mash with a little hot milk. The texture is no different, but the vitamin value is increased.

3 lbs.	parsnips	1.5 kgs	
½ cup	butter	125 mL	*PARSNIP*
½ cup	whipping cream	125 mL	*ROAST*
6 oz.	Cheddar cheese, grated	170 g	
	salt and pepper		
	paprika		

Slice parsnips and cook in salted water until tender. • Mash well. • Beat in the butter, cream and ⅔ of the cheese. Season well with salt and pepper. • Transfer to a greased casserole dish. • Cover with remaining cheese and sprinkle with paprika. • Brown in 425°F (220°C) oven for 10-15 minutes. • Extremely good with turkey or as a vegetarian dish served with baked potatoes and a crisp green salad.

2-3	medium turnips	2-3	*TURNIP*
1 cup	applesauce	250 mL	*CASSEROLE*
6 tbsp.	butter	90 mL	
4 tsp.	sugar	20 mL	
1 tbsp.	salt	15 mL	
¼ tsp.	pepper	1 mL	*Great with turkey.*
1¾ cups	bread crumbs	425 mL	
2 tbsp.	melted butter	30 mL	

Cook and mash the turnip. • Combine with applesauce, butter, sugar, salt, pepper and 1 cup (250 mL) bread crumbs. Pour into a 2-quart (2 L) greased casserole dish. • Mix together ¾ cup (175 mL) bread crumbs and the melted butter. Pat crumbs on top of the turnip mixture. • Bake, uncovered, at 350°F (180°C) for 30-60 minutes.

6	medium tomatoes (2 lbs. [1 kg])	6	*BAKED*
¼ cup	minced green pepper	50 mL	*STUFFED*
¼ cup	grated Parmesan cheese	50 mL	*TOMATOES*
⅓ cup	croutons	75 mL	
1 tsp.	salt	5 mL	
	parsley sprigs OR crisp bacon, crumbled for garnish		

Wash tomatoes and remove stem ends. Remove pulp from each tomato, leaving a ½" (1.3 cm) wall. Chop pulp to measure ⅓ cup (75 mL). • Stir together tomato pulp and remaining ingredients except garnish. • Fill tomatoes with tomato-cheese mixture. • Place filled tomatoes in an ungreased 12" x 8" (3 L) baking dish. • Bake at 350°F (180°C) for 20-25 minutes or until tomatoes are heated through. • Garnish with parsley or bacon.

93

SCALLOPED TOMATOES

19 oz.	can tomatoes	540 mL
2 tbsp.	chopped onion	30 mL
1 tbsp.	chopped green pepper	15 mL
3 tbsp.	chopped celery	45 mL
3 tbsp.	flour	45 mL
4 tsp.	sugar	20 mL
1 tsp.	salt	5 mL
¼ tsp.	pepper	1 mL
½ cup	soft bread crumbs	125 mL
2 tbsp.	butter	30 mL

Combine all vegetables in a mixing bowl. • Mix together flour, sugar, salt and pepper and stir into vegetables. • Turn into a greased 1½-quart (1.5 L) baking dish. Top with bread crumbs and dot with butter. • Bake at 350°F (180°C) for 45 minutes. • Serves 4-6.

AUNT FANNY'S BAKED SQUASH

*Gluten-Free **

3 lbs.	yellow summer squash**	1.5 kg
½ cup	chopped onion	125 mL
2	eggs	2
½ cup	butter	125 mL
1 tbsp.	sugar	15 mL
	salt and pepper	
½ cup	cracker OR bread crumbs*	125 mL

Wash, peel if necessary, and cut up squash. Boil until tender, drain thoroughly, and mash. • Add all ingredients, except ¼ cup (50 mL) of butter and crumbs, to squash. • Melt remaining butter. Pour squash mixture in baking dish, then spread melted butter over top and sprinkle with cracker OR bread crumbs. • Bake at 375°F (190°C) for approximately 1 hour or until brown on top. • * For gluten-free diets, substitute crushed cornflakes for crumbs. • ** Yams may be used in place of squash. Bake in microwave until tender, peel and mash as squash.

SWEET POTATO BALLS

Gluten-Free

¼ cup	butter	50 mL
¾ cup	brown sugar	175 mL
2 tbsp.	orange juice	30 mL
1 tsp.	grated orange rind	5 mL
¼ tsp.	salt	1 mL
3 cups	baked and mashed sweet potato	750 mL
½ cup	crushed cornflakes	125 mL

Add butter, sugar, orange juice, orange rind and salt to sweet potatoes. • Using about ¼ cup (50 mL) potato each, form into balls and roll in cornflakes to cover. • Place balls in a buttered baking dish and bake for 20 minutes at 350°F (180°C). • **Variation:** Potato may be shaped around a large marshmallow for added interest. Serve with turkey, chicken or ham.

6	medium carrots, sliced	6
¼ tsp.	ginger	1 mL
1 tsp.	brown sugar	5 mL
1 tbsp.	butter	15 mL

GINGER CARROTS

In a microwave dish, cover and cook sliced carrots on HIGH for 3 to 4 minutes, stir, then cook 2 more minutes. • Mix together ginger, brown sugar and butter. • Stir ginger mixture into carrots, cover, and cook on HIGH for another 1-2 minutes. • Serves 4. • These are unusual and very good.

¼ cup	chopped onion	50 mL
¼ cup	butter OR margarine	50 mL
¼ cup	flour	50 mL
¼ tsp.	dry mustard	1 mL
1 tsp.	salt	5 mL
⅛ tsp.	pepper	0.5 mL
2 cups	milk	500 mL
12	medium carrots, sliced and cooked	12
2 cups	grated sharp Cheddar cheese	500 mL
1 cup	buttered bread crumbs*	250 mL

SCALLOPED CHEESE AND CARROTS

Gluten-Free

Sauté onions in butter, stir in flour, mustard, salt and pepper. Cook over medium heat for 1 minute stirring constantly. • Remove from heat and gradually add milk. • Return to heat, bring to a boil and stir for 1 minute. • Alternate carrots, cheese and sauce, and top with bread crumbs. Bake at 350°F (180°C) for 35-45 minutes. • Serves 6-8. • *For a gluten-free variation, substitute crushed cornflakes for bread crumbs.

3	kohlrabi	3
3	carrots	3
3	potatoes	3
3 tbsp.	peanut oil	45 mL
½ cup	fresh peas	125 mL
4 tbsp.	water (or a little more) salt and pepper to taste	60 mL

WHAT TO DO WITH KOHLRABI

Peel kohlrabi and cut into long slices French-fry style. • Cut carrots and potatoes the same way. • Heat oil over intense heat and stir-fry vegetables. During cooking, the ingredients must be kept in constant motion, stirring vigorously. • Pour in water and cover. Shake pan and turn heat to simmer. Cook 10 minutes or until done. • Serve with a roast, veal, steak or cold cuts.

CREAMED BEETS

3 cups	mashed beets	750 mL
¼ tsp.	salt	1 mL
⅛ tsp.	pepper	0.5 mL
¼ cup	vinegar	50 mL
2 tbsp.	butter	30 mL
½ cup	cream	125 mL

Cook beets until fork tender. • Mash and add salt, pepper, vinegar and butter. Allow to sit for ½ hour. • Add cream, stirring quickly. • Bake at 350°F (180°C) for ½ hour. • Serves 4.

SAUCE FOR HARVARD BEETS

1 tbsp.	butter	15 mL
2 tbsp.	vinegar	30 mL
½ cup	water	125 mL
1 tsp.	cornstarch	5 mL
1 tbsp.	cold water	15 mL

Combine butter, vinegar and water and bring to a boil. Add cornstarch mixed with cold water and cook until clear.

"CAN-CAN" BAKED BEANS

6 cups	canned baked beans	1.5 L
1 cup	seasoned tomato sauce	250 mL
1 cup	chopped onion	250 mL
¼ cup	brown sugar	50 mL
½ cup	ketchup	125 mL
2 tbsp.	prepared mustard	30 mL
1 tsp.	salt	5 mL
1 tbsp.	molasses	15 mL
6 slices	bacon, cooked and crumbled	6

In a 2-quart (2 L) casserole, combine beans, tomato sauce, onion, brown sugar, ketchup, seasonings and bacon. • Bake, uncovered, at 300°F (150°C) for 3½-4 hours. Towards the end of the cooking time, stir carefully with a fork and bring bacon to the top. • Serves 6-18, depending on the bean-lovers at your table.

Hint: When cooking vegetables, cover those that grow underground, such as onions, potatoes, etc. and leave uncovered all vegetables that grow above the ground.

6	large potatoes, in ¼" (1 cm) slices	6
2 tbsp.	butter OR margarine	30 mL
½ tsp.	garlic powder OR more to taste	2 mL
1 tsp.	chili powder OR more	5 mL
1 tsp.	salt	5 mL
1 tsp.	pepper	5 mL
2	onions, sliced, rings	2
4 oz.	grated Parmesan	115 g
½ lb.	grated Cheddar	250 g

PIZZA POTATOES

Zesty!

Place potatoes in single layers on greased cookie sheets; put a bit of butter on each slice. • Sprinkle with garlic powder, chili powder, salt and pepper. • Lay an onion ring on each slice and sprinkle with cheeses. • Bake for 30-40 minutes, until soft, in a 400°F (200°C) oven. • Serves 6-8.

½ cup	all-purpose flour	125 mL
½ tsp.	salt	2 mL
¼ tsp.	freshly grated nutmeg	1 mL
¼ tsp.	black pepper	1 mL
½ cup	water	125 mL
4 tbsp.	unsalted butter	60 mL
2	large eggs	2
1½ cups	Potato Duchesse (fine potato purée)	375 mL

POTATOES DAUPHINE

Combine flour, salt, nutmeg and pepper. • Bring water and butter to a boil, until butter is melted and is foamy. Add flour mixture all at once and mix until dough forms a ball. • Take off stove and let cool for 5 minutes. • Beat in eggs, 1 at a time, until dough is right consistency. • If too dry, add 1 tbsp. (15 mL) of additional beaten egg at a time, until you have a soft dough. • Add Potato Duchesse. Mix well. • Drop the dough by tablespoonsful (15 mL) into very hot fat, 375°F (190°C). Cook 5 minutes, until nicely browned. • Serve hot.

4 cups	thinly sliced potatoes	1L
⅔ cup	minced onion	150 mL
2 tbsp.	flour	30 mL
1 tsp.	salt	5 mL
⅛ tsp.	pepper	0.5 mL
2 tbsp.	butter OR margarine	30 mL
1½ cups	scalded milk paprika	375 mL

OLD-TIME SCALLOPED POTATOES

Layer ½ the potatoes in a greased 2-quart (2 L) casserole. • Cover with ½ of the onions. • Combine flour, salt and pepper. • Sprinkle onion layer with ½ of the flour mixture. • Dot with ½ of the butter. • Repeat layers, ending with butter. • Pour milk over all. • Sprinkle with paprika. • Bake, covered, at 375°F (190°C) for 45 minutes; uncover and bake for 15 minutes longer. • Serves 4.

BAKED POTATOES AND TOMATOES

Delicious!

8	large baking potatoes	8
2	garlic cloves, minced	2
2 tsp.	salt	10 mL
½ tsp.	black pepper	2 mL
½ tsp.	dried rosemary leaves	2 mL
½ cup	olive oil	125 mL
6	large ripe tomatoes, peeled OR canned	6
1 tbsp.	chopped Italian parsley or flakes	15 mL

Cut peeled potatoes lengthwise into wedges. Place in a bowl with half the garlic, half the salt, half the pepper and all the rosemary. Add ¼ cup (50 mL) oil and toss to distribute the dressing evenly. ● Cut each tomato into 6 or 8 pieces and place in another bowl. Season with the remaining garlic, salt, pepper and oil. Add parsley. ● Spread the potatoes in a large ungreased baking dish. ● Top with tomatoes and bake, uncovered, at 375°F (190°C) for 1 hour. ● Serves 6.

PEROGIE

5	eggs	5
2 cups	sour cream	500 mL
1 tsp.	salt	5 mL
5 cups	flour	1.25 L

POTATO-CHEESE

8	medium potatoes	8
1 cup	grated Cheddar cheese	250 mL

CABBAGE-BACON

1	small head cabbage	1
4	green onions, chopped	4
6	slices bacon, well cooked	6

PLUM-PLUM

plums, halved
sugar to garnish

Whip eggs, sour cream and salt and add flour until soft dough is formed. ● Roll out on lightly floured counter until about ¼" (1 cm) thick and cut with a tumbler. ● Put your choice of filling on ½ of circle, close and pinch-press to seal. ● If the dough sticks, dip fingers in flour before pinching edges. ● Potato-Cheese Filling: Cook potatoes until soft, mash with potato masher and add cheese until well mixed. ● Cabbage-Bacon Filling: Boil cabbage until soft, drain and squeeze out all water. Slice cabbage very finely; add bacon and green onion. ● Plum-Plum Filling: Put ½ plum in center and press shut. Cook as usual but sprinkle with sugar. ● To cook perogies, bring 2-quarts (2 L) of water or more to a boil and put in 6-8 perogies. Boil until perogies come to the top of the water. ● Drain perogies and put in pan with butter and/or add green onions and bacon. ● These Perogies are Ukrainian and Polish.

---

1 cup	cornmeal	250 mL	
3	slices bacon	3	
1 cup	chopped onion	250 mL	
4 cups	chicken broth	1 L	
dash	salt	dash	
2 tsp.	sugar	10 mL	
1 tsp.	parsley	5 mL	

NACHYNKA CORNMEAL CASSEROLE

Gluten-Free

Heat cornmeal in 300°F (150°C) oven for 15 minutes. • Cut bacon in cubes, fry until crisp, then add onions and fry until they are golden. • Stir cornmeal into bacon and onions. Add seasoning. Pour chicken broth over cornmeal and stir well. • Place in a 2-quart (2 L) casserole and bake at 350°F (180°C) for 30 minutes.

---

1 tsp.	salt	5 mL
¼ cup	sugar	50 mL
⅓ cup	shortening	75 mL
2 cups	hot water	500 mL
1 cup	cold water	250 mL
7 cups	white flour	1.75 L
2	eggs	2
3 tbsp.	Fermipan yeast	45 mL

PIROSHKY

(Pee-rosh-key).

1 lb.	ground beef	500 g
2	onions, finely grated	2
1	medium cabbage, finely grated	1
8	hard-boiled eggs, finely chopped	8
	salt, pepper, garlic to taste	

FILLING

To make filling, brown the ground beef and onions, then drain off any fat. • Sauté the cabbage, add to the ground meat. Stir in the hard-boiled eggs. Season with salt, pepper and garlic to taste. Mix well. • It sounds awful, but it is good! • Make this a few hours before you are going to use it as a stuffing so it is cool. • To make dough, heat together salt, sugar, shortening and hot water until the shortening melts. Add cold water. Beat in 4 cups (1 L) flour. Add eggs, 1 cup (250 mL) flour and yeast. Add approximately 2 cups (500 mL) of flour, kneading until the dough feels smooth to touch. • This recipe is using dough hooks. Kneading by hand would be the same but takes longer. • Place in a large greased bowl and cover with a cloth in a warm oven with the light bulb on for heat. Let rise for about 20 minutes or until double in size. • • Make dough balls the size of a golf ball. Roll out into a pancake 6" (15 cm) in diameter. • Fill with the filling, pinch closed. • Put on a floured surface, sealed side down. • Let rise and deep-fry until golden brown. • Depending on the "golf ball" size, this makes 65-70 Piroshky or whatever it takes for 9 holes!!

BAKED PYROHY

½ cup	warm water	125 mL
2 tsp.	sugar	10 mL
1 tbsp.	yeast (7 g pkg.)	15 mL
2	eggs	2
½ cup	sugar	125 mL
1 tbsp.	vinegar	15 mL
1 cup	oil	250 mL
1 tsp.	salt	5 mL
2 cups	scalded milk, cooled	500 mL
1½ cups	water	375 mL
10 cups	flour	2.5 L

FILLING

16 oz.	dry cottage cheese	500 g
6 cups	mashed potatoes	1.5 L
1	large onion, minced	1
2	egg yolks	2
	salt and pepper	

To make dough, combine warm water, 2 tsp. (10 mL) sugar and yeast; let stand about 10 minutes. Combine eggs, ½ cup (125 mL) sugar, vinegar, oil and salt. Beat eggs and then add milk, water and yeast. Add 4 cups (1 L) of flour and beat very well. Continue adding flour by hand, then knead until dough is smooth and elastic. Put in buttered bowl, turn buttered side to the top and put in a warm place to rise until double in bulk. • Mix together all filling ingredients. • Roll dough out in small portions ½" (1.3 cm) thick. Cut in rounds and put potato and cheese filling in the center. Bring dough up around the filling and pinch to seal, forming a little bun. • Put on cookie sheet; bake in 375°F (190°C) oven until lightly browned. • Serve with sour cream and sautéed onions.

KASHA

1 cup	coarse kasha (buckwheat groats)	250 mL
1	egg, lightly beaten	1
1 tsp.	salt	5 mL
½ cup	butter	125 mL
2-3 cups	boiling water	500-750 mL
2 cups	finely chopped onions	500 mL
½ lb.	fresh mushrooms, finely chopped	250 g

Coat kasha with the egg. • Transfer to hot skillet, stirring until toasted and dry. • Add salt, 3 tbsp. (45 mL) butter, and 2 cups (500 mL) boiling water. Stir, cover pan and reduce heat to low. Simmer, stirring occasionally, for about 20 minutes. If not tender and dry cook 10 minutes longer, or until grains are separate and fluffy. Remove pan from heat and let kasha rest for 10 minutes. • Melt 3 tbsp. (45 mL) butter in a skillet. Add onion and fry until soft and pale gold. Stir into kasha. • In the same skillet, melt 2 tbsp. (30 mL) butter. Cook mushrooms on moderate heat 2-3 minutes, then on high heat until all the liquid is gone. • Add to kasha. • Season to taste. • Serve at once or prepare this ahead and reheat at 250°F (120°C) or by steaming for 20 minutes. • Serves 6-8.

1 cup	wild rice	250 mL	
10 oz.	beef broth	284 mL	
10 oz.	water	284 mL	
1 cup	cooked white rice *	250 mL	
3 tbsp.	butter	45 mL	
½ cup	chopped onion	125 mL	
1 cup	chopped mushrooms	250 mL	
½ cup	chopped celery	125 mL	
	toasted almonds		

WILD RICE CASSEROLE

Soak wild rice overnight in water. • Drain off water. • Boil wild rice in beef broth and water until rice grains open, approximately 30 minutes. • Melt butter in a frying pan and sauté vegetables until soft. • Combine wild rice, white rice and vegetables in a casserole dish. • Sprinkle with toasted almonds. • Keep warm until served. • Serves 6 - 8. • * An additional ½ cup(125 mL) wild rice may be used instead of the white rice for an all wild-rice casserole. • See photograph, page 144A.

6 oz.	wild rice	170 g
1 cup	boiling water	250 mL
1 cup	grated Cheddar cheese	250 mL
1 cup	canned tomatoes	250 mL
1 cup	sautéed mushrooms	250 mL
½ cup	butter OR margarine	125 mL
1 tsp.	salt	5 mL

GOURMET WILD RICE CASSERROLE

Place wild rice in a double boiler, cover with boiling water and cook for 1 hour or until the rice is tender. • Drain rice, if necessary, and add the remaining ingredients. • Place in a 2-quart (2 L) buttered casserole and bake for 1 hour at 350°F (180°C). • **Note:** This may be prepared the day before and baked just before serving.

6 oz.	wild rice	170 g
4 cups	water	1 L
1 tsp.	salt	5 mL

HOW TO COOK WILD RICE

Wash the wild rice in a wire strainer under cold running water and then combine all ingredients in a heavy saucepan. • Heat to a boil. Cover and simmer over low heat for 40-50 minutes or until the rice is tender. • After 30 minutes of cooking, check rice to see that it is not sticking to the pan. If necessary, an additional ¼ cup (50 mL) water may be added. • Remove the cover and fluff rice with a fork and cook for 5 minutes longer. • Serves 6. • **Note:** Wild rice swells to approximately 4 times its size. Some cooks prefer to soak wild rice for several hours before cooking.

PICKLES PLUS

MOM'S SPECIAL DILLS

2 qts.	water	2 L
½ cup	pickling salt	125 mL
1 qt.	vinegar	1 L
	fresh cucumbers	
1	sprig fresh dill	1
1	garlic clove, if desired	1
⅛ tsp.	alum	0.5 mL
⅛ tsp.	cream of tartar	0.5 mL

Combine water, salt and vinegar. Bring to a boil and cool. ● Wipe cucumbers with damp cloth, DO NOT WASH, snip off bud end. Place in sealer with dill. Add garlic if desired. Add alum and cream of tartar. ● Fill jar to top with brine, make sure cucumbers are completely covered. Seal.

KOSHER DILL PICKLES

1 lb.	small firm cucumbers	500 g
pinch	alum	pinch
3	sprigs fresh dill	3
1	garlic clove	1
1 tsp.	mixed pickling spice, including 1 dried pepper	5 mL

BRINE

5 qts.	water	1.25 L
1 cup	coarse salt	250 mL
1 cup	vinegar	250 mL

Cucumber and spice amounts are given per quart (1 L). ● Use only fresh, small firm cucumbers. Wash well in cold water. Soak a few hours or overnight with a pinch of alum in water. ● Line up sterilized sealers. In the bottom of each jar, place a small piece of fresh dill, 1 garlic clove, 1 tsp. (5 mL) mixed pickling spices which include 1 dried red pepper. Pack neatly with cucumbers. Add more dill in centre, more cukes, and a small piece of dill on top. ● Combine brine ingredients and bring to a boil. Pour boiling brine over cucuumbers. Seal jars. Turn jars up and down several times. ● Store in cool place for several days. Turn upside down on newspapers to check for leakage. Re-tighten. ● Ready for use (in half-sour stage) in about 10 days. Can be kept at this stage if stored in refrigerator, otherwise store in cool place.

½ cup	mustard powder	125 mL
5 cups	white sugar	1.25 L
6 cups	vinegar	1.5 L
1 tsp.	salt	5 mL
1 tsp.	turmeric	5 mL
1 cup	flour	250 mL
2 tsp.	celery seed	10 mL
5 qts.	sliced or diced cooked hot beets	5 L

MUSTARD BEET PICKLE

Mix first 4 ingredients with part of the vinegar. Heat remaining vinegar and add to mustard mixture. Add salt and celery seed. Cook until thick. • Pour over cooked hot beets. Fill sterilized jars and seal.

---

6 lbs.	pickling onions	2.5 kg
1½-2 cups	coarse salt	375-500 mL
4½ cups	boiling water	1.125 L
1 tbsp.	alum	15 mL
4½ cups	white sugar	1.125 L
4½ cups	vinegar	1.125 L
2 tsp.	pickling spice	10 mL
	food coloring (optional)	

PICKLED ONIONS

Pour boiling water over onions. Cool and peel. • Put onions in crock and cover with boiling water and ½ cup (125 mL) coarse salt. Weight onions down with plate. Change salt and water 2 or 3 times in 1 week. Drain and rinse in clear water. Cover with boiling water and alum. Let cool. Drain and rinse with clear water and drain again. • Pack in jars and cover with syrup made with equal parts white sugar and vinegar simmered for about 5 minutes with pickling spice. • **Optional:** Add 3 drops red or green food coloring per 16-oz. (500 mL). Makes 7-8, 16-oz. (500 mL) containers.

---

	carrots	
1 tbsp.	pickling salt	15 mL
	garlic, to taste	
	dill, to taste	
½ cup	vinegar	125 mL

DILLED CARROTS

Measurements are given per quart (1 L). • Clean carrots and fill quart (1 L) jars. Add spices. You may add green pepper for color and pickling spices for flavor. • Fill the jars with ice-cold water and seal. (The quarts actually do not seal because of the cold water.) • Carrots will be ready to eat in 6 weeks.

Hint: To peel tiny white onions for boiling or cooking, pour boiling water over them and let stand for 3 minutes. Drain and cover with cold water. Cut off stem and root ends. Skins will peel off almost in 1 piece.

PICKLED CARROTS

1 lb.	carrots, sliced	500 g
1	medium onion, sliced in rings	1
1	green pepper, sliced in strips	1
SAUCE		
5 oz.	tomato soup, (½ can)	142 mL
¼ cup	white sugar	50 mL
¼ cup	oil	50 mL
¼ cup	vinegar	50 mL
½ tsp.	dry mustard	2 mL
½ tsp.	salt	2 mL
¼ tsp.	pepper	1 mL

Boil carrots for 7 minutes only; they must be crisp. Mix together the onion rings and green pepper strips. • To make sauce, combine all ingredients. • Add the sauce to the onion and green pepper. Stir in the hot drained carrots. • Bottle in sterile jars. This recipe keeps well in the refrigerator.

ZUCCHINI RELISH

4⅓ lbs.	zucchini, chopped (16½ cups [4 L])	2 kg
4	large onions, chopped (5 cups [1.25 L])	4
1	sweet red pepper, chopped	1
1	green pepper, chopped	1
3 tbsp.	salt	45 mL
2½ cups	white OR cider vinegar	625 mL
1 cup	honey OR 2 cups (500 mL) white sugar	250 mL
½ tsp.	nutmeg	2 mL
2 tsp.	celery seed	10 mL
1 tsp.	turmeric	5 mL
1 tsp.	dry mustard	5 mL
½ tsp.	black pepper	2 mL

Chop vegetables by hand or in a food processor. • Mix with salt in a large bowl and let stand for several hours or overnight to extract moisture. • Drain, rinse with cold water, and drain thoroughly. (A salad spinner can be used for drying.) • Combine vegetables with remaining ingredients in a 5-quart (5 L) pot and bring to a boil. Simmer, uncovered, for 20 minutes, stirring occasionally. • Ladle into warm sterilized 8-oz (250 mL) or 16-oz. (500 mL) jars, leaving ¼″-½″ (1-1.3 cm) headspace. • Process in a steam canner or boiling water bath for 10 minutes. • Makes 6, 16-oz. (3 L) containers.

Hint: *To clean small intricate designs on silver, brass or copper pieces use a mascara brush to dip into your cleaner.*

6	medium, firm, ripe tomatoes, peeled	6
2 oz.	pkg. powdered fruit pectin	57 g
4½ cups	sugar	1.125 L
1	lemon, quartered and thinly sliced	1
	paraffin	

OLD-FASHIONED TOMATO PRESERVES

Place tomatoes in a large saucepan. Do not add water or cover pan. Heat to boiling; simmer 10 minutes. • Measure tomatoes, then return 3 cups (750 mL) to pan. Stir in pectin. Heat quickly, stirring several times, to boiling. Stir in sugar and lemon and heat again, stirring constantly until mixture comes to a boil. Cook for 1 minute. • Ladle into hot sterilized jars and top with a thin layer of melted paraffin. • Makes 5, 8-oz. (250 mL) jars.

5 lbs.	green tomatoes, thinly sliced	2.2 kg
2½ lbs.	onions, thinly sliced	1.25 kg
¼ cup	salt	50 mL
3 cups	white vinegar	750 mL
3 cups	white sugar	750 mL
¼ cup	pickling spice	50 mL
1 tsp.	dry mustard	5 mL
¼ tsp.	cayenne pepper	1 mL

GREEN TOMATO RELISH

In a large bowl, layer sliced tomatoes and onions alternately, sprinkling each layer with salt. Add cold water to cover and let stand overnight. • Next day drain off the water. • In a large pot, bring vinegar and sugar to a boil. Add the spices, tied in a cloth bag, tomatoes and onions. Boil 1¼ hours. Vegetables will be transparent. Do not let all the fluid evaporate. Just before removing from heat, add mustard and cayenne. • Seal in hot, sterilized jars. • Delicious with cold roast beef. • Makes 7, 16-oz (500 mL) containers.

10 lbs.	tomatoes	5 kg
4 lbs.	brown sugar	2 kg
1 qt.	white vinegar	1 L
1 tsp.	allspice	5 mL
1 tsp.	cinnamon	5 mL
1 tsp.	ground cloves	5 mL
1 tsp.	salt	5 mL

TOMATO BUTTER

A tart, spicy old-fashioned treat.

Wash, peel and cut tomatoes into small pieces. • Place tomatoes in a large enamel or stainless steel saucepan. Add brown sugar and vinegar; cook slowly, stirring occasionally, for 3-4 hours. • When tomato mixture coats the spoon and has a jam-like consistency, stir in all spices. Blend well. • Remove from heat and pour hot into sterilized, self-sealing jars. • Wonderful on toast or as a condiment with roast beef, pork or venison.

HAMBURGER RELISH

7 cups	sliced cucumber	1.75 L
1 cup	chopped celery	250 mL
1	green pepper	1
3 cups	chopped onion	750 mL
2	red peppers	2
6 cups	water	1.5 L
¾ cup	salt	175 mL
4 cups	vinegar	1 L
4 cups	sugar	1 L
2 tbsp.	mustard seed	30 mL
2 tbsp.	celery seed	30 mL

Grind the first 5 ingredients together. • Let stand in water and salt overnight. Drain and rinse in cold water. • To prepare brine, combine the remaining ingredients. Bring to a boil, add vegetables and let mixture boil for 10 minutes. Bottle and seal.

SANDWICH SPREAD

2 cups	green tomatoes	500 mL
2	red peppers	2
2	green peppers	2
2 tbsp.	pickling salt	30 mL
1 cup	water	250 mL
½ cup	vinegar	125 mL
¾ cup	sugar	175 mL
2 tbsp.	flour	30 mL
1 cup	sour cream, beaten	250 mL
1 tsp.	dry mustard	5 mL
3	eggs, well beaten (optional)	3

Put tomatoes and peppers through a food chopper, sprinkle with salt and let stand for ½ hour. Drain. • Add water and simmer until tender. • Mix vinegar, sugar, mustard, flour, sour cream and eggs. Add to vegetables and simmer until thick. • Place in sterilized jars. • Keeps indefinitely in a cool, dry area.

CHERRY OLIVES

2 qts.	Bing cherries	2 L
3 cups	vinegar	750 mL
1 cup	water	250 mL
½ cup	sugar	125 mL
1 tbsp.	cinnamon	15 mL
1 tbsp.	white mustard seed	15 mL
1 tsp.	allspice	5 mL
½ tsp.	whole cloves	2 mL
1 tsp.	salt	5 mL

Clip cherry stems short. Pack in clean hot sterilized jars. Boil vinegar, water, sugar and spices for 8 minutes. Pour over cherries and seal. • Let stand 6 weeks.

9-10	green apples, cored and sliced	9-10
1 cup	apple juice OR cider	250 mL
1½ cups	sugar	375 mL
½ tsp.	allspice	2 mL
1 tsp.	cinnamon	5 mL
¼ tsp.	cloves	1 mL
⅛ tsp.	salt	0.5 mL

BEULAH'S APPLE BUTTER

Combine apples and juice in a large heavy saucepan. Cover, bring to a boil and cook until the apples are mushy, about 15 minutes. • Press mixture through a fine sieve or strainer. • Return strained mixture to saucepan. Add sugar, spices and salt. Simmer 30-40 minutes, until apple butter is thick. • Seal in sterilized 6-8 oz. (175-250 mL) jars. • Wonderful with meat and irresistible on toast.

12	firm, tart apples water	12
1 cup	sugar	250 mL
1 tsp.	EACH pepper, cloves, mustard	5 mL
2 tsp.	cinnamon	10 mL
2	onions, finely chopped	2
1 tbsp.	salt	15 mL
2 cups	vinegar	500 mL

APPLE KETCHUP

Great with pork — slightly tart flavor.

Peel and quarter apples, stew until soft, in as little water as possible. Put the pulp through a sieve. • To 1 quart (1 L) of apple pulp add sugar, pepper, cloves, mustard, cinnamon and onions. Stir together. Add salt and vinegar. Boil for 1 hour and pour, hot, into sterilized bottles.

8 cups	quartered, seeded crabapples	2 L
2 cups	sugar	500 mL
2 tsp.	black pepper	10 mL
2 tsp.	cloves	10 mL
2 tsp.	cinnamon	10 mL
3	large onions, finely chopped	3
2 tsp.	salt	10 mL
1 cup	EACH, pickle vinegar and white vinegar OR 2 cups (500 mL) white vinegar	250 mL

CRABAPPLE KETCHUP

Wash the apples then cut the fruit off around the seeds, which is easier than quartering. Stew crabapples until tender in as little water as possible. • If you wish you can put this through a sieve. For a chutney-like consistency do not put through sieve. • Add sugar, spices, onions, salt and vinegar. Simmer for 1 hour over low heat. • Pour into sterilized jars and seal. • This is great with cold roast beef or on sandwiches. • **Variation:** apples may be used.

SWEET MUSTARD SAUCE

1 cup	sugar	250 mL
3-4 tbsp.	mustard	45-60 mL
⅔ cup	vinegar	150 mL
2	eggs, well beaten	2

Blend sugar and mustard. Stir in vinegar and eggs. • Cook mixture slowly until it has thickened. • Cool and store in the refrigerator. • This keeps for ages. It is particularly good with ham, but can also be served with other meats.

BARBECUE MUSTARD SAUCE

2 tbsp.	butter	30 mL
2 tbsp.	barbecue sauce	30 mL
2 tsp.	Worcestershire sauce	10 mL
2 tsp.	dry mustard	10 mL
2 tbsp.	cream	30 mL

Melt butter and add all ingredients except cream. Cook for 5 minutes on medium heat. Add cream and heat through. • Very good over oven-baked chicken.

TASTY SWEET MUSTARD

16 oz.	jar prepared mustard	500 mL
1⅓ cups	brown sugar	325 mL
½ cup	molasses	125 mL
1 tsp.	celery seed	5 mL

Combine all ingredients in a saucepan. • Bring mixture to a boil, stirring constantly. Boil for 2 minutes. • Remove from heat. • When sauce is cool pour into bottles and store in the refrigerator.

SAUCE FOR BARBECUED FISH

¼ cup	vegetable oil	50 mL
¼ cup	vinegar	50 mL
1	garlic clove	1
½ tsp.	salt	2 mL
½ cup	chili sauce	125 mL
½ tsp.	finely chopped onion	2 mL
½ tsp.	Worcestershire sauce	2 mL
2 tbsp.	brown sugar	30 mL

Mix all ingredients together in a glass jar. Cover; shake well and refrigerate for 2 hours. • Meanwhile, prepare fish fillets. Place between wire racks (toaster or other barbecue device) and set over hot coals. Brush lavishly with the sauce several times while cooking, on both sides of the the fillets. • This is especially good on salmon, Dolly Varden, rainbow trout or any other large fish.

I made my favorite thing for dinner tonight . . . A RESERVATION.

¾ cup	chopped green pepper	175 mL	
¼ cup	chopped jalapeño peppers	50 mL	
1 cup	apple cider vinegar	250 mL	
5 cups	sugar	1.25 L	
6 oz.	liquid pectin	170 mL	
	green food coloring (optional)		

JALAPEÑO JELLY

Place peppers and vinegar in a blender. Blend well and then add sugar. • Transfer to a pan over medium-high heat and bring mixture to a boil. Boil for 5 minutes. Remove from heat, add the pectin, return to heat and boil again for 1 minute. • You may add a few drops of green food coloring. • Seal in jars. Makes 5, 1-cup (250 mL) jars. • This is great served on crackers spread with cream cheese. • **Optional:** You can use ⅓ cup (75 mL) juice from hot jalapeño pickles instead of the chopped jalapeño peppers, and you can also substitute red pepper for green pepper or use both.

2 cups	brown sugar	500 mL
1 cup	white sugar	250 mL
4 tbsp.	corn syrup	60 mL
1½ cups	hot water	375 mL
½ tsp.	vanilla	2 mL
1½ tsp.	maple flavoring	7 mL

PANCAKE SYRUP

Boil sugars, corn syrup and hot water together for 7 minutes. • Add the vanilla and maple flavorings. • Pour over your favorite pancakes or waffles. • This recipe has been in my family for generations, it's quick and excellent.

3 cups	chokecherry juice	750 mL
1 cup	crabapple juice	250 mL
2 tsp.	lemon juice (optional)	10 mL
3 cups	sugar	750 mL

FRUIT SYRUP

Combine the juices over medium-high heat. Bring to a boil that cannot be stirred down and boil for 5 minutes. • Add the sugar (¾ cups [175 mL] per cup of juice). Bring to a boil again for 5 minutes more and then ladle mixture into sterilized jars and seal. • Makes about 3, 1½-cup (375 mL) jars.

4 cups	plums (heaping cups)	1 L
½ cup	water	125 mL
3 cups	sugar (level)	750 mL

PLUM JAM

Wash, pit and quarter plums. • Place in large kettle. Add approximately ½ cup (125 mL) water to prevent burning. Cook until plums are soft, stirring often. • Add sugar (sugar may be preheated in oven if desired). Bring to a hard boil. Keep at rolling boil for 20 minutes. • Seal in sterile jars. • Do not make large quantities, it is the short boiling process which gives the fresh plum flavor.

BEET-GRAPE JELLY

Delicious - believe it or not!

3 cups	beet juice (from boiled beets)	750 mL
3 tbsp.	lemon juice	45 mL
2 oz.	box Certo powder	579 g
4 cups	sugar	1 L
1/5 oz.	pkg. grape Kool-Aid (unsweetened)	6 g

Mix beet juice and lemon juice together. Bring to a boil and stir in the Certo. Add the sugar and bring to a rapid boil; boil for 6 minutes. Skim off the white foam and stir in the Kool-Aid. • Pour into sterilized glass jars and let it set. It will be ready for breakfast tomorrow morning. • You can substitute your favorite Kool-Aid flavor for the grape.

HEAVENLY JAM

2	oranges	2
2	lemons	2
	water to cover	
6	peaches	6
6	pears	6
6	apples	6
	sugar	
19 oz.	can crushed pineapple	540 mL
6 oz.	bottle maraschino cherries	170 mL

Squeeze juice from oranges and lemons. Grind up rind. Cover with water and let stand overnight. • Simmer orange and lemon rind until translucent. • Peel peaches, pears and apples, cut in small pieces. Measure and add equal parts of sugar. • Simmer all together until thick. Add maraschino cherries. • Seal while hot.

MARMALADE

2	grapefruit	2
2	oranges	2
2	lemons	2
	water	
	sugar	

Wash whole fruit thoroughly. Put it through a food chopper. • For each 1 cup (250 mL) of pulp, add 3 cups (750 mL) water. Cover and let stand overnight. • Bring to a boil, until fruit is clear. For 1 cup (250 mL) of fruit add 1 cup (250 mL) of sugar. Boil until it thickens. This may take ¾ hour and you must stir every few minutes so that it does not adhere to the bottom of the pan and burn. • Pour into sterilized jars. • My school chum for many years was the daughter of a widow. This lady earned a living by making marmalade in a large pot on her kitchen stove. She sold it exclusively to Jenkins Groceteria. When she died and her daughter left town I inherited the big pot which I still use for making jams and marmalade.

ENTRÉES

BEEF PLUS

SPICED BEEF

5-7 lb.	point beef brisket	2.2-3 kg
2 tsp.	saltpeter (potassium nitrate)	10 mL
3 tsp.	salt	15 mL
5 tsp.	mixed pickling spices	25 mL
5 tsp.	sugar	25 mL
¼ tsp.	cinnamon	1 mL
5-7	garlic cloves, crushed OR 2 tbsp. (30 mL) garlic powder	5-7

This needs to be prepared 12-14 days ahead of serving time. • Place meat on heavy waxed paper. Score meat or puncture it thoroughly with a fork. Rub mixed spices into the meat. Wrap in waxed paper, then seal with foil. • Put in the refrigerator, turning every 2 days for 12-14 days (best at 14 days). • Remove brisket from foil. Bake at 300°F (150°C) with ½" (1.3 cm) of water for 5 hours, uncovered. • Cover with foil and bake for 2 more hours. Add water if necessary. • Cool beef for 24 hours before slicing. • A butcher can slice it for you if you wish. • This may be divided and frozen then used as needed.

MARINATED ROAST BRISKET

3-4	onions	3-4
4-5 lb.	point brisket	2-2.2 kg
2 tsp.	salt	10 mL
¼ tsp.	pepper	1 mL
1 tbsp.	paprika	15 mL
1 tsp.	dry mustard	5 mL
4	garlic cloves, crushed	4
½ cup	soy sauce	125 mL
2-3 tbsp.	honey OR maple syrup	30-45 mL

Slice onions thinly and place in the botton of a roasting pan. • Rub brisket on all sides with salt, pepper, paprika and mustard, and place in pan. • Combine garlic with soy sauce and honey. Pour mixture over brisket and rub into the meat on all sides. • Cover pan with foil. Marinate 1 hour at room temperature, or overnight in the refrigerator. • Roast, covered, in a 325°F (160°C) oven, allowing 45 minutes per pound, or until meat is fork tender. • Uncover for the last hour and baste occasionally. • Let stand for 20-30 minutes before slicing. • Reheat for a few minutes in pan gravy. • Serves 8-10. • Freezes well.

Beef on Sizzling Rice, page 117

2	small carrots, cut into small sticks	2	
2	celery stalks, cut into small sticks	2	
½	small turnip, cut into small sticks	½	
8	small potatoes	8	
	other seasonal vegetables as green beans, snow peas, Brussels sprouts, banana squash, broccoli, cauliflower		
8	green onions	8	
4 x 7 oz.	beef tenderloins, trimmed	4 x 200 g	
4 cups	strong beef stock or consommé	1 L	
2	bay leaves	2	
1	small fresh ginger root cut into julienne	1	

BEEF TENDERLOIN ON A STRING WITH VEGETABLES

Light and healthy.

Chef Zimmerman
Westin Hotel, Calgary

Clean, wash and cut up vegetables. ● Wrap a butcher string around each tenderloin and leave about 8" (20 cm) string end on each. ● Bring beef stock to a boil and add bay leaves. Add root vegetables and celery and boil 2-5 minutes. Add the rest of your choice of vegetables, boil for another 3-5 minutes and add whole green onions. ● Add tenderloins with string ends hanging out of the pot and bring back to boil. Add ginger strips. ● Turn power off and put cover on pot. ● Check clock for desired doneness as per schedule: 10-12 minutes - rare; 12-16 minutes - medium rare; 16-20 minutes - medium; 20-24 minutes - medium rare; 24 minutes - well done. ● Tenderloins may be pulled out at any time, individually. ● Potatoes are best cooked separately. To serve, simply arrange vegetables on plates, add potatoes and place tenderloins in center. ● Grain mustard, soy sauce, horseradish, Worcestershire or other preferred sauces may be served with this.

Hint: Cauliflower will remain white if a little milk is added while cooking.

STUFFED MEAT ROLLS

1½ lbs.	round steak, ¼" (1 cm) thick	750 g
1½ tbsp.	Dijon mustard	22 mL
3	medium dill pickles, cut in ¼s lengthwise	3
3	slices bacon, cut in half	3
1	large onion, chopped	1
	salt, pepper and paprika to taste	
4 tbsp.	butter OR bacon fat	60 mL
1½ cups	beef broth OR dry red wine	375 mL
2 tbsp.	tomato paste	30 mL
1-2 tbsp.	flour	15-30 mL

Cut round steak into 6 pieces and pound to tenderize. Spread with mustard. Place 2 pieces of pickle, 1 slice of bacon and some chopped onion on top. Sprinkle with salt, pepper, and paprika. Roll up and fasten with toothpicks. • Dredge rolls in flour. • In an ovenproof pan, melt the butter, place the rolls evenly in the pan and brown them on the top of the stove. Mix broth or wine with tomato paste and pour over the rolls. • Cover and place in 350°F (180°C) oven for 2-3 hours. Check occasionally and add a little water if needed. • Make a light gravy from the drippings by whisking in flour and stirring until thickened. • Serve with rice, potatoes or dumplings. • Serves 4 - 6. • **Variation:** Substitute ½ pkg. (¾ oz. [20 g]) onion soup mix and a little water for beef broth and tomato paste.

SIMPLY ELEGANT STEAK AND RICE

Good family dinner.

1½ lbs.	boneless, inside-of-round steak	750 g
1½ tbsp.	oil	22 mL
2	large onions, cut into ½" (1.3 cm) slices, separated in rings	2
10 oz.	can cream of mushroom soup	284 mL
10 oz.	can sliced mushrooms and liquid	284 mL
½ cup	dry sherry (optional)	125 mL
1½ tsp.	garlic salt	7 mL

Cut steak into thin strips. • In a large skillet brown meat in hot oil. Add onions and sauté until tender-crisp. • Blend together soup, liquid from mushrooms, sherry and garlic salt and pour over steak. Add the mushrooms. • Reduce heat, cover and simmer mixture for 1 hour or until tender. • Serve with fluffy rice.

1½-2 lbs.	boneless round steak, cut ½" (1.3 cm) thick, well trimmed	750 g-1 kg
½ tsp.	salt	2 mL
¼ tsp.	pepper	1 mL
¼ cup	flour	50 mL
2 tbsp.	vegetable oil	30 mL
2	large onions, sliced in rings	2
1½-2 cups	sliced carrots	375-500 mL
2	garlic cloves, minced	2
16 oz.	can tomatoes, drained and chopped	500 mL
½-⅔ cups	picante sauce	125-150 mL
½ cup	beef broth	125 mL
2 tbsp.	chopped parsley	30 mL

SOUTH-WESTERN-STYLE SWISS STEAK

Cut meat into serving pieces; sprinkle with salt and pepper. Pound all flour into meat. • Heat oil in large heavy skillet. Brown meat thoroughly. Sprinkle onions, carrots and garlic over meat. Pour tomatoes, picante sauce and beef broth over all. Cover tightly and simmer 50-60 minutes. • Remove meat to serving platter. Cook remaining liquid over high heat until thickened, about 5-7 minutes. Pour over meat and sprinkle with picante sauce. • Serves 6.

½ cup	fine bread crumbs	125 mL
¼ cup	grated Parmesan cheese	50 mL
1 tsp.	oregano	5 mL
1 tsp.	salt	5 mL
½ tsp.	black pepper	2 mL
4	pieces veal (pounded thin)	4
1	egg, beaten	1
¼ cup	cold water	50 mL
¼ cup	olive oil	50 mL
2 cups	spaghetti sauce OR tomato sauce	500 mL
4	slices mozzarella cheese	4
4	thin slices cooked ham	4

VEAL SCALOPPINI

Mix bread crumbs, Parmesan cheese, oregano, salt and pepper on waxed paper. • Mix egg and water and dip veal pieces into egg mixture, then into bread crumbs. • Slowly heat oil in skillet and sauté veal until golden brown. • Pour ½ of the tomato sauce in a 9" x 13" (4 L) pan. Place veal on top, then ham, then cheese of slice. Cover with the remaining sauce and sprinkle with Parmesan cheese. • Bake at 350°F (180°C) for 10-15 minutes. • Serve immediately. • Serves 4.

BAKED VEAL AND HAM BIRDS

2 lbs.	veal round (pork may be substituted)	1 kg
8	slices ham	8
8	slices Swiss cheese	8
1	egg	1
2 tbsp.	milk	30 mL
1 cup	fine bread crumbs	250 mL
10 oz.	can cream of mushroom soup	284 mL
2 tbsp.	cooking sauterne OR sherry	30 mL
½ cup	milk OR light cream	125 mL

Cut meat into 8 slices and pound to ⅛″ (0.5 cm) thick. • Top each piece with a slice of ham and then cheese. • Roll up and secure with toothpicks. • Thoroughly combine egg and milk. Brush rolls with egg mixture and roll in crumbs. • Place seam-side-down in 9″ x 13″ (4 L) baking dish. • Combine soup, sauterne and milk. Heat until bubbling, and pour mixture over the meat rolls. • Cover baking dish with foil. Bake at 350°F (180°C) for 50 minutes or until tender. Uncover the dish for the last 10 minutes to crisp coating. • Serves 8.

GA LAY KGOW YUK

Curried Beef.

4 tbsp.	vegetable oil	60 mL
2 lbs.	tender beef, cut in thin strips	1 kg
1 tsp.	salt	5 mL
½ tsp.	pepper	2 mL
2	slices of fresh ginger OR 1 tsp. (5 mL) ginger	2
dash	M S G	dash
2	medium onions, sliced	2
3 tsp.	curry powder	15 mL

SAUCE

1 tbsp.	chicken base	15 mL
1½ cups	water	375 mL
1 tbsp.	soy sauce	15 mL
1½ tbsp.	cornstarch	22 mL
2 tbsp.	sugar	30 mL

Heat 2 tbsp. (30 mL) oil in Dutch oven, add beef; fry 2-3 minutes. Add salt, pepper, ginger, M S G, mix well, remove from pan. • Fry onions in 2 tbsp. (30 mL) oil until slightly cooked, add curry powder, stirring constantly for 1 minute. Combine sauce ingredients. Add beef and sauce, cover, let simmer for 10 minutes. Serve hot with boiled rice.

¾ lb.	beef tenderloin, thinly sliced, cut in 1½" (4 cm) lengths	365 g
1 oz.	carrot, sliced (2 tbsp. [30 mL])	30 g
1 oz.	bamboo shoot, sliced (2 tbsp. [30 mL])	30 g
1 oz.	baby corn (2 tbsp. [30 mL])	30 g
2	water chestnuts	2
2 oz.	mushroom, sliced (4 tbsp. [60 mL])	60 g
1 oz.	snow peas	30 g
3 oz.	broccoli, chopped	85 g
1	egg white	1
1 tsp.	soy sauce	5 mL
¼ tsp.	sugar	1 mL
dash	white pepper	dash
1 tsp.	oil	5 mL
1 tsp.	cornstarch	5 mL
2 tbsp.	vegetable oil	30 mL
2	slices ginger	2
3-4	slices of garlic	3-4
2 cups	chicken broth	500 mL
2 tsp.	oyster sauce	10 mL
½ tsp.	sugar	2 mL
⅛ tsp.	salt	0.5 mL
2 tsp.	cornstarch	10 mL
1 tbsp.	water	15 mL
2 cups	vegetable oil	500 mL
5 oz.	dry rice crusts, (1 cup [250 mL]) see below	140 g

BEEF ON SIZZLING RICE

Lily and Nicky Chan
Lily Restaurant, Calgary

MARINADE

SAUCE

Prepare beef and vegetables. Combine marinade ingredients. Marinate beef for 20 minutes. Heat 1 tbsp. (15 mL) oil in wok. Stir-fry beef in oil. Drain well.   •   Wash all vegetables. Drain well.   •   Heat 1 tbsp. (15 mL) oil in wok. Add ginger and garlic and stir-fry until brown.   •   Add chicken broth, oyster sauce, salt and sugar. Add all vegetables and boil for 2 minutes. Add beef then stir in cornstarch dissolved in water. Cook until sauce thickens.   •   Put 2 cups (500 mL) of oil in a wok. Heat to 450°F (230°C). Add Rice Crust. Deep-fry until puffy. Drain well.   •   Put Rice Crusts in a big serving bowl. Put beef and vegetables over rice. The rice will start sizzling and singing, happy with the beef. **Note:** Dry rice has to be cooked at the last minute.   •   To make Dry Rice Crusts: Use cooked long-grain rice. Let it cool. Spread cooked rice on a cookie sheet. Bake in 250°F (120°C) oven for 1 hour or until the rice becomes very very dry.   •   See photograph, page 112.

CURRIED BEEF

An East Indian Dish.

2 lbs.	stewing beef	1 kg
2 tbsp.	brown sugar	30 mL
1 tsp.	parsley flakes	5 mL
1 tsp.	ground thyme	5 mL
2 tsp.	garlic salt	10 mL
2 tsp.	soy sauce	10 mL
4	garlic cloves, minced	4
2½ tbsp.	curry powder	37 mL
1	onion, finely minced	1
2	tomatoes, sliced	2
2 cups	hot water	500 mL
2	medium potatoes, cut in pieces	2
3 tbsp.	oil	45 mL
½ cup	water	125 mL

Wash and cut meat into cubes. Season with sugar, parsley, thyme, garlic salt and soy sauce; marinate for 1 hour. • To very hot oil add garlic and curry powder; stir for 2 minutes. Add the meat mixture, stirring well for 15-20 minutes, until the curry coats all the meat. Stir in minced onion and tomatoes then simmer for 5 minutes. • Add hot water. Bring mixture to a boil and cook until meat is nearly done. Add the potatoes and ½ cup (125 mL) of water. Cook until meat and potatoes are tender. • Serve with Chapati or Roti, see page 18, "Among Friends" Volume I.

PEPPER STEAK I

*Gluten-Free**

1 lb.	steak, round or sirloin	500 g
2 tbsp.	Worcestershire sauce	30 mL
1 tbsp.	lemon juice	15 mL
1 tbsp.	Tamari soy sauce	15 mL
dash	freshly-ground pepper	dash
1 tbsp.	whole-wheat flour OR cornstarch *	15 mL
1 tbsp.	oil	15 mL
½ cup	red wine OR water	125 mL
1 cup	slivered green peppers	250 mL
1	small onion, sliced	1
1 cup	sliced mushrooms	250 mL
2	tomatoes, cut in wedges	2

Cut meat into thin strips. • Combine Worcestershire sauce, lemon juice, soy sauce and pepper. • Add meat and flour, stir to coat meat. Allow to marinate 2-3 hours. Drain meat well. • Sauté meat in hot oil until browned. Stir in wine and marinade, cover and simmer for 1½ hours. • Add green pepper, onion and mushrooms, simmer gently until peppers are tender but still crunchy. Remove from heat and stir in tomatoes. Place on heat source again and cook for 5 minutes. • Serve over rice. • This meat is always tender and the peppers and tomatoes create an attractive entrée. • Serves 4. • *For gluten-free diets substitute cornstarch for flour.

1¼ lbs.	beef, top round OR sirloin steak	625 g	
¼ cup	salad oil	50 mL	
1 cup	water	250 mL	
1 tsp.	medium onion, cut in ¼″ (1 cm) slices	5 mL	
½ tsp.	garlic salt	2 mL	
1	minced fresh ginger OR ¼ tsp. (1 mL) ground ginger	1	
2	medium green peppers, in ¾″ (2 cm) strips	2	
1 tbsp.	cornstarch	15 mL	
2-3 tsp.	sugar (optional)	10-15 mL	
2 tbsp.	soy sauce	30 mL	
2	medium tomatoes cooked rice for 4-5	2	

PEPPER STEAK II

Gluten-Free

Trim fat from meat and cut into thin strips, 2″ x 1″ (5 x 2.5 cm). • Heat oil in a large skillet and add meat, stirring frequently for approximately 5 minutes or until meat is browned. • Stir in water, onion, garlic salt and ginger. Bring to a boil then reduce heat. Cover and simmer 12-15 minutes for round steak, 5-8 minutes for sirloin steak. Add the green pepper strips during the last 5 minutes. • Blend cornstarch, sugar and soy sauce and stir into meat mixture. Cook, stirring constantly, until mixture boils and thickens. Boil and stir 1 minute more. • Cut each tomato into eighths and place on meat mixture. Cover and cook over low heat until tomatoes are heated through, about 3 minutes. • Serve with rice.

FAITH (In Yourself)

I.   *Personal achievement begins in the form of THOUGHT, and is limited only by the person in whose mind the thought is. FAITH removes limitations. Remember this whenever you bargain with life for the price that you ask for having passed this way. You can do what you have faith to do.*

II.   *If you think you are beaten you are,*
      If you think you dare not you don't,
      If you like to win but you think you can't
      It's almost certain you won't.
      If you think you'll lose, you're lost
      For out of the world we find,
      Success begins with a fellow's will
      And it's all in the state of the mind.
      If you think you're outclassed you are,
      You've got to think high to rise,
      You've got to be sure of yourself
      Before you can win a prize.

ZESTY MEAT LOAF

*Gluten-Free **

¾ cup	dry bread crumbs OR cracker crumbs *	175 mL
1 cup	milk	250 mL
2	eggs, slightly beaten	2
1	onion, chopped, parboiled, drained	1
½ cup	chopped mushrooms (optional)	125 mL
1½ lbs.	hamburger	750 g
1 tsp.	salt	5 mL
1 tsp.	pepper	5 mL
1-2	garlic cloves, minced	1-2
1 tsp.	Worcestershire sauce	5 mL
1½ tsp.	poultry seasoning	7 mL

SAUCE

1½ cups	boiling water	375 mL
4 tbsp.	brown sugar	60 mL
5 tbsp.	ketchup	75 mL
1 tsp.	nutmeg	5 mL
½ tsp.	dry mustard	2 mL

Mix crumbs with milk. Soak for a few minutes and then add eggs. To this add the onion, mushroom and hamburger. Mix well. Stir in the seasonings. Pack into a 9" x 5" (2 L) loaf pan. ● Combine sauce ingredients and pour over loaf. ● Bake at 325°F (160°C) for 1½-1¼ hours. ● **Variations:** To basic meatloaf mixture add ¼ cup (50 mL) blue cheese, 2-3 green onions chopped and ½ tsp. (2 mL) dry or Dijon mustard. ● Other tasty additions include oregano, thyme, chili powder, chili sauce, anchovy paste, capers, sliced stuffed olives, chopped fresh chives or parsley. ● * For gluten-free diets, substitute crushed cornflakes for bread crumbs.

A MEAL IN A MEATBALL

1 lb.	ground beef	500 g
½ cup	raw rice	125 mL
½ cup	water	125 mL
⅓ cup	chopped onion	75 mL
1 tsp.	salt	5 mL
½ tsp.	celery salt	2 mL
1	garlic clove, minced	1
⅛ tsp.	pepper	0.5 mL
14 oz.	can tomato sauce	398 mL
1 cup	water	250 mL
2 tsp.	Worcestershire sauce	10 mL

Mix meat, rice, ½ cup (125 mL) water, onion, salts, garlic and pepper. Shape mixture into ice-cream-scoop-sized balls. ● Place meatballs in an 8" x 8" (2 L) ungreased baking dish. ● Stir together remaining ingredients and pour over meatballs. ● Cover and bake at 350°F (180°C) for 45 minutes. Uncover, and bake 15 minutes longer. ● Serves 4-6.

SICILIAN MEAT ROLL

*Gluten-Free **

2	eggs, beaten	2
½ cup	tomato juice	125 mL
¾ cup	soft bread crumbs *	175 mL
2 tbsp.	chopped fresh parsley	30 mL
½ tsp.	oregano	2 mL
¼ tsp.	salt	1 mL
¼ tsp.	pepper	1 mL
1	garlic clove, minced	1
2 lbs.	ground beef	1 kg
4-6 oz.	thinly sliced cooked ham	115-170 g
6 oz. pkg	sliced mozzarella cheese	170 g

Mix together eggs and tomato juice. Stir in bread crumbs, spices and ground beef and mix well.   •   On waxed paper pat meat into an 8″ x 10″ (20 x 25 cm) rectangle. Arrange ham slices on top of meat, leaving a small margin around the edges. Place the cheese over the ham, reserving 1 slice.   •   Starting from the short end, carefully roll up the meat, using the paper to lift; seal edges and ends.   •   Place roll, seam-side-down, in a 9″ x 13″ (4 L) baking dish and bake at 350°F (180°C) for approximately 1¼ hours. Cut the remaining slice of cheese into 4 triangles, and overlap on the meat; return to oven until cheese melts.   •   Center of the roll will be pink because of the ham.   •   Serves 8.   •   * For gluten-free diets, substitute crushed cornflakes for bread crumbs.

BEEF CRUST PIE

*Gluten-Free **

1 lb.	ground beef	500 g
½ cup	rolled oats *	125 mL
¼ cup	chopped onion	50 mL
¼ cup	diced green pepper	50 mL
2 tbsp.	parsley	30 mL
1 tsp.	salt	5 mL
⅛ tsp.	pepper	0.5 mL
¼ tsp.	savory	1 mL
1	egg, beaten	1
½ cup	tomato juice	125 mL
1 tbsp.	ketchup	15 mL
1 tsp.	Worcestershire sauce	5 mL

FILLING

2 cups	cooked rice	500 mL
7½ oz.	can tomato sauce	218 mL
⅛ tsp.	pepper	0.5 mL
1 cup	grated Cheddar cheese	250 mL
⅛ tsp.	basil	0.5 mL

Combine the first 12 ingredients and press in the bottom and sides of a 9″ (1 L) deep pie plate.   •   To make the filling, combine the rice, tomato sauce, seasonings and ¼ cup (50 mL) of the cheese.   •   Spread filling over the meat mixture, cover and bake at 350°F (180°C) for 45 minutes. Uncover, sprinkle with the remaining cheese and bake for 10-15 minutes or until the cheese melts.   •   * For gluten-free diets replace rolled oats with crushed corn or rice cereal.

CHEESE-BURGER PIE

9"	unbaked pastry shell	23 cm
1 lb.	ground beef	500 g
½ tsp.	oregano	2 mL
1 tsp.	salt	5 mL
¼ tsp.	pepper	1 mL
¼ cup	chopped onion	50 mL
¼ cup	chopped green pepper	50 mL
½ cup	fine bread crumbs	125 mL
7½ oz.	can tomato sauce	213 mL
1 cup	grated cheese	250 mL
1	egg	1
¼ cup	milk	50 mL
½ tsp.	salt	2 mL
½ tsp.	mustard	2 mL
dash	Worcestershire sauce	dash

Prepare pastry shell. • Combine the next 8 ingredients, ending with the tomato sauce and put into pie shell. • Combine remaining 6 ingredients and top pie with this cheese mixture. • Bake for 30 minutes at 425°F (220°C).

BROCCOLI-BEEF SQUARES

2 cups	chopped, fresh broccoli	500 mL
1 lb.	ground beef	500 g
10 oz.	can mushroom stems and pieces, drained	284 mL
2 cups	shredded Cheddar cheese	500 mL
⅓ cup	chopped onion	75 mL
2 cups	buttermilk pancake mix	500 mL
½ cup	cold water	125 mL
¼ cup	grated Parmesan	50 mL
1 tsp.	salt	5 mL
dash	pepper	dash
½ cup	milk	125 mL
4	eggs	4

Cook broccoli until almost tender, about 5 minutes, and drain thoroughly. Cook and stir gound beef in a 10" (25 cm) skillet until brown; drain thoroughly. Stir in mushrooms, 1½ cups (375 mL) Cheddar cheese and onion. • Combine baking mix, water and remaining Cheddar cheese until soft dough forms, then beat vigorously 20 strokes. • With floured hands, pat dough into a greased 13" x 9" (4 L) baking dish , pressing dough ½" (1.3 cm) up the sides. • Spread beef mixture over dough and sprinkle with broccoli. • Combine remaining ingredients and pour over broccoli. • Cook, uncovered, at 400°F (200°C) for 25-30 minutes or until golden brown and knife inserted near the center comes out clean. •
Serves 6-8.

TAMALE PIE AND CORN BREAD TOPPING

1 lb.	lean ground beef	500 g
½ cup	chopped onion	125 mL
1 cup	kernel corn	250 mL
10 oz.	can tomato soup OR 5½ oz. (156 mL) tomato paste	284 mL
2 cups	water	500 mL
1 tsp.	salt	5 mL
½-1 tsp.	chili powder	2-5 mL

TOPPING

1 cup	yellow cornmeal	250 mL
½ cup	flour	125 mL
1 tbsp.	sugar	15 mL
1 tsp.	salt	5 mL
2 tsp.	baking powder	10 mL
¾ cup	milk	175 mL
1	egg, beaten	1
2 tbsp.	melted shortening	30 mL
1 cup	grated Cheddar cheese	250 mL

Sauté meat and onions, stirring to break up meat. Add corn, soup, water and seasonings, simmer for 8-10 minutes. Pour mixture into a 9″ x 13″ (4 L) baking dish. • To make the topping, mix remaining ingredients except for the grated cheese. • Quickly pour topping over the meat mixture and bake at 350°F (180°C) for 20-25 minutes. Sprinkle grated cheese over top and return to oven for 5 minutes or until the cheese melts. • Serves 4-6.

FAVORITE CASSEROLE

1 lb.	lean ground beef	500 g
1	medium onion, sliced	1
10 oz.	can mushrooms, drained	284 mL
1	garlic clove, crushed	1
½ tsp.	oregano	2 mL
10 oz.	pkg. frozen, chopped spinach, thawed	283 g
3 tbsp.	quick-cooking rice	50 mL
10 oz.	can cream of celery soup	284 mL
1 cup	sour cream	250 mL
dash	salt	dash
dash	pepper	dash
6 oz.	mozzarella cheese	170 g

Brown meat, onion, mushrooms, garlic and oregano. Drain meat thoroughly. • Stir in spinach, rice, soup, sour cream, salt and pepper. Blend well, and place mixture in a 9″ x 13″ (4 L) casserole and top with cheese. • Bake at 350°F (180°C) for 35-45 minutes. • This recipe may be prepared in the morning, and refrigerated until needed; it also freezes very well. • Serve with a tossed salad and hot rolls.

GERRY'S CURRY AND RICE

Gerry's favorite will be yours, too!

2 lbs.	hamburger	1 kg
1	large onion, chopped	1
3 tbsp.	curry powder	45 mL
2 tsp.	vinegar	10 mL
½ cup	ketchup	125 mL
2 tbsp.	brown sugar	30 mL
1½ cups	ketchup	375 mL
1	apple, peeled, chopped (optional)	1
1 cup	raisins (optional)	250 mL
1 tbsp.	cornstarch mixed in ½ cup (125 mL) cold water (optional)	15 mL
	cooked rice for 6	
	sliced banana for garnish	
	coconut for garnish	

Brown hamburger and onion. Drain thoroughly. • Add curry powder, vinegar, and ½ cup (125 mL) ketchup. Cover and simmer for 10 minutes. • Add the brown sugar, remaining ketchup, apple, raisins and enough water to cover. Simmer for 1½ hours. • If desired, this may be thickened with cornstarch mixed in water and brought back to a boil. • Serve over hot, cooked rice. • Garnish with sliced bananas and coconut. • Serves 6.

ORIENTAL BEEF

1 tbsp.	cooking oil	15 mL
1 lb.	ground beef	500 g
1	green pepper, slivered	1
2 cups	thinly sliced celery	500 mL
3	green onions with tops, chopped	3
10 oz.	can cream of celery soup	284 mL
10 oz.	can mushrooms, drained and sliced	284 mL
¼ cup	light cream	50 mL
1 tbsp.	soy sauce	15 mL
¼ tsp.	pepper	1 mL
½ cup	fine dry bread crumbs	125 mL
½ cup	slivered almonds	125 mL
2 tbsp.	melted butter	25 mL

Heat oil in a heavy skillet, add beef and brown well stirring constantly. Drain and put beef into a 2-quart (2 L) casserole. • Sprinkle with green pepper, celery and onions. • Combine soup, mushrooms, cream, soy sauce and pepper. Pour over beef mixture. • Combine crumbs, almonds and butter. Sprinkle over beef mixture. • Bake 45 minutes at 375°F (190°C) or until bubbling and browned. • Vegetables will still be crisp. • Serves 6.

6	large tomatoes	6	
2 tbsp.	butter	30 mL	
1	onion, chopped	1	
1 lb.	lean minced beef	500 g	
4 oz.	mushrooms, chopped	115 g	
1 tbsp.	chopped parsley	15 mL	
6 tbsp.	dry white wine	90 mL	
	salt and pepper		
¼ cup	bread crumbs	50 mL	
	lemon wedges		

BEEF-AND-MUSHROOM-STUFFED TOMATOES

Halve the tomatoes; scoop out and chop up the flesh. • Melt butter in a skillet and fry the onion until transparent. Add the beef and fry for 5 minutes. Add mushrooms, parsley, chopped tomato, wine, salt and pepper. Cover and cook for 10 minutes. Stir in the bread crumbs. • Spoon the mixture into the tomato halves. • Arrange in an ovenproof dish and bake at 350°F (180°C) for 25-30 minutes until the tops are brown and crisp. • Garnish with lemon wedges and serve with rice or mashed potatoes. • Serves 3-4.

1	medium onion	1	
2 tbsp.	oil	30 mL	
1 lb.	lean ground beef	500 g	
1 tbsp.	flour	15 mL	
1-3 tsp.	curry powder	5-15 mL	
1½ cups	beef broth	375 mL	
2	chilies, fresh or dried	2	
1-2 tbsp.	chutney, mango or sweet	15-30 mL	
6	medium green peppers OR 4 large	6	
	cornstarch (optional)		

SPICED GREEN PEPPERS

Sauté onion in oil; add the meat and fry until browned. Drain. • Add flour and curry powder, stir and cook gently for 2 minutes. • Remove from heat and slowly add broth, stirring constantly. Finally add chilies and chutney and simmer gently for 40 minutes. • Wash the green peppers. Cut a slice off the stalk end, about ½" (1.3 cm) deep. Carefully remove seeds and pith; save the tops. • Remove chilies, if fresh, from the curry. • Strain ground beef from the sauce. Put meat into green peppers and replace tops. • Put the peppers into a 2-quart (2 L) casserole. • Pour sauce around the peppers. • Cover and cook at 350°F (180°C) for 35 minutes. • Thicken sauce with cornstarch if necessary. • Serves 4-6. • Serving suggestions: Serve with rice and a green salad. Garnish with mango chutney, sliced tomato, sliced onion, yogurt or sour cream, and coconut. • **Hints:** When buying green peppers choose the freshest, crispiest and most regular-shaped.

SWEET AND SOUR CABBAGE ROLLS

1	large head cabbage	1
2 lbs.	hamburger	1 kg
1 cup	raw rice	250 mL
1	large onion, chopped	1
	salt and pepper to taste	
1	garlic clove, minced	1
2 x 10 oz.	cans tomato soup	2 x 284 mL
2	lemons, juice of	2
½ cup	water	125 mL
4 tbsp.	white sugar	60 mL

Wilt cabbage leaves either by steaming or by freezing the cabbage for 24 hours and defrosting for 12 hours. • Combine hamburger, rice, onion, salt, pepper and garlic and roll into wilted cabbage leaves. • Pack rolls into a large greased roasting pan or casserole. • Combine tomato soup, lemon juice, water and white sugar and pour mixture over the rolls. • Cover and cook 4 hours at 325°F (160°C). • Serves 6-8.

STUFFED CABBAGE ROLLS

3 lbs.	lean ground beef	1.5 kg
2 tsp.	salt	10 mL
¾ tsp.	pepper	3 mL
2 tsp.	celery salt	10 mL
½ cup	ketchup	125 mL
2	eggs	2
½ cup	crushed unsalted crackers	125 mL
2	heads green cabbage	2
3 cups	chopped onion	750 mL
2 cups	chili sauce	500 mL
1 cup	grape jelly	250 mL
¼ cup	water	50 mL

In a large bowl, combine ground beef, salt, pepper, celery salt, ketchup, eggs and crackers. Mix until well combined. • Put cabbage leaves in hot water to soften. • Form meat mixture into 28 rolls, to fit the cabbage leaves, and roll up. • Line the bottom of a large greased roasting pan or casserole with the chopped onion and then place cabbage rolls on top. • In a 2-quart (2 L) saucepan combine chili sauce, grape jelly and water. Heat until jelly melts. • Pour over cabbage rolls and cover pan with foil; bake for 2 hours at 375°F (190°C). Brush rolls with sauce and bake 40 minutes longer, uncovered. • Makes 28 cabbage rolls. • Serves 14.

Hint: Marinate liver in lemon juice for 30 minutes before cooking. Adds a delicate flavor.

2	large onions	2
½ cup	butter	125 mL
½ cup	dry red wine	125 mL
¼ cup	chopped parsley	50 mL
1	bay leaf	1
1 tsp.	thyme	5 mL
½ cup	flour	125 mL
1 tsp.	salt	5 mL
	freshly ground pepper	
½ cup	water	125 mL
6	slices of calf OR beef liver	6

BAKED LIVER AND ONIONS

Cut onions into ½" (1.3 cm) slices. Arrange in baking dish. Dot with butter. Add wine, parsley, bay leaf, thyme, salt, pepper and ½ cup (125 mL) water. Cover and bake at 350°F (180°C) for 30 minutes. • Coat liver in flour. Place on top of onion slices, cover and bake 30 minutes, basting 2-3 times. • Remove cover, bake for 10 minutes. We like this with whipped mashed potatoes, green vegetables and hot rolls. • Serves 6. • **Note:** Beef and calf livers do not require scalding but lamb or pork livers do. To scald, drop into boiling water for approximately 1 minute. Drain immediately. Lamb or pork may be substituted for calf liver in any recipe and prepared in the same way.

3 tbsp.	flour	45 mL
¼ tsp.	M S G (optional)	1 mL
¼ tsp.	salt	1 mL
¼ tsp.	dry mustard	1 mL
dash	pepper	dash
½ lb.	liver sliced into ½" (1.3 cm) strips	250 g
2 tbsp.	butter OR margarine	30 mL
1 tsp.	finely chopped onion	5 mL
¾ cup	water	175 mL
1 tsp.	liquid meat extract OR 1 bouillon cube	5 mL
¼ cup	sour cream	50 mL

LIVER STROGANOFF

Mix flour, M S G, if used, salt, dry mustard and pepper in a bag. • Shake liver pieces, a few at a time, in bag until well-coated. • Heat butter in a large skillet and add the onion and liver. Fry, stirring occasionally, until browned, approximately 4 minutes. • Slowly stir in water and meat extract. Stir constantly until thickened. Cover and reduce heat; simmer for 5 minutes. • Stir in sour cream and heat through but do NOT let mixture come to a boil or the sour cream will curdle. • Serves 2.

SWEETBREAD EN BROCHETTE

3	pair sweetbreads	3
1	egg	1
1 tbsp.	dry white wine	15 mL
½ tsp.	salt	2 mL
	freshly ground pepper	
½ cup	bread crumbs	125 mL
6	slices bacon, cut in pieces	6
24	mushroom caps	24
3	medium green peppers, cut in 1" (2.5 cm) squares	3
½ cup	butter, melted	125 mL
	Château Sauce, recipe follows.	

Parboil sweetbread and cut each into 4 pieces. ● Dip into egg beaten with wine, salt and pepper. Then dip into bread crumbs. ● Thread on skewers, alternating sweetbreads with bacon, mushrooms and peppers. ● Broil under low heat, basting with melted butter, until golden brown. ● Serve with Château Sauce. ● Serves 6.

CHÂTEAU SAUCE

1 cup	chopped onion	250 mL
2 tbsp.	chopped shallots	30 mL
¾ cup	butter	175 mL
4 tbsp.	flour	60 mL
¼ cup	tomato paste	50 mL
2 tbsp.	strong beef stock	750 mL
2 tbsp.	bottled meat extract	30 mL
¼ cup	chopped mushrooms	50 mL
¼ cup	dry white wine	50 mL

Sauté onion and shallots in 4 tbsp. (60 mL) butter until golden. Add flour and cook until deep brown, stirring constantly. Add tomato paste, stock and meat extract. Cook until thickened, stirring constantly. ● Combine mushrooms with wine and cook over high heat for 5 minutes. Stir into thickened sauce. ● Melt the remaining ½ cup of butter and stir it into the sauce with a wire whisk or rotary beater until thoroughly blended. ● Makes 4 cups (1 L).

Hint: Can your hollandaise be saved? If the sauce curdles, remove it from heat, beat in boiling water, a teaspoonful (5 mL) at a time, until smooth.

1 lb.	veal heart, diced	500 g
1 lb.	veal kidneys, diced	500 g
½ lb.	pork liver (calves if desired)	250 g
½ cup	flour	125 mL
4 tbsp.	butter	60 mL
½ cup	celery leaves	125 mL
1 tbsp.	chopped chives	15 mL
½ cup	chopped parsley	125 mL
1	garlic clove, minced	1
2	cloves	2
1	bay leaf, crumbled	1
½ tsp.	thyme	2 mL
1 tsp.	salt	5 mL
	ground black pepper	
2 cups	dry red wine	500 mL
½ lb.	mushrooms, sliced	250 g

VEAL HEART AND RED WINE STEW

Roll veal heart, kidney and pork liver in flour. Sauté in butter in large saucepan, for 10 minutes or until lightly browned, stirring constantly. • Add celery, chives, parsley, garlic, cloves, bay leaf, thyme, salt and pepper, plus enough water to cover. Bring to a boil, reduce heat, cover pan and simmer for 3 hours, stirring occasionally. • Add wine and mushrooms and simmer for 15 minutes, stirring occasionally. • The stock may be thickened with cornstarch. Mix cornstarch with water, add a little hot stock and stir cornstarch mixture into stew. • Serve over noodles or rice with salad and French bread. • Serves 6-8.

---

2 lbs.	sweetbreads	1 kg
3 qts.	water	3 L
2	carrots, sliced	2
2	celery stalks	2
1	onion, peeled	1
	bouquet garni	
5 tsp.	coarse salt	25 mL
	flour	
4 tbsp.	butter	60 mL
15 oz.	can salsifies	450 mL
¼ cup	vermouth	50 mL
	salt and pepper	
1 cup	whipping cream	250 mL

SWEETBREADS WITH SALSIFIES

*Bernard and Fernando
Versailles Dining Room,
Calgary*

Place the sweetbreads in a large pot of cold water. Soak for 2 hours. • Change the water and add carrots, celery, onions, bouquet garni and salt. Bring to a boil and let simmer for 3 minutes. Drain and rinse in cold water. Drain again and press the sweetbreads between 2 plates overnight. • Take off the thin membrane surrounding sweetbreads. • Roll them in flour. Heat butter in a high-sided frying pan and brown sweetbreads for 6 minutes, turning them as necessary. • Add the salsifies and cook for 3 minutes. Add vermouth and cream, cook until the sauce is thick enough. • Serves 6.

LAMB IN PUFF PASTRY

Bernard and Fernando
Versailles Dining Room,
Calgary

Always delicious!

3 tbsp.	butter	45 mL
1	shallot, sliced	1
2	slices bacon	2
1¾ oz.	mushroom, chopped (¼ cup [50 mL])	50 g
2 tbsp.	olive oil	30 mL
½	lemon, juice of	½
	chopped parsley	
1½ tbsp.	bread crumbs	22 mL
1	garlic clove, peeled and crushed	1
½ tsp.	savory	2 mL
	salt and pepper to taste	
6	small racks of lamb, boneless	6
1	sheet puff pastry, 14" x 28" (35 x 71 cm)	1
2	egg yolks	2
2 tbsp.	water	30 mL

Heat 1 tbsp. (15 mL) butter in a saucepan. Add sliced shallots and sauté on medium-high for 3-4 minutes. Add bacon and cook for 2 minutes; add chopped mushrooms and cook for 3 minutes. Let cool. • Add olive oil, lemon juice, chopped parsley, bread crumbs, garlic and savory. Add salt and pepper to taste. • Melt 2 tbsp. (30 mL) butter in a frying pan, and cook the racks of lamb for 8 minutes, until they are pink. Let cool. • Place the sheet of puff pastry on the table and cut into 6 pieces. Place a rack of lamb on each piece of puff pastry. Place 1 spoonful of mushroom mixure on the top of each rack of lamb. • Fold the puff pastry over the lamb. Combine egg yolks and water. Seal the pastry edges with egg mixture. Brush yolk mixture over the puff pastry. • Bake at 500°F (260°C) for about 10-12 minutes. • Serves 6.

GIFTS FOR THE RIGHT PEOPLE

To your enemy — forgiveness
To your opponent — tolerance
To a friend — your heart
To a customer — service
To all men — charity
To every child — a good example
To yourself — respect

TIPS FOR DRESSING GAME

Chef Williams
Palliser Hotel, Calgary

To dress game, tie the hind legs together and hang remaining rope over a branch. Pull, to haul the beast up, and secure the rope, then make your incision. • Once opened to expose the rib cage, discard insides and place a stick between the rib cages. If available, pack with snow for faster cooling. • When carrying the beast, tie hind legs, then front legs and place a strong branch between legs. You and your partner take one end each and exit the beast from the field.

8 tsp.	red current jelly	40 mL	
¼ cup	port wine	50 mL	
1 tsp.	mustard	5 mL	
¼ tsp.	cayenne pepper	1 mL	
¼ tsp.	ground ginger	1 mL	
½ tsp.	lemon rind, blanched	2 mL	
½ tsp.	orange rind, blanched	2 mL	
2	oranges, juice of	2	
1	lemon, juice of	1	

COLD SAUCE FOR VENISON

Chef Williams
Palliser Hotel, Calgary

Heat the jelly in a small saucepan until it dissolves. • Stir in the port and add all remaining ingredients. Mix well. • Serve cold.

HOW TO KILL A PROFESSIONAL ORGANIZATION IN 13 EASY STEPS.

1. *Stay away from meetings*
2. *If you do come, find fault.*
3. *Decline office or appointment to a committee.*
4. *Get sore if you aren't nominated or appointed.*
5. *After you are named, don't attend board or committee meetings.*
6. *If you get to one, despite your better judgement, clam up until it's over. Then sound off on how things really should be done.*
7. *Do no work if you can help it. When the "OLD" reliables pitch in, accuse them of being a clique.*
8. *Oppose all banquets, parties, and shindigs as being a waste of members' money.*
9. *If everything is strictly business, complain that the meetings are dull and officers a bunch of old sticks.*
10. *Never accept a place at the head table.*
11. *If you aren't asked to sit there, threaten to resign because you aren't appreciated.*
12. *Don't rush to pay your dues. Let the Executive Committee sweat; after all, they wrote the budget.*
13. *Read mail from headquarters only now and then; don't reply if you can help it.*

PORK

BAKED CROWN ROAST OF PORK

STUFFING

Gluten-Free and delicious.

SAUCE

1	12-chop crown roast of pork	1
2½ cups	cornbread, crumbled (your own or corn muffins from bakery)	625 mL
1 cup	cooked white rice	250 mL
½ cup	chopped onion, sautéed in 3 tbsp. (45 mL) butter	125 mL
2 tbsp.	grated fresh ginger	30 mL
½ tsp.	freshly ground pepper	2 mL
2 tsp.	grated orange peel	10 mL
½ cup	chopped celery	125 mL
1 cup	orange juice (fresh is best)	250 mL
½ cup	liquid honey	125 mL
2 tsp.	fresh ginger, grated	10 mL

Get butcher to prepare a 12-chop crown roast of pork tied in a circle, with the bone partly cut at the bottom. • Mix all stuffing ingredients together well. Add more melted butter if crumbs are very dry. Put stuffing in middle of crown roast. • Roast in open pan at 325°F (160°C) for 1½-2 hours. Use foil to cover if some parts get too brown. • Combine orange juice, honey and ginger. Baste roast with the orange sauce during the last hour of cooking. • Let roast stand for about 10 minutes before cutting into individual pork chops to serve. Spoon stuffing beside chops. • Serves 6-8. • See photograph on front cover.

Hint: If you find the meal you have prepared isn't going to be filling enough try dressing up the bread this way: Whip an egg white stiff and fold in plenty of shredded cheese. Spread on bread slices and toast in hot oven until browned. this is very good with a vegetable meal.

6	pork chops	6
1 tbsp.	cooking oil	15 mL
3	medium carrots	3
3	celery stalks	3
3	medium potatoes	3
2	green onions, chopped	2
2 cups	apple juice	500 mL
2 tsp.	curry powder	10 mL
1 tsp.	salt	5 mL
¼ tsp.	pepper	1 mL
¼ cup	raisins	50 mL

FRUIT CURRIED PORK CHOPS

For the Slow-Cooker.

Brown chops in cooking oil. • Cut carrots into sticks and cut up celery and potatoes. • Place vegetables in bottom of a slow-cooker and add meat. Sprinkle onions over meat. • Mix apple juice, curry powder, salt and pepper together and pour over contents in slow-cooker. Sprinkle with raisins. • Cook 6-8 hours on low. • Serve over pilaf or brown rice. • Serves 6.

---

	pork chops	
¼ cup	orange juice	50 mL
¼ cup	ketchup	50 mL
sprinkle	brown sugar	sprinkle
	equal amounts of juice and ketchup to make up desired amount of sauce	

HARVEST PORK CHOPS

Trim chops of excess fat. Brown on both sides in a hot skillet. Drain off the excess liquid. • Combine juice, ketchup, and brown sugar. Pour over chops, cover and simmer, or place in a casserole and finish cooking at 350°F (180°C) until pork chops are cooked through. • Serve with rice. • If more sauce is needed mix equal amounts of juice and ketchup and pour over chops. • This recipe can be adapted to serve as many people as you like.

6	pork chops	6
3 tbsp.	bacon dripping	45 mL
2	medium onions, chopped	2
1	can sauerkraut	1
2	large apples, sliced	2
½ cup	sugar	125 mL

PORK, KRAUT AND APPLE SKILLET

In heavy skillet or Dutch oven, brown chops in drippings. Add onions and cook several minutes. • Mix sauerkraut and apples and spoon over meat. • In separate pan, heat sugar, stirring constantly, until rich caramel color. • Pour over sauerkraut mixture. Cover tightly and cook over low heat 30 minutes. • Serves 6.

CHINESE PORK AND RICE

⅔ cup	uncooked regular rice	150 mL
½ cup	chopped onion	125 mL
2 tbsp.	vegetable oil	30 mL
2 cups	cut-up cooked pork (1″ [2.5 cm]) pieces	500 mL
1½ cups	chicken OR beef broth	375 mL
2 tbsp.	soy sauce	30 mL
1 cup	diagonally sliced celery	250 mL
1 cup	chopped green pepper cashews (optional)	250 mL

Cook and stir rice and onion in oil in a 10″ (25 cm) skillet over medium heat until the rice is golden brown. • Stir in pork, broth and soy sauce. Pour into a ungreased 2-quart (2 L) casserole or 12″ x 8″ (3 L) baking dish. • Cover and cook in 375°F (190°C) for 35 minutes. • Stir in celery and green pepper. • Cover and cook until rice is tender and liquid is absorbed, about 10 minutes longer. • Sprinkle with cashews, if desired. • Serves 4.

CAJUN SPARERIBS

SAUCE

3 lbs.	ribs, * cut-up	1.5 kg
½ cup	brown sugar	125 mL
½ cup	ketchup	125 mL
1 tbsp.	dry mustard	15 mL
1 tsp.	chili powder	5 mL
1 tsp.	salt	5 mL
1 tsp.	pepper	5 mL
1 cup	water	250 mL
2 tsp.	Worcestershire sauce	10 mL
6-8	drops Tabasco sauce	6-8
1 tbsp.	flour	15 mL
1	large onion, sliced	1
1	green pepper, chopped (optional)	1

Do not brown ribs! • Combine all ingredients, except the onions and peppers, in a large casserole. • Bake for 1 hour at 325°F (160°C). • Add onion and green pepper and bake for 1½ hours at 300°F (150°C). Always have cover on casserole. • ENJOY!! • This sauce may also be used on meatloaf, see recipes page 120. • * Beef or pork ribs may be used.

Hint: To make copper shine like new, clean with salt and vinegar.

3-5 lbs.	pork ribs, * cut up	1.5-2.2 kg
½ cup	vinegar	125 mL
1 cup	water	250 mL
3 tbsp.	cornstarch	45 mL
6 tbsp.	cold water	90 mL
¾ cup	ketchup	175 mL
¾ cup	brown sugar	175 mL
1½ tsp.	soy sauce	7 mL
¾ tsp.	salt	3 mL

SPARERIBS TAHITI

Bake first 3 ingredients together, covered, for 1 hour at 325°F (160°C). Drain off liquid and save for sauce. • Combine cornstarch and cold water. Add reserved liquid plus all the remaining ingredients. Bring to a boil to thicken. • Pour over ribs in a shallow pan. • Bake at 325°F (160°C) for 30 minutes or until brown. •
* Use country-style ribs, if possible.

---

3 lbs.	pork side spareribs, in 2 pieces	1.5 kg
½ cup	butter OR margarine	125 mL
2 cups	chopped onions	500 mL
1 tsp.	salt	5 mL
½ tsp.	pepper	2 mL
¼ tsp.	paprika	1 mL
½ tsp.	poultry seasoning	2 mL
½ tsp.	dried sage	2 mL
½ cup	cooked pork sausage (optional)	125 mL
3 cups	dry bread cubes OR crumbs	750 mL
1	egg, lightly beaten chicken OR beef stock (optional)	1

STUFFED PORK SPARERIBS

BREAD STUFFING

Use 4 or 5 cups of your favorite stuffing recipe or use the recipe above. Melt butter in frying pan and sauté onions until translucent. Mix in remaining ingredients. Add a little stock to moisten stuffing, if necessary. • Place 1 piece of the spareribs, hollow-side-up, on a rack in a shallow roasting pan. Spread with the bread stuffing. Cover with the second piece of sparerib, hollow-side-down. Skewer or tie ribs together (can use white thread). • For individual servings, cut into 3" (7 cm) pieces, 5-6 ribs each, stuff, roll and tie. • Bake, uncovered, at 325°F (160°C) for 2 hours. • Serves 4-6.

Hint: A steaming microwave — if condensation builds up on the walls and glass of the microwave: Wipe off and check that the vents on the microwave are not obstructed.

TOAD IN THE HOLE

1 lb.	pork or beef sausages	500 g
2	eggs	2
1 cup	milk	250 mL
1 cup	flour	250 mL
dash	salt	dash
5 tbsp.	butter OR margarine (optional)	75 mL

Bake sausages in a 9" (23 cm) square, covered pan in 375°F (190°C) oven for 30 minutes. • Have remaining ingredients at room temperature or they will not puff properly. • Mix the next 4 ingredients into a batter. Beat together until smooth. • Remove sausages from pan and drain off most of the fat. Leave about 5 tbsp. (75 mL) of hot fat, or use hot butter, in the pan. Return sausages to the pan and cover with the batter. • Return to oven and bake for 30 minutes.

PORK HOCKS

4	pork hocks	4
	water	
1	onion, sliced	1
1 tbsp.	garlic salt	15 mL
	pepper to taste	
2	bay leaves	2
6	cloves	6
3 tbsp.	lemon juice	45 mL
¼ cup	brown sugar	50 mL
	water	

GLAZE

1 cup	honey	250 mL
2 tsp.	dry mustard	10 mL
½ cup	beer	125 mL
¼ cup	fat drippings from the hocks	50 mL

Rinse the pork hocks thoroughly, making sure that the skin is well-scraped. Leave the skin and fat on. • In a large pot, cover the pork hocks with water. Add the remaining ingredients, except for the glaze ingredients, and bring mixture to a boil. Simmer for 2½ hours or until pork hocks are tender. • To make the glaze, mix together all ingredients. Arrange the hocks in a baking pan, and coat them with the glaze. Broil until crisp, turning until browned on all sides or place pan into a 400°F (200°C) oven and cook until browned. • **Note:** The volumes in this recipe are easily increased as required. Basically you are simply seasoning to taste. • A good complementary dish to go with pork hocks is sauerkraut. A slight variation is to put drained and heated sauerkraut on the bottom of the baking dish and place the boiled hocks on top before putting in the oven. Retain just enough broth to keep the mixture wet. Some folks add dumplings too.

CHICKEN

6.5 oz.	3-4 pieces, flattened, skinless, boneless chicken breast	180 g	
⅓ oz.	butter (2 tsp. [10 mL])	10 g	
1 tsp.	red wine vinegar	5 mL	
¾ tsp.	soy sauce	3 mL	
1 tsp.	honey	5 mL	
¼ tsp.	finely chopped garlic (1 mL)	1 g	
½ tsp.	finely chopped ginger (2 mL)	2 g	

GLACÉD CHICKEN BREAST WITH STRAWBERRIES

Chef Zimmerman
Westin Hotel, Calgary

Heat butter in skillet. Season chicken with salt and pepper and sauté on both sides, until meat is white throughout. Remove chicken and set aside. • Deglacé pan with red wine vinegar (stir wine vinegar into pan juices). Add soy sauce, honey, garlic, and ginger, stir well. Add chicken and glacé in residue. • Add strawberries, but just heat - don't cook. • Serve immediately with sautéed wild rice with pine nuts. • Serves 2. • See photograph, page 144A.

¼ cup	butter OR margarine	50 mL
5	small onions	5
1	garlic clove, minced	1
3 lbs.	chicken pieces	1.5 kg
14 oz.	can whole tomatoes	398 mL
1 cup	dry red wine	250 mL
½ tsp.	basil	2 mL
	salt and pepper to taste	

ITALIAN CHICKEN CASSEROLE

Melt butter in a skillet and add 1 finely chopped onion, garlic and chicken pieces. Cook, turning often, until chicken is brown. • Transfer to an ovenproof dish and add the undrained tomatoes, wine, basil, peeled whole onions, salt and pepper. • Cover and bake at 325°F (160°C) for 40 minutes or until the chicken is tender. • Serves 4.

Hard work is often just the easy work you didn't do at the right time.

EASY CHICKEN CACCIATORE

Delicious!

	flour	
3 lbs.	cut up frying chicken	1.5 kg
	butter	
3 cups	tomato juice	750 mL
½ cup	chopped onion	125 mL
1	garlic clove, minced (optional)	1
1 tbsp.	dried parsley	15 mL
¼ tsp.	thyme	1 mL
dash	paprika	dash
dash	Tabasco sauce	dash
	salt and pepper to taste	
2	green peppers, cut in chunks	2
1½ cups	sliced mushrooms	375 mL

Flour chicken; melt butter in a frying pan and brown chicken. Transfer to a casserole dish. • To make sauce, combine all remaining ingredients in saucepan, except peppers and mushrooms, and cook slowly for about ½ hour. • Add sauce to chicken and cook at 350°F (180°C) for ½ hour, then add peppers and mushrooms and cook an additional ½ hour. • Serve with rice and French green beans.

CHICKEN PILAF TIMOTHY

½ cup	butter OR margarine	125 mL
2 cups	strips of cooked chicken, ham or other meat	500 mL
¼ cup	diced onion	50 mL
2 tsp.	salt	10 mL
⅛ tsp.	pepper	0.5 mL
½ tsp.	oregano OR thyme	2 mL
1 cup	uncooked rice	250 mL
2½ cups	chicken stock	625 mL
½ cup	chopped tomatoes, drained	125 mL
½ cup	chopped walnuts	125 mL

Melt the butter OR margarine in a large saucepan. Add meat and onion and cook until the onion is tender. Add salt, pepper and oregano, then add the rice and cook, stirring occasionally, for 5 minutes. • Slowly add the chicken stock, tomatoes and walnuts; bring to a boil, cover and simmer for about 20 minutes, or until the rice is tender. Do not stir while cooking. • Serve very hot with crisp hot bread, a green salad, and a fruit dessert. • Serves 8.

⅓ cup	oil	75 mL	
1	whole chicken, cut into 2" (5 cm) pieces	1	**EASY**
1	clove garlic, minced	1	**SPANISH RICE**
1	medium onion, chopped	1	**PAELLA**
1	tomato, cut into pieces	1	
1 tbsp.	chopped parsley	15 mL	
12	medium shrimp	12	
	salt to taste		
2 oz.	can Spanish red peppers	55 g	
4½ cups	chicken broth	1.125 L	
½ tsp.	saffron, for color*	2 mL	
1½ cups	uncooked long-grain rice	375 mL	
½ cup	sliced, hard Spanish or Italian sausage (optional)	125 mL	

In a hot skillet heat oil and cook chicken pieces until tender; add garlic, onion, tomato and parsley; simmer for 10-15 minutes. • Add the shrimp, salt and red peppers and cook for a few minutes longer on low heat. • Add chicken broth, saffron, rice and sausage and simmer, covered, for 30 minutes. • Stir gently and simmer for another 15 minutes, uncovered. • Serves 6. • * If you don't have saffron on hand, substitute turmeric to color this dish.

3	large chicken breasts, halved	3	**HERBED**
	salt and pepper to taste		**CHICKEN EN**
¼ cup	butter OR margarine	50 mL	**CASSEROLE**
10 oz.	can cream of chicken soup	284 mL	
¾ cup	white wine	175 mL	
⅔ cup	sliced water chestnuts	150 mL	
⅔ cup	sliced mushrooms	150 mL	
2 tbsp.	chopped green pepper	25 mL	
¼ tsp.	crushed thyme	1 mL	

Lightly season chicken with salt and pepper. • Melt butter in a skillet and brown chicken slowly. • Arrange browned chicken, skin side up, in a 8" x 12" (3 L) baking dish. • For the sauce, add soup to drippings in the skillet. Slowly add the wine, stirring smoothly; add the remaining ingredients and heat until boiling. • Pour sauce over chicken. • Cover with foil and bake at 350°F (180°C) for 25 minutes. Uncover and continue to bake for 25-35 minutes or until chicken is tender. • Serve with hot fluffy rice. • Serves 6.

CHICKEN IN LEMON SAUCE

1 pkg.	EACH chicken thighs and chicken legs	1 pkg.
½ cup	liquid honey	125 mL
¼ cup	ketchup	50 mL
2 tbsp.	soy sauce	30 mL
2 tbsp.	lemon juice	30 mL

Place chicken in a 8" x 12" (3 L) dish. • Mix together honey, ketchup, soy sauce and lemon juice and pour over chicken. • Marinate about 3 hours. • Cover with foil and cook at 350°F (180°C) for 45 minutes. Remove foil and cook another 45 minutes or until chicken is cooked. • Serves 4. • **Note:** If doubling this recipe, do NOT double soy sauce.

CHICKEN FILLETS IN MUSHROOM SAUCE

3	whole chicken breasts (6 halves)	3
	cornstarch	
	salt and pepper	
	vegetable oil	
2	egg whites, lightly beaten	2
1 tbsp.	butter OR margarine	15 mL

SAUCE

½ lb.	mushrooms	250 g
2 tbsp.	butter OR margarine	30 mL
1 tbsp.	flour	15 mL
2 tsp.	beef bouillon (dry crystals)	10 mL
1-1½ cups	cream	250-375 mL
2	egg yolks	2

Cut each breast in half and bone. Flatten slightly with a mallet. • Lay breasts in a single layer in a pan and sprinkle both sides with cornstarch, salt and pepper. Leave 20 minutes, then sprinkle both sides with oil. Leave 20 minutes and then coat with egg white. • Melt butter in a nonstick pan and brown breasts. • Put in oven and bake, uncovered, 20 minutes at 300°F (150°C). • To make the sauce, sauté mushrooms in melted butter. Stir in flour. Add bouillon and 1 cup (250 mL) cream. Cook to thicken. • Beat yolks, adding a little sauce to warm them. Return this mixture to pan, stirring constantly, and cook slowly for a few minutes. Add more cream if necessary. Sauce should be fairly thick. • Top each breast with sauce. • Serves 6.

Although having a telephone answering device in our home was pretty expensive, we really do miss her now that she's gone off to college.

4	whole chicken breasts	4	
½ cup	flour	125 mL	
1 tsp.	salt	5 mL	
⅛ tsp.	pepper	0.5 mL	
½ tsp.	paprika	2 mL	
¼ cup	butter	50 mL	
1 cup	sliced mushrooms	250 mL	
1½ cups	thick sour cream	375 mL	
1 cup	water	250 mL	
1 tsp.	thyme	5 mL	

MUSHROOM CHICKEN IN CREAM

Split breasts in half, bone if desired. ● Combine flour, salt, pepper and paprika. ● Dredge breasts in the flour mixture and then brown in butter. ● Transfer to an ovenproof dish, add mushrooms and 1 cup (250 mL) sour cream with the water. Sprinkle with thyme, cover tightly, and bake at 325°F (160°C) for 1 hour. Stir in the remaining cream and return to oven for 5 minutes. Serve immediately. ● Serves 8.

1	roasting chicken, cut in serving pieces	1
3-4	onions, chopped	3-4
	garlic cloves to taste	
	salt and pepper to taste	
	potatoes	

DUTCH-OVEN ONION CHICKEN

Rinse chicken pieces, pat dry. Rub all sides with cut garlic cloves. ● Arrange generous layer of chopped onion on bottom of Dutch oven or roaster. Season onions with salt and pepper and remainder of garlic cloves, crushed. ● Rub each chicken piece with a handful of seasoned onion. Place chicken pieces on top of onions. Roast, covered, in 350°F (180°C) oven, turning and basting with pan juices until almost golden. If liquid is absorbed, a small amount of water may be added. ● Peel and quarter enough potatoes for required servings; place around chicken. Continue baking until chicken and potatoes are golden brown. The browner, the better.

Hint: An excellent cheap furniture polish: take equal parts of boiled linseed oil, turpentine, and vinegar. Mix together and shake well before using. Pour a little on a soft cloth to apply and wipe completely dry with a clean soft cloth. Use every 6 months, very sparingly, with lots of elbow grease.

CHICKEN AND DUMPLINGS

2	whole chicken breasts, split, boned and skinned	2
1 cup	plus 2 tbsp. flour	280 mL
1 tsp.	poultry seasoning	5 mL
1 tsp.	ground coriander	5 mL
½ tsp.	salt	2 mL
1 tbsp.	vegetable oil	15 mL
1	large onion, coarsely chopped	1
1	garlic clove, minced	1
2 cups	chicken broth	500 mL
¼ cup	water	50 mL
1 cup	sliced mushrooms OR halved or quartered	250 mL
1½ cups	sliced carrots	375 mL
½ cup	plus 2 tbsp. picante sauce	155 mL
1	red pepper, cut into 1" (2.5 cm) pieces	1
1 tsp.	baking powder	5 mL
½-⅓ cup	milk	75-125 mL

Cut chicken into 1" (2.5 cm) pieces. • Combine 2 tbsp. (30 mL) of flour, poultry seasoning, coriander and salt in plastic bag. • Shake chicken in flour to coat. • Heat oil in Dutch oven or large saucepan over medium heat. Brown chicken in oil on all sides. Add any remaining flour mixture from bag, onion and garlic; cook 1 minute. Add broth, water, mushrooms, carrots and ½ cup (125 mL) picante sauce. Bring to boil, reduce heat. Cover and simmer 5 minutes. Stir in red pepper. • Combine remaining 1 cup (250 mL) flour and baking powder. Add milk and 2 tbsp. (30 mL) picante sauce. Stir just until moistened. Drop batter by heaping teaspoons (7 mL) into simmering chicken mixture. Serve with additional picante sauce. • Serves 6.

SAUCY CRANBERRY CHICKEN

½ cup	chopped onion	125 mL
2 tbsp.	butter OR margarine	30 mL
¼ cup	butter OR margarine	50 mL
1½ cups	canned cranberries	375 mL
⅔ cup	ketchup	150 mL
½ cup	brown sugar	125 mL
2 tbsp.	vinegar	30 mL
1 tsp.	dry mustard	5 mL
3 lbs.	chicken pieces	1.5 kg

In a medium skillet, sauté onion in 2 tbsp. (30 mL) butter. Stir in remaining ingredients, except for chicken, bring to a boil and simmer, uncovered, for 15 minutes. • Spoon cranberry mixture over chicken and bake at 350°F (180°C) for 30-40 minutes or until chicken is done.

2	broiler/fryer chickens, quartered	2
6 tbsp.	butter OR margarine	90 mL
1 cup	chopped onion	250 mL
8 slices	bacon, finely diced	8
2 tbsp.	flour	30 mL
1 tbsp.	curry powder	15 mL
10 oz.	can beef broth	284 mL
¼ cup	orange or ginger marmalade	50 mL
2 tbsp.	ketchup	30 mL
2 tbsp.	lemon juice	30 mL

GLAZED CURRY PARTY CHICKEN

Wash chicken quarters, pat dry, skin if desired. • Melt butter in a large shallow baking pan. Dip chicken in butter to coat both sides, then arrange, meaty side up, in a single layer, in the same pan. Bake at 400°F (200°C) for 20 minutes or until the chicken is a light golden brown. • To make glaze, combine remaining ingredients in a medium-sized saucepan, stirring constantly; bring to a boil then let simmer, stirring often, for 15 minutes or until thick. • Spoon half of glaze over chicken to make a thick coating. Continue baking for 20 minutes. • Spoon on rest of the glaze. Bake 20 minutes longer or until chicken is tender and richly glazed. • Serves 6-8.

3 lb.	frying chicken, cut up flour, salt, pepper for dredging	1.5 kg
¼ cup	shortening or vegetable oil	50 mL
1	large white onion	1
1	green pepper, cut in strips	2
19 oz.	can peach halves	540 mL
1 tbsp.	cornstarch	15 mL
1 tbsp.	soy sauce	15 mL
3 tbsp.	white vinegar	45 mL
2	ripe medium tomatoes	2

POLYNESIAN CHICKEN

Wash chicken and pat dry. Coat with seasoned flour. Heat oil in electric frying pan to 350°F (180°C) and brown the chicken pieces on all sides. Lower heat to 250°F (120°C), cover and cook for 20 minutes, turning occasionally. • Drain off excess fat. • Quarter the onion and separate into pieces. Add the onion and green pepper to the frying pan. Cook until onion is transparent and chicken is tender. • Drain syrup from peaches. Measure 1 cup (250 mL), adding water if necessary, and blend in the cornstarch. Add soy sauce and vinegar. • Stir into chicken and cook until liquid is clear and slightly thickened, stirring often. Add peaches and tomatoes. Heat 5 minutes. • Serve with rice. • Serves 4.

2 x 3 lb.	frying chickens, cut up OR 5 lbs. (2.2 kg) boned chicken breasts	1.5 kg
1 cup	all-purpose flour	250 mL
1 tsp.	salt	5 mL
¼ tsp.	pepper	1 mL
¼ cup	butter OR margarine	50 mL
½	medium onion, finely chopped	½
1	garlic clove, minced	1
⅓ cup	green pepper, diced	75 mL
½ tsp.	dry mustard	2 mL
1 tbsp.	soy sauce	15 mL
⅓ cup	chili sauce	75 mL
14 oz.	can unsweetened pineapple chunks	398 mL
10 oz.	can mandarin orange segments	284 mL
	dry white table wine	

SPICY POLYNESIAN CHICKEN

Wash chicken pieces and pat dry on paper towels. • In paper bag, mix flour, salt and pepper. Shake chicken pieces in bag until coated. • Melt butter in heavy frying pan and sauté chicken pieces until golden brown. Remove to 2½-quart (2.5 L) casserole. • Drain off excess fat, leaving about 1 tbsp. (15 mL). Sauté onion, garlic, green pepper for about 5 minutes. Remove from heat. • Dissolve dry mustard in soy sauce. Add, with chili sauce, to frying pan. Drain juices from pineapple and oranges into measuring cup. Bring liquid to 12 oz. (340 mL) by addition of dry white wine. Add to frying pan, mix, bring to a boil and stir to dissolve brown bits in pan. Reduce heat and simmer for 5 minutes. • Spoon sauce over chicken in casserole. Bake, covered at 350°F (180°C) for 45 minutes. Add drained fruit and baste with liquid in casserole. Bake, uncovered, for additional 15 minutes. • This may be made ahead and frozen - but add fruit later.

Finger Print Experts

Fine furniture is all hand rubbed
Repeatedly, I've read it.
The finest then let ours be dubbed
and give our tots the credit.

by Virginia Moody Hagan

Glacéd Chicken Breast with Strawberries, page 137
Gourmet Wild Rice Casserole, page 101

1	large pineapple	1	
1 tsp.	soy sauce	5 mL	
dash	white pepper	dash	
¾ lb.	boneless chicken, cut in 1″ (2.5 cm) cubes	365 g	

SWEET AND SOUR CHICKEN

BATTER

½ cup	all-purpose flour	125 mL
¼ cup	cornstarch	50 mL
1	egg	1
½ cup	water	125 mL
1 tbsp.	oil	15 mL

SAUCE

2 tsp.	vegetable oil	10 mL
2 tbsp.	white wine vinegar	30 mL
3 tbsp.	ketchup	45 mL
1¼ tbsp.	sugar	18 mL
¼ tsp.	salt	1 mL
3 oz.	fresh pineapple, cut in 1″ (2.5 cm) squares	85 g
1	small tomato, cut in 1″ (2.5 cm) squares	1
2 oz.	green bell pepper, cut in 1″ (2.5 cm) squares	55 g
2 tsp.	cornstarch	10 mL
1 tbsp.	water	15 mL

Lily and Nicky Chan
Lily Restaurant, Calgary

Cut pineapple in quarters, lengthwise. Remove fruit. Save the shells. ● Add soy sauce and pepper to chicken. Mix well. Let sit for 15 minutes. ● To make batter, put flour, cornstarch, egg, water and oil in a big bowl; mix well. ● Heat 2 cups oil in wok over high heat. Dip chicken in batter. Deep-fry until golden brown. Drain well. ● To make sauce, heat 2 tsp. (5 mL) vegetable oil over medium-high heat. Add vinegar, ketchup, sugar, salt, pineapple, tomato and green pepper. Cook for 2 minutes. ● Mix cornstarch with water and add to sauce. Cook until sauce is thick. Add chicken, stir well and serve on pineapple shells.

Home Recipe for Wall Cleaner

1 cup	ammonia	250 mL
½ cup	vinegar	125 mL
¼ cup	baking soda	50 mL
1 gallon	warm water	4 L

Combine all ingredients in an acid-resistant container, plastic is fine. Cleaner will not dull paint or streak.

HAWAIIAN CHICKEN

1	large chicken, cut up	1
¼ cup	flour	50 mL
½ tsp.	paprika	2 mL
½ cup	melted margarine OR butter	125 mL
1	onion, finely chopped	1
1⅓ cups	ketchup	325 mL
2 cups	pineapple juice	500 mL
1 tsp.	salt	5 mL
⅛ tsp.	pepper	0.5 mL
4 tsp.	Worcestershire sauce	20 mL
1 cup	brown sugar	250 mL
½ cup	lemon juice	125 mL

Dust chicken with flour and paprika. • Brown the chicken in the butter in a large skillet and remove to a shallow ovenproof dish. • To make sauce, sauté onions in pan drippings until translucent, add the remaining ingredients and stir to remove all bits from the bottom of the pan. When well blended and hot, pour the sauce over the chicken. • Bake, uncovered, at 325°F (160°C) for 2 hours. • Serves 6.

MANDARIN CHICKEN

Very quick and easy to prepare.

1	whole chicken breast, skinned, boned	1
3 tbsp.	soy sauce	45 mL
½ tsp.	dried dillweed	2 mL
3 tbsp.	peanut oil	45 mL
½ cup	thinly sliced celery	125 mL
8 oz.	can water chestnuts, drained, thinly sliced	227 mL
10 oz.	can mandarin orange sections, drained, liquid reserved	284 mL
1 tbsp.	cornstarch	15 mL

Cut chicken into bite-sized pieces. • Combine 2 tbsp. (30 mL) soy sauce and dillweed. • Pour over chicken and let stand for 30 minutes. • Heat 1 tbsp. (15 mL) oil in a wok or a large skillet. Add celery and water chestnuts. Stir-fry for 2 minutes or until celery turns bright green. Remove from wok and set aside. • Heat remaining oil in wok and add the chicken; stir-fry for about 3 minutes then add celery and water chestnuts. • Blend liquid from mandarin orange sections with cornstarch and 1 tbsp. (15 mL) soy sauce. Slowly stir into wok and cook until bubbly. Add orange sections and cook until heated through. • Makes 2 servings.

OVEN-BARBECUED CHICKEN

Gluten-Free *

6 lbs.	frying chicken parts	2.5 kg
⅓ cup	lemon juice	75 mL
¼ cup	soy sauce	50 mL
1 tbsp.	chopped parsley	15 mL
¾ cup	vegetable oil	175 mL
6	drops Tabasco sauce	6
⅛ tsp.	salt	0.5 mL
⅛ tsp.	pepper	0.5 mL
1½ tsp.	garlic salt OR 1 garlic clove, crushed	7 mL
1 cup	bread crumbs OR flour*	250 mL

Wash and dry chicken parts. • Combine the remaining ingredients except for the bread crumbs. Pour mixture over chicken and let stand for 4 hours, turning pieces occasionally. • Drain chicken and roll lightly in the bread crumbs OR flour. • Arrange in a shallow pan and bake at 350°F (180°C) for 2 hours or until chicken is tender. • * For gluten-free diets, substitute crushed cornflakes for crumbs or flour.

DEEP-FRIED CHICKEN DRUMSTICKS

8	drumsticks	8
2	eggs, beaten	2
2	garlic cloves, minced	2
½ tsp.	minced fresh ginger	2 mL
2 tbsp.	pale dry sherry	30 mL
2 tbsp.	soy sauce	30 mL
1 tsp.	sugar	5 mL
2 tbsp.	cornstarch	30 mL
¼ cup	all-purpose flour	50 mL

Marinate drumsticks in a mixture of eggs, garlic, ginger, sherry, soy sauce and sugar for 30 minutes or more. • Remove chicken and add cornstarch and flour to the marinade. Lightly coat the chicken with marinade and deep-fry, in oil heated to 375°F (190°C), for 10 minutes; drain and place on baking sheet. • Keep warm by covering with foil, until all deep-frying is completed. • Bake drumsticks in a preheated 300°F (150°C) oven for 20 minutes or until tender, turning drumsticks over after 10 minutes. • Serve on a heated platter.

Hint: To mend a leaky vase, melt some paraffin and pour a thick layer into the bottom. Allow to harden.

SMOKED CHICKEN

1	roasting OR stewing chicken	1
2 tbsp.	whole peppercorns	30 mL
2 tbsp.	salt	30 mL
½ cup	white sugar	125 mL
½ cup	black dry Chinese Keemun tea leaves	125 mL
	sesame seed oil	
	parsley for garnish	

Prepare the chicken by removing as much fat from inside the cavity and under the skin as is feasible and saving it. • Toast whole peppercorns until hot, then crush them coarsely and mix with salt. Rub the chicken with this mixture, inside and out, and let stand for 3 hours. • In the bottom of a roasting pan, place a sufficiently large sheet of foil to totally enclose chicken. Sprinkle sugar and Keemun tea leaves onto the foil. Place a rack, on the foil and place the saved chicken fat on the rack. Place the chicken on the rack and seal the foil. • Cook in a preheated 375°F (190°C) oven for 25-30 minutes per lb. • When cooked, uncover the chicken and brush with sesame seed oil; return to the oven and roast, uncovered, for 5-10 minutes more or until golden brown. • Cut the chicken into serving pieces, serve hot and garnish with parsley. • **Note:** The results of this recipe are as good with stewing chickens as with roasting chickens.

RABBIT AND CALVADOS

Chef Williams
Palliser Hotel, Calgary

1	medium rabbit	1
	flour, salt and pepper	
4 oz.	butter (8 tbsp. [120 mL])	115 g
2	medium onions finely chopped	2
2	garlic cloves, chopped	2
¼ cup	Calvados	50 mL
2 cups	English cider	500 mL
1 tbsp.	flour	15 mL
½ cup	32% cream	125 mL

Prepare rabbit and cut into pieces. Dust with a little flour and season. • Heat butter in a large frying pan. Cook rabbit in the butter until golden brown on both sides. • Add the onions and cook until transparent, then add garlic. Add the Calvados and flambé. Stir in cider and simmer for 30-45 minutes. • Add cream and simmer to reduce by one-third the cooking liqueur. Correct seasoning and consistency. • Serve hot with accompanying vegetables and potato. • Serves 4.

Be not anxious about what you have, but what you are.

FISH

1 lb.	fresh shrimp	500 g	**DEEP-FRIED**
½ tsp.	powdered ginger	2 mL	**SHRIMP**
dash	M S G	dash	
½ cup	flour	125 mL	
1 tbsp.	sugar	15 mL	*BATTER*
¼ cup	cornstarch	50 mL	
1 tsp.	salt	5 mL	*Gon Jaw Har Kew.*
½ tsp.	baking powder	2 mL	
½ cup	water	125 mL	

Wash shrimp in cold water, shell, devein, wash and drain. • Cut shrimp in half, lengthwise, sprinkle ginger, and M S G over shrimp. Mix lightly. Combine all dry ingredients, add water. Add 2 tbsps. (30 mL) more water if batter is too thick. Beat until smooth. • Dip shrimp in batter and deep-fry, at 370°F (190°C), until golden brown.

2 tbsp.	cooking oil	30 mL	**TOMATO**
2 tbsp.	chopped green pepper	30 mL	**SAUCE FOR**
2 tbsp.	chopped green onion	30 mL	**SHRIMP**
5½ oz.	can tomato sauce	156 mL	
1½ cups	water	375 mL	
1 tsp.	salt	5 mL	
1 tbsp.	sugar	15 mL	
1 tsp.	Worcestershire Sauce	5 mL	
1 tsp.	mustard powder	5 mL	

Heat oil. Fry green onions and peppers for 3 minutes. Add rest of ingredients. Simmer 10 minutes. Strain. Serve with shrimp.

Hint: Do not starch linens that are to be stored as the starch may cause them to rot.

SPICED SHRIMP

3 tbsp.	oil	45 mL
1 lb.	large raw deveined shrimp	500 g
1 tbsp.	sherry	15 mL
½ tsp.	salt	2 mL
pinch	white pepper	pinch
2	garlic cloves	2
1	slice ginger root, chopped	1
1	green onion, chopped	1
¼ cup	tomato ketchup	50 mL
1 tbsp.	Worcestershire sauce	15 mL
dash	Tabasco	dash
2 tsp.	sugar	10 mL
1 tsp.	cornstarch	5 mL
1 tbsp.	water	15 mL

Heat oil in wok. Add shrimp, sherry, salt and pepper and stir-fry until shrimp are pink. Remove from wok using slotted spoon. • Add garlic, ginger and green onion to wok and stir-fry for 30 seconds, then add ketchup, sauces and sugar and stir-fry for 1 minute. • Dissolve cornstarch in water, add and simmer, stirring until thickened. Return the shrimp and toss until heated through. • Serve hot.

CURRIED SHRIMP

1 lb.	shelled raw shrimp, fresh or frozen	500 g
2 tbsp.	butter OR margarine	30 mL
1	medium onion	1
1	small bay leaf	1
dash	thyme	dash
1 tbsp.	curry powder, or to taste	15 mL
6-8	mushrooms, sliced	6-8
10 oz.	can cream of chicken soup	284 mL
½ cup	light cream OR milk	125 mL

Clean and cook shrimp. • Melt butter in a saucepan, and cook onion until soft but not brown. Add bay leaf, thyme, curry powder and mushrooms, mixing well. Stir in soup and cream. Bring to a boil for 2-3 minutes, stirring constantly, until sauce is thick and smooth. Add the shrimp and heat thoroughly. • Serve with hot rice and small dishes of chutney, toasted almonds, raisins and coconut. • Serves 4-6.

"The best way out is through". (Robert Frost)

½ cup	chopped green onions	125 mL
2-3	garlic cloves, minced	2-3
⅓ cup	vegetable oil	75 mL
¼ cup	flour	50 mL
7½ oz.	can tomato sauce	213 mL
1¼ cups	7-Up	300 mL
1 lb.	shelled shrimp, cooked	500 g
2	bay leaves	2
1 tsp.	salt	5 mL
2 tsp.	thyme	10 mL

SHRIMP CREOLE

Brown onions and garlic in heated oil for 5 minutes, stirring occasionally. • Stir in flour, then add tomato sauce and 7-Up, cooking until mixture boils. • Add shrimp, bay leaves, salt and thyme. Cook over low heat for 15 minutes. • Remove bay leaves and serve over rice.

¼ cup	butter	50 mL
¼ cup	minced onion	50 mL
½ lb.	scallops	250 g
½ lb.	shrimp	250 g
½ lb.	oysters	250 g
1 tbsp.	butter	15 mL
½ lb.	fresh mushrooms, sliced or quartered	250 g
1 tbsp.	flour	15 mL
1½ cups	sour cream at room temperature	375 mL
1¼ tsp.	salt	6 mL
dash	pepper	dash

SEAFOOD STROGANOFF

In a large skillet melt butter, add onion and sauté for 5 minutes or until soft. • Add all the seafood and sauté another 5 minutes. • Transfer this to a heated dish and put in oven on warm. • Add remaining butter to skillet and add mushrooms. Cook on medium heat until browned. • Sprinkle in flour and stir together for 2 minutes. • Reduce heat to medium low and add sour cream, seafood mixture, salt and pepper. Cook, stirring constantly, until seafood is heated through. DO NOT BOIL! • Serve with rice or noodles, garnish with parsley and lemon slices. • Serves 8.

"For it is in giving that we receive."

LOBSTER CASSEROLE

Very simple but elegant and delicious.

2 x 5 oz.	cans lobster	2 x 142 g
10 oz.	can tomato soup	284 mL
10 oz.	can green pea soup	284 mL
1 cup	sour cream	250 mL
½ tsp.	curry	2 mL
¼ tsp.	cayenne	1 mL
3 tbsp.	sherry	45 mL

Combine ingredients and heat for 30 minutes. • Serve with rice. • Serves 6. • **Variation:** For a similar and equally delicious soup see page 70.

SEAFOOD CASSEROLE

2 cups	chopped onion	500 mL
3 cups	chopped celery	750 mL
2 cups	sliced mushrooms	750 mL
3 tbsp.	butter OR margarine	45 mL
1 tsp.	salt	5 mL
¼ tsp.	pepper	1 mL
5 cups	milk	1.25 L
½ cup	butter	125 mL
¾ cup	all-purpose flour	175 mL
1 lb.	mild Cheddar cheese, grated	500 g
2 x 5 oz.	cans lobster meat	2 x 142 g
½ lb.	crab meat cooked	250 g
¾ lb.	shrimp cooked	365 g
1 lb.	scallops, cooked, quartered	500 g

Sauté onion, celery and mushrooms in butter; add salt and pepper. • Heat milk until very hot, but DO NOT BOIL. Whisk in combined butter and flour; add the onion, celery, mushrooms and cheese. Using a whisk, stir occasionally and cook until cheese has melted and the sauce has thickened slightly. • Add more hot milk if sauce is too thick. Add all the seafood and place in a large casserole or individual casserole dishes. • Heat in 350°F (180°C) oven until bubbly and brown, approximately 25-30 minutes. • Do not overbake or scallops may be tough. • Serve on rusks with a tossed salad. • Serves 8-10. • **Note:** If frozen seafood is used, it must be steamed before adding to the sauce.

It is not what comes into your life that makes the pattern.
It is the use you make of it that counts.

6-8	salmon fillets *	6-8	SIMPLE
1 tsp.	anise seeds	5 mL	SALMON
1 tsp.	black peppercorns	5 mL	
½ tsp.	salt	2 mL	
pinch	fresh OR dry parsley	pinch	

SIMPLE SALMON

Preheat broiler. ● Arrange fillets in a single layer on a lightly oiled broiler pan. ● Combine the seasonings, grind to a coarse mixture and spread on the fillets lightly, to your taste. ● Broil fillets for 4-6 minutes. Do not overcook. ● To serve, garnish with lemon slices or chives or mayonnaise mixed with lemon or lime juice (1 part juice to 2 parts mayonnaise). ● * Or any other firm-textured fish.

1 cup	butter OR margarine	250 mL
1	garlic clove, minced	1
¼ cup	ketchup	50 mL
4 tsp.	prepared mustard	20 mL
¼ tsp.	Worcestershire sauce	1 mL
¼ tsp.	pepper	1 mL
1 tbsp.	lemon juice	15 mL
4-5 lbs.	salmon	2-2.5 kg

BAKED SALMON

Combine all ingredients, except the salmon. Heat to a simmer, but do not boil. ● Place the prepared salmon on a foil-lined cookie sheet. Crimp foil loosely around fish. ● Pour sauce over salmon and bake at 350°F (180°C) for 1 hour, or until salmon flakes easily.

1 tbsp.	butter OR margarine	15 mL
¼ cup	chopped celery	50 mL
¼ cup	diced carrots	50 mL
1	small onion, chopped	1
10 oz.	cream of celery soup	284 mL
2 x 7.5 oz.	cans salmon, drained	2 x 225 g
¼ tsp.	basil	1 mL
¼ tsp.	rosemary	1 mL
¼ tsp.	thyme	1 mL
7 oz.	uncooked flat noodles, cooked	200 g
½ cup	grated Cheddar cheese	125 mL

SALMON CASSEROLE

Melt butter in a frying pan; sauté celery, carrots and onion until browned lightly. ● Mix in soup. Flake salmon, and blend well into soup mixture. Add herbs and stir frequently. ● Lightly grease a 1¼-2-quart (1.5-2 L) casserole. ● Spread ½ of soup and vegetable mixture on the bottom, then add the noodles and spread remaining soup mixture on top. ● Sprinkle grated cheese on top. ● Bake at 350°F (190°C) for 30 minutes. ● Serves 4-6.

FILLET OF SOLE WITH SHRIMP SAUCE

4	fillets of sole	4
3 tbsp.	flour	45 mL
½ tsp.	salt	2 mL
⅓ cup	butter, melted	75 mL
1 cup	Shrimp Sauce, recipe follows	250 mL
	parsley for garnish	
	lemon wedges for garnish	

WHITE SAUCE

2 tbsp.	butter	15 mL
2 tbsp.	flour	30 mL
1 cup	half and half (creamilk)	250 mL
1 tsp.	chicken base	5 mL
	salt and pepper to taste	

SHRIMP SAUCE

Delicious

1 cup	White Sauce, recipe above	250 mL
1 tbsp.	butter	15 mL
¼ cup	chopped onion	50 mL
1 cup	Norwegian baby shrimp OR small shrimp	250 mL
1 tbsp.	white wine	15 mL

Roll fillets in flour, sprinkle with salt. Place them in shallow baking pan. Sprinkle melted butter on fish. Bake at 350°F for 20 minutes. • Place on a platter. Cover with warm Shrimp Sauce, sprinkle with parsley. Garnish with lemon wedges. • To make White Sauce, melt butter in a saucepan over medium heat. Blend in flour; stir in cream. Cook quickly, add chicken stock, stirring constantly until mixture thickens and bubbles. Remove from heat. Makes 1 cup (250 mL) of White Sauce. Use for various sauces. • Prepare Shrimp Sauce while making White Sauce. Melt butter, add onion, fry until translucent. When White Sauce is ready, add shrimp and white wine. • Use Shrimp Sauce for whitefish, such as fillets of sole, cod OR for vegetables.

There is a time when you have to explain to your children why they're born and its a marvelous thing if you know the reason by then. (Hazel Scott, American pianist — 1920).

3 lbs.	dressed, split, whole whitefish*	1.5 g	# BAKED STUFFED FISH
2 tbsp.	melted butter OR margarine	30 mL	
	salt and pepper to taste		

3 cups	soft bread crumbs (6 slices)	750 mL	## DILL CHEESE STUFFING
1 cup	cottage cheese (½ lb. [255 oz.])	250 mL	
½ cup	chopped dill pickle	125 mL	
¼ cup	chopped onion	50 mL	
1	egg, lightly beaten	1	
1 tsp.	salt	5 mL	
¼ tsp.	pepper	1 mL	

Clean and prepare fish. • To make stuffing, combine first 6 ingredients in order given. Makes 3 cups (750 mL). • Place half of fish, skin-side-down, in a greased large shallow baking dish and spread with the stuffing. • Place the other half of fish, skin-side-up, over stuffing and fasten with skewers or wooden picks. • Brush top with butter and sprinkle with salt and pepper. Bake in a 450°F (230°C) oven for 10 minutes per inch of fish at thickest part. • * You could also use striped bass, haddock, cod or bluefish.

2 tsp.	paprika	10 mL	# FISH AU GRATIN
¼ tsp.	ground cumin	1 mL	
½ tsp.	turmeric	2 mL	
½ tsp.	salt	2 mL	
2 tsp.	vinegar	10 mL	
	water		
1 lb.	fish fillets	500 g	
3 tbsp.	butter	45 mL	
6 tbsp.	white flour	90 mL	
3 cups	milk	750 mL	
3	eggs (beat whites first, then add yolks)	3	
½ lb.	cheese, grated	500 g	

Mix spices, salt and vinegar to make a paste. If necessary, add a little water. • Cut fish into fairly big pieces. • Apply paste to the fish and let it stand for at least 1 hour. • In a saucepan heat butter, add flour and brown it. Add milk slowly, stirring constantly. Add beaten eggs. Keep on stirring until sauce thickens. Do not boil as sauce will curdle. • Add ¼ of the grated cheese and mix well. Remove from heat. • Grease a casserole dish and spread a layer of the sauce on the bottom and then a layer of fish. Alternate layers of sauce and fish, ending with sauce. • Top with a heavy sprinkling of grated cheese, to form a thick crust when baked. • Bake at 350-375°F (180-190°C) for 45-60 minutes.

A TELEVISION FISH DISH

1 lb.	fish fillets	500 g
1 cup	milk	250 mL
1 cup	water	250 mL
	salt to taste	

SHRIMP SAUCE

3 tbsp.	softened butter OR margarine	45 mL
3 tbsp.	flour	45 mL
1 cup	cream	250 mL
1 cup	milk	250 mL
1	bay leaf	1
½ cup	finely chopped celery	125 mL
¼ cup	diced onions	50 mL
	salt and pepper	
½ lb.	fresh or frozen shrimp OR 2 x 4.5 oz. (128 g) cans	250 g

Roll fillets and secure with toothpicks. • Place milk, water and salt in a saucepan and bring to a boil. • Add fish rolls and reduce heat to simmer gently for 10 minutes. • To make the sauce, combine butter and flour and blend well. Gradually stir in the cream and milk. Add bay leaf, celery, onions, salt and pepper. • Boil sauce gently, stirring constantly to a creamy thickness. Add shrimp and heat for 1 minute. • To serve, cover fish rolls with sauce. • Serve hot.

FISH WITH SWEET AND SOUR SAUCE

½ cup	flour	125 mL
1 tsp	EACH salt, paprika, pepper	5 mL
	oil for frying	
1 lb.	fish fillets, fresh or frozen	500 g

SWEET AND SOUR SAUCE

¾ cup	chopped onion	175 mL
1 tbsp.	vegetable oil	15 mL
1 cup	water	250 mL
2 tbsp.	vinegar	30 mL
1 tbsp.	sugar	15 mL
1 tsp.	ground ginger	5 mL
¼ tsp.	salt	1 mL
¼ cup	cold water	50 mL
1 tsp.	cornstarch	5 mL
½ cup	ketchup	125 mL

Mix flour and seasonings in bag and dredge fish fillets with flour mixture. • Fry fish in hot oil, 6-8 minutes, or until fish flakes easily. • Drain on absorbent paper. • To make the sauce, cook onion in oil until tender. Add 1 cup (250 mL) water, vinegar, sugar, ginger and salt. Boil 10 minutes. • Combine cold water and cornstarch. Add cornstarch mixture and ketchup to saucepan. Cook until thick, stirring constantly. • Serve hot over cooked fish.

---

3 tbsp.	butter	45 mL
½ cup	chopped green pepper OR pimiento	125 mL
2	slices onion, chopped	2
6 tbsp.	flour	90 mL
½ tsp.	salt	2 mL
3 cups	milk	750 mL
2 x 6.5 oz.	cans tuna, solid or flaked, drained	2 x 184 g
1 tbsp.	lemon juice	15 mL
½ tsp.	salt	2 mL

TUNA PINWHEEL PIE

1½ cups	flour	375 mL
1 tbsp.	baking powder	15 mL
½ tsp.	salt	2 mL
dash	cayenne	dash
3 tbsp.	shortening	45 mL
½ cup	milk	125 mL
¾ cup	grated Cheddar cheese	175 mL
2	pimientoes, chopped	

CHEESE ROLLS

Melt butter, add green pepper and onion and cook until soft. Add flour and stir until blended. Slowly add salt and milk, stirring constantly. Bring mixture to a boil for 2 minutes. • Add tuna and lemon juice, mix well and pour into a 1-quart (2 L) baking dish or casserole. • To make cheese pinwheels, sift together first 4 roll ingredients, then cut in shortening. Add milk to make a soft dough. • Turn lightly onto a floured board. Roll out 8″ x 12″ (20 x 30 cm). • Sprinkle with grated cheese and pimiento. Roll up like a jelly roll and slice in 8 slices, (or as many servings as you need). Flatten slightly and place on top of the tuna mixture. • Bake at 450°F (230°C) for approximately 30 minutes. • Serves 4. • This is a good lunch dish for hungry children or a good light supper dish.

---

1 cup	flaked tuna	250 mL
1 cup	mashed potatoes	250 mL
6-8	capers (optional)	6-8
½	garlic clove, minced	½
1 tsp.	grated onion	5 mL
1 tbsp.	minced parsley	15 mL
	salt and pepper to taste	
1 tsp.	brandy or dry sherry	5 mL
1 tsp.	dried basil (optional)	5 mL
½ cup	butter OR oil	125 mL
¾ cup	ground walnuts	175 mL

TUNA FISH BALLS

Combine all but the last 2 ingredients. • Shape the mixture into 1″ (2.5 cm) balls. • Sauté balls for 2-3 minutes in butter or oil. • Drain the balls and roll them in the ground nuts. • Makes about 4 servings.

PASTA

HEARTY LASAGNE

1 lb.	ground beef	500 g
1	small onion, diced	1
½	small green pepper, minced (optional)	½
1 cup	sliced mushrooms	250 mL
28 oz.	can tomatoes	796 mL
13 oz.	can tomato paste	369 mL
1 tbsp.	white sugar	15 mL
1½ tsp.	salt	7 mL
½ tsp.	crushed oregano leaves	2 mL
½ tsp.	thyme leaves	2 mL
½ tsp.	crushed red pepper	2 mL
1	garlic clove, minced	1
1	bay leaf	1
16 oz.	pkg. lasagne noodles (use 14 noodles)	500 g
2	eggs	2
2 cups	ricotta cheese OR dry cottage cheese	500 mL
½ cup	Parmesan cheese	125 mL
10 oz.	pkg. frozen chopped spinach (optional)	283 g
1 lb.	mozzarella cheese, grated	500 g

In a 5-quart (5 L) Dutch oven, cook ground beef, onion, green pepper and mushrooms, stirring frequently, until all pan juices evaporate and beef is well browned. • Add tomatoes, tomato paste, sugar, salt, oregano, thyme, pepper, garlic and bay leaf. Heat to boiling, stirring to break up tomatoes, reduce heat to low, cover and simmer for 30 minutes. • Spoon off fat. • Cook lasagna noodles and drain well. • Arrange half of the noodles in a 9" x 13" (4 L) baking dish. • Combine eggs, cottage cheese, Parmesan cheese and spinach if using. Spoon ½ the mixture over the noodles. • Spread ½ the mozzarella cheese over and top with ½ of the sauce. • Repeat layers. • Bake at 375°F (190°C) for 45 minutes or until heated thorough. • Remove and let stand 10 minutes for easier serving.

LASAGNE

TOMATO SAUCE

1	large onion	1
1	garlic clove	1
¼ cup	shortening OR margarine	50 mL
28 oz.	can tomatoes	796 mL
4 oz.	can tomato paste	113 mL
2	bay leaves	2
1 tsp.	salt	5 mL
¼ tsp.	pepper	1 mL
½ cup	water	125 mL
1 lb.	lean ground beef	500 g

CHEESE SAUCE

1	small onion	1
4 tbsp.	shortening	60 mL
3 tbsp.	flour	45 mL
¾ cup	Parmesan cheese	175 mL
	salt to taste	
2 cups	milk	500 mL
2	egg yolks	2

1 lb.	pkg. lasagne noodles	500 g

To make tomato sauce, chop onion and garlic and fry in shortening. Add tomatoes, tomato paste, bay leaves, salt, pepper, water and mix. Crumble ground beef and add to this. Cover and cook over low heat 45 minutes, stir occasionally. • To make cheese sauce, chop small onion finely and cook in melted shortening 1 minute. Blend in the flour, add Parmesan cheese and salt. Gradually stir in milk and continue cooking over low heat, stirring constantly until sauce is thick as heavy cream. Mix a small amount of hot cheese mixture into the slightly beaten egg to prevent curdling. Then mix all cheese mixture and yolks together and cook over low heat 10 minutes more. Remove from heat. • Cook noodles according to package directions and drain. • Grease a large glass baking dish. Put a layer of noodles on the bottom of the dish, then pour over enough tomato sauce to cover noodles and add some of the cheese sauce. Continue layering the ingredients ending with the cheese sauce. Be sure to remove bay leaves. • Bake at 350°F (180°C) for 20 minutes then broil for 4 minutes. • Serves 6-8.

Hint: To prevent gummy or soggy noodles, rice, macaroni and spaghetti, add 2 tsp. (10 mL) of cooking oil to the water before cooking.

HOT NOODLES

Zesty flavor!

1 tsp.	sugar	5 mL
2 tbsp.	water	30 mL
1 tbsp.	light soy sauce	15 mL
1 tbsp.	oyster sauce	15 mL
2 tsp.	curry powder or to taste	10 mL
10 oz.	dry wheat noodles	285 g
3 tbsp.	peanut oil	45 mL
	finely chopped green/red/yellow sweet peppers for garnish	

Combine the first 5 ingredients and set aside. Adjust to suit your taste. Curry powder will add heat, oyster sauce flavor. ● Cook noodles as directed or 8-10 minutes in boiling water. Rinse with cold water and allow to drain, 15-20 minutes. ● Heat a wok or pan large enough to allow stirring of the noodles, add peanut oil and noodles, stirring until they are well-coated. ● Add sauce mixture and stir until hot. ● Serve on a heated platter; garnish with peppers. ● Serves 3-4. ● See photograph opposite.

PARTY CASSEROLE

Zesty flavor!

2 x 10 oz.	pkgs. frozen spinach, cooked	2 x 283 g
1 cup	chopped onion	250 mL
5 tbsp.	butter OR margarine	75 mL
½ cup	tomato sauce	125 mL
½ cup	red wine	125 mL
2 tsp.	salt	10 mL
1 tsp.	sugar	5 mL
2 lbs.	ground beef	1 kg
6 tbsp.	butter OR margarine	90 mL
1 tbsp.	flour	15 mL
3 cups	milk	750 mL
¼ tsp.	nutmeg	1 mL
12 oz.	mild Cheddar cheese, grated	340 g
3	eggs, lightly beaten	3
½ cup	grated Parmesan	125 mL
12 oz.	uncooked wide egg noodles, cooked	340 g

Boil spinach in salted water and drain when cooked. ● Sauté onion in 1 tbsp. (15 mL) butter in a small frying pan. ● Add 4 tbsp. (60 mL) butter, tomato sauce, red wine, salt, and sugar and heat through. ● Brown ground beef and add onion mixture. ● Melt remaining butter in a small saucepan, stir in flour, then slowly add milk to make a white sauce. Add nutmeg, Cheddar and eggs and mix thoroughly. ● Place half of the noodles in a large greased 12" x 16" (30 x 41 cm) casserole dish. Cover with all of the ground beef mixture, then add the remaining noodles. Cover noodles with spinach and pour the sauce over spinach. Sprinkle with Parmesan cheese. ● Bake for 1 hour at 350°F (180°C).

Hot Noodles, page 160

6 oz.	spaghetti	170 g
2 tbsp.	butter OR margarine	30 mL
2	eggs, beaten	2
⅓ cup	grated Parmesan cheese	75 mL
1 cup	creamed cottage cheese (8 oz. [250 g])	250 mL
1 lb.	ground beef OR bulk pork sausage	500 g
½ cup	chopped onion	125 mL
¼ cup	chopped green pepper	50 mL
7½ oz.	can tomatoes, cut up	213 mL
5½ oz.	can tomato paste	156 mL
1 tsp.	sugar	5 mL
1 tsp.	crushed dried oregano	5 mL
½ tsp.	garlic salt OR 1 garlic clove, crushed	2 mL
	salt to taste	
½ cup	shredded mozzarella cheese (20 oz. [55 g])	125 mL

SPAGHETTI PIE

Cook spaghetti according to package directions, and drain (should amount to approximately 3 cups [750 mL]).   •   Stir butter or margarine into hot spaghetti, then stir in beaten eggs and Parmesan cheese.   •   Form spaghetti mixture into a "crust" in a greased 10" (1 L) pie plate. Spread with cottage cheese.   •   In skillet, cook ground meat, onion and green pepper until meat is brown and vegetables are tender. Drain off fat.   •   Stir in undrained tomatoes, tomato paste, sugar, oregano, garlic and salt and heat through.   •   Turn meat mixture into spaghetti crust.   •   Bake, uncovered, at 350°F (180°C) for 20 minutes.   •   Sprinkle with mozzarella cheese, bake until melted, about 5 minutes.   •   Makes 6 servings.

Dancing Snowballs — Christmas Table Centrepiece

1	apothecary jar or goldfish bowl	1
1	tall red candle	1
	modelling clay	
¾ cup	mothballs	1
	water to fill jar	
¼ cup	vinegar	50 mL
1 tsp.	baking soda	5 mL

First anchor candle to bottom of jar with modelling clay.   •   Then add mothballs, and for each cup of water needed to fill jar, add vinegar and baking soda.   •   The mothballs will dance merrily about the candle for over an hour.   •   Renew baking soda and vinegar as needed.

CHEESE AND PASTA IN A POT

Quick, easy and tastes great.

8 oz.	large shell macaroni	250 g
2 lbs.	ground beef	1 kg
2	medium onions, chopped	2
1	garlic clove, minced	1
14 oz.	can tomatoes	398 mL
14 oz.	can spaghetti sauce	398 mL
10 oz.	can mushroom pieces and juice	284 mL
2 cups	sour cream	500 mL
½ lb.	medium Cheddar cheese	250 g
¼ lb.	mozzarella cheese	125 g

Cook macaroni according to package directions. Rinse with cold water. Drain and set aside. • Brown beef in frying pan. Drain and put into a large saucepan, such as a Dutch oven. • Add onions, garlic, tomatoes, spaghetti sauce, and mushrooms with juice. Bring mixture to a boil and allow to simmer for 20 minutes, until onions are tender. Stir occasionally while boiling. Remove from heat. • Using a 4-quart (4 L) casserole, pour ½ macaroni into the bottom of the casserole, pour ½ of meat sauce over top and spread with ½ of the sour cream. • Slice Cheddar cheese thinly and layer ½ on top. • Repeat layers. • Cover and bake at 350°F (180°C) for 45 minutes. Remove cover and top with thin slices of mozzarella cheese. Continue cooking until cheese melts. • Serves 12.

PIZZA CASSEROLE

1	medium onion, chopped	1
1 lb.	ground beef	500 g
3 cups	penne macaroni	750 mL
1 tsp.	salt	5 mL
½ tsp.	pepper	2 mL
2 x 7.5 oz.	cans tomato sauce	2 x 213 mL
1 lb.	pepperoni, sliced	500 g
1 lb.	mozzarella cheese, grated	500 g
10 oz.	can sliced mushrooms, drained	284 mL
2 x 14 oz.	jars pizza sauce	2 x 398 mL
1	large green pepper, chopped	1

Brown onion with ground beef and drain thoroughly. • Cook macaroni according to directions on package. • In a very large pan, combine salt, pepper, tomato sauce, ½ lb. (250 g) pepperoni, mozzarella cheese, ½ can mushrooms, 1 jar pizza sauce and all of the green pepper, except 2 tbsp. (30 mL). • Stir in meat mixture and macaroni. • Pour into a 9" x 13" (4 L) lasagne pan. • On top spread remaining mushrooms, green pepper, pepperoni and pizza sauce. • Bake at 350°F (180°C), uncovered, for 1 hour. • Serves 6-8.

1 lb.	ground beef	500 g	# HAMBURGER-NOODLE BAKE
¾ cup	chopped onions	175 mL	
¼ cup	chopped green pepper	50 mL	
4 oz.	medium noodles	115 g	
10 oz.	can condensed tomato soup	284 mL	
1 cup	shredded cheese	250 mL	
¼ cup	chili sauce	50 mL	*Easy to make and good to eat!*
2 tbsp.	chopped pimiento	30 mL	
½ tsp.	salt	2 mL	
½ tsp.	chili powder	2 mL	
dash	pepper	dash	
½ cup	water	125 mL	
1¼ cups	soft bread crumbs	300 mL	
2 tbsp.	melted butter	30 mL	
	green pepper rings (optional)		

In a large skillet, cook beef, onions and green pepper until the meat is brown. Drain off fat. • Cook noodles according to package directions and drain well. Return noodles to kettle. • Stir in meat mixture, tomato soup, cheese, chili sauce, pimiento, salt, chili powder, pepper and water. Mix well and put into a 9″ x 9″ (2.5 L) casserole. • Toss bread crumbs with melted butter and sprinkle on top of casserole. • Garnish with green pepper rings, if desired. • Bake, un-covered, at 350°F (180°C) until heated through, approximately 45 min-utes. • Serves 4.

---

2 tbsp.	lard	30 mL	# INTERESTING SPAGHETTI SAUCE
2-3 lbs.	steak, in bite-sized pieces	1-1.5 kg	
2	pork chops, in bite-sized pieces	2	
13 oz.	tomato paste	369 mL	
14 oz.	tomato sauce	398 mL	
2	garlic cloves, crushed	2	
2 x 10 oz.	cans whole mushrooms, drained	2 x 284 mL	
1	large green pepper, cut into chunks	1	
3 x 28 oz.	cans tomatoes	3 x 796 mL	
½-¾ cup	dry sherry	125-175 mL	
1-2 tbsp.	crushed chilies	15-30 mL	

In a large heavy pot melt the lard and brown steak and pork chops pieces. Drain off the fat and add remaining ingredients. Mix well and bring to a boil. Lower heat and simmer 3-4 hours. • Making this sauce a day ahead enhances the flavor.

SPAGHETTI TETRAZZINI

8 oz.	pkg. fine noodles	250 g
1 cup	sliced fresh mushrooms	500 mL
¼ cup	butter OR margarine	50 mL
1	medium onion, chopped	1
3 tbsp.	flour	45 mL
2 tsp.	salt	10 mL
dash	pepper	dash
dash	cayenne pepper	dash
2½ cups	milk	625 mL
2 cups	thin strips of cooked meat, ham, chicken, etc.	500 mL
2 tbsp.	grated Parmesan cheese	30 mL

Cook the noodles until chewy but not quite tender; drain. • Wash fresh mushrooms by dousing up and down in salted water, drain on a towel, then slice. • Melt butter in a skillet, add mushrooms and onion and cook until tender but not brown. Stir in the flour until smooth, add the seasonings, then gradually stir in the milk. Cook, stirring constantly, until the sauce is smooth and bubbling. • Add meat, and cheese. • Arrange noodles in a thick border around the edge of a buttered shallow baking dish. • Pour meat sauce in the center. • Bake at 400°F (200°C) for about 15-20 minutes. • Serves 6.

HAM NOODLE FLORENTINE

2 cups	uncooked egg noodles	500 mL
10 oz.	pkg. frozen chopped spinach, cooked, drained	283 g
8 oz.	pkg. ham cut in strips	250 g
10 oz.	can cream of mushroom soup	284 mL
1 cup	grated cheese	250 mL
2 tbsp.	milk	30 mL
1 tbsp.	mustard	15 mL
¼ cup	bread crumbs	60 mL

Cook noodles and combine with spinach and ham. • Place in a 2-quart (2 L) casserole. • Combine soup, cheese, milk, and mustard and mix lightly with noodles. Top with bread crumbs. • Bake for 30 minutes at 350°F (180°C). • Serves 6.

Hint: *For smoother spaghetti sauce, throw all the ingredients into a blender before cooking or heating the sauce.*

CHICKEN OR TURKEY NOODLE CASSEROLE

2 cups	broad noodles	500 mL
1½ cups	sliced broccoli OR 10 oz. (284 mL) pkg. of frozen sliced broccoli	375 mL
2 tbsp.	flour	30 mL
2 tbsp.	butter	30 mL
1 cup	chicken stock	250 mL
5 oz.	scalded cream	150 mL
8 oz.	Swiss cheese, grated	250 g
¼ tsp.	dry mustard	1 mL
¼ tsp.	salt	1 mL
¼ tsp.	pepper	1 mL
2½ cups	thinly sliced chicken OR turkey	625 mL
	slivered almonds (optional)	

Cook noodles in boiling salted water. Cook fresh broccoli just until color turns bright green. Frozen broccoli does not need to be precooked. • Meanwhile, make a roux by melting butter in a frying pan and stirring in flour; add stock, scalded cream, cheese, mustard, salt and pepper; whisk until smooth. Let cook for a few minutes. • Butter a large casserole. • Place cooked noodles and half the sauce in the bottom, then broccoli and chicken. • Top with the remainder of the sauce. • Sprinkle with slivered almonds, if desired. • Bake approximately 1 hour at 350°F (180°C). • Serves 6-8.

HAM AND MAC BAKE

3½ oz.	elbow macaroni (1 cup [250 mL])	92 g
¼ cup	butter OR margarine	50 mL
¼ cup	all-purpose flour	50 mL
2 tbsp.	brown sugar	30 mL
2 tbsp.	prepared mustard	30 mL
¼ tsp.	salt	1 mL
dash	pepper	dash
2 cups	milk	500 mL
2 cups	cubed, cooked ham	500 mL
2	medium apples, peeled, thinly sliced	2
1½ cups	soft bread crumbs	375 mL
2 tbsp.	butter OR margarine	30 mL

Cook macaroni in boiling salted water until tender, 8-10 minutes; drain. • In a large saucepan, melt butter, blend in flour, brown sugar, mustard, salt and pepper. Add milk all at once, cook and stir until thickened and bubbly. • Stir in cooked macaroni, ham and apple slices. • Turn mixture into a 2-quart (2 L) casserole. • Combine crumbs and melted butter, sprinkle over casserole. • Bake, uncovered, at 350°F (180°C) for 35 minutes. • Serves 6.

BACON AND EGG LASAGNE

12	lasagane noodles, cooked and drained	12
1 lb.	bacon, cut into 1" (2.5 cm) strips	500 g
⅓ cup	bacon drippings	75 mL
1 cup	chopped onion	250 mL
⅓ cup	flour	75 mL
½ tsp.	salt	2 mL
¼ tsp.	pepper	1 mL
4 cups	milk	1 L
12	hard-boiled eggs, sliced	12
2 cups	shredded Swiss cheese	500 mL
⅓ cup	grated Parmesan cheese	75 mL
2 tbsp.	chopped parsley	30 mL

Prepare lasagne noodles. • In a large skillet, cook bacon until crisp, drain, reserving ⅓ cup (75 mL) bacon fat. Set bacon aside. • Cook onion in fat until tender, add flour, salt and pepper. Stir until mixture forms a paste. Add milk, cook and stir until the mixture comes to a boil and thickens. • Spoon small amount of this white sauce into the bottom of a greased 9" x 13" (4 L) baking dish. • Divide noodles, bacon, white sauce, eggs and Swiss cheese into thirds. Spread in pan in 3 layers. • Sprinkle with Parmesan cheese. • Bake for 25-30 minutes at 350°F (180°C). • Sprinkle with parsley. • Let stand 10 minutes before serving.

BACHELOR MACARONI AND CHEESE

Microwave Recipe.

¼ lb.	bacon	125 g
1½ cups	raw macaroni	375 mL
1 tbsp.	finely chopped onion (optional)	15 mL
1½ cups	milk	375 mL
1 tsp.	Worcestershire sauce	5 mL
½ cup	water	125 mL
10 oz.	can Cheddar cheese soup	284 mL
½ tsp.	salt	2 mL
1 cup	shredded Cheddar cheese	250 mL

Place bacon in 2-quart (2 L) casserole, cover with paper towelling and microwave on full power for 5-6 minutes or until bacon is crisp. • Remove bacon, crumble and set aside. • Add macaroni, onion, milk, water, soup, salt and Worcestershire sauce to bacon drippings. Blend ingredients well. • Cover with lid and microwave on MEDIUM (70%) power for 20 minutes or until macaroni is tender. Stir in cheese and crumbled bacon. • Let stand for 5 minutes. • Serves 6.

10 oz.	pkg. large macaroni shells *	284 g
¼ cup	butter OR margarine	60 mL
8 oz.	fresh mushrooms, sliced	250 g
2 x 6.5 oz.	cans tuna, drained, flaked	2 x 184 g
10 oz.	pkg. frozen green peas	283 g
¼ cup	all-purpose flour	60 mL
1 tsp.	salt	5 mL
½ tsp.	dried dillweed	2 mL
¼ tsp.	white pepper	1 mL
2 cups	light cream OR whole milk	500 mL
1 cup	chicken broth	250 mL
3 tbsp.	dry sherry, or more (optional)	45 mL
½ cup	fresh breadcrumbs	125 mL
2 tbsp.	melted butter	30 mL

TUNA CASSEROLE SUPREME

Cook macaroni according to package directions, until tender but firm to the bite and drain. Rinse with cold water to prevent sticking, drain well. • In a large skillet, melt butter, add mushrooms and sauté over high heat for 3-5 minutes or until tender. • Arrange ½ of the macaroni over the bottom of a buttered 2-quart (2 L) casserole. • Top with ½ of tuna and ½ of peas. • Using a slotted spoon, remove mushrooms from skillet, leaving drippings in skillet. Spoon mushrooms over peas. Top with remaining macaroni, tuna and peas. • Whisk flour into drippings in skillet until blended. Stir in salt, dillweed, white pepper, cream or milk, and broth; bring to a boil, whisking constantly until thickened. Whisk in sherry, if using. • Pour sauce over mixture in casserole. • In a small bowl, combine breadcrumbs and melted butter; sprinkle over sauce in casserole. • Bake, uncovered, 30-40 minutes at 350°F (180°C) or until browned and bubbly. • Serves 6. • * You may use an equal weight of any shape noodles or macaroni.

"Who so neglects learning in his youth loses the past and is dead for the future." (Euripides)

CHEESE AND BEAN ENCHILADAS

3 tbsp.	olive OR vegetable oil	45 mL
½	large onion, chopped	½
3-4	garlic cloves, crushed	3-4
2 oz.	diced green chilies OR green pepper (chilies preferred)	55 g
1 lb.	cooked, peeled and chopped tomatoes OR 14 oz. (398 mL) can tomatoes, chopped (not stewed)	500 g
1 cup	tomato juice OR juice from canned tomatoes	250 mL
¼ tsp.	powdered oregano	1 mL
¼ tsp.	basil	1 mL
1 cup	strong vegetable broth OR bouillon	250 mL
1½ tbsp.	cornstarch dissolved in cool water	22 mL

FILLING

8	flour or corn tortillas	8
8-10 oz.	grated old Cheddar cheese	250-285 g
14 oz.	can refried pinto beans	398 mL
½ cup	sliced pitted black olives	125 mL
2-3	scallions OR green onions, chopped parsley, for garnish sour cream or yogurt (optional) taco sauce (optional)	2-3

To prepare sauce, heat olive oil in skillet, add onions and garlic and sauté. When onion is quite transparent, add peppers, tomatoes, tomato juice and herbs. Let simmer for a few minutes, then add broth. • Dissolve cornstarch in water and stir slowly into sauce. Let cook VERY SLOWLY for at least 10 minutes. • To assemble, lightly oil a rectangular baking dish with sides at least 2" (5 cm) high. • Take 1 tortilla at a time, and place it gently ON the heated sauce. Draw tortilla off when warm. • On saucy side of tortilla, arrange beans, in a fat, off-center line. Place cheese on top of beans and sprinkle other ingredients on top. Roll tortilla tightly around filling and place in the baking dish. • Use the same procedure for each tortilla, placing them side by side. • Pour the remaining sauce over them. • Bake for 15-20 minutes at 350°F (180°C). • Garnish with parsley. Serve with sour cream or plain yogurt and taco sauce if desired. • Serves 4.

Desserts

CHEESECAKE PLUS

RHUBARB CRISP CHEESECAKE

1½ cups	crushed vanilla wafers (40)	375 mL
⅓ cup	melted butter	75 mL
½ tsp.	cinnamon	2 mL

FILLING

1 lb.	cream cheese	500 g
½ cup	granulated sugar	125 mL
2	eggs	2
¼ cup	whipping cream	50 mL
1 tbsp.	grated orange rind	15 mL
1 tsp.	vanilla	5 mL
2 tbsp.	all-purpose flour	30 mL

RHUBARB TOPPING

4 cups	chopped rhubarb (1 lb. [500 g])	1 L
⅓ cup	packed brown sugar	75 mL
⅓ cup	granulated sugar	75 mL
1 tsp.	cinnamon	5 mL

CRISP TOPPING

½ cup	all-purpose flour	125 mL
⅓ cup	packed brown sugar	75 mL
1 tsp.	cinnamon	5 mL
¼ cup	butter	50 mL
1 tbsp.	icing sugar	15 mL

To prepare crust, combine crushed wafers with butter and cinnamon. Press into foil-lined 9″ (23 cm) pan. ● To prepare filling, beat cream cheese until smooth; beat in sugar, eggs, cream, orange rind and vanilla until smooth. Sprinkle with flour. Beat well. Pour over crust. Bake at 350°F (180°C) for 30-35 minutes. Let cool at least 10 minutes. ● To prepare rhubarb topping, in large saucepan combine rhubarb with sugars and cinnamon. Cook over medium heat until thick. Spread over cooled cheesecake. ● To prepare crisp topping, combine flour with sugar and cinnamon. Cut in butter until crumbly. Sprinkle over rhubarb. Broil, watching closely, just to golden brown. Let cool and dust with icing sugar. ● Makes 8-10 servings.

1½ cups	graham wafer crumbs	375 mL	
¼-½ cup	butter OR margarine	50-125 mL	
2 tbsp.	sugar	30 mL	
pinch	cinnamon	pinch	
16 oz.	cream cheese	500 g	
½ cup	sugar	125 mL	
1 tbsp.	lemon juice	15 mL	
pinch	salt	pinch	
1 tsp.	vanilla	5 mL	
3	eggs	3	
2 cups	sour cream	500 mL	
⅓ cup	sugar	75 mL	
1 tsp.	vanilla	5 mL	
	blueberries, fresh OR frozen		

FRUIT-FILLED CHEESECAKE

Combine crumbs, butter, sugar and cinnamon. Line a 9" x 13" (4 L) square pan with the crumb mixture, building up the sides. • Beat cream cheese until fluffy, add sugar, lemon juice, salt and vanilla. Beat after each addition. Add eggs, 1 at a time, beating after each addition. Pour filling into crust. • Bake at 325 °F (160°C) for 25-30 minutes. • Combine sour cream, sugar and vanilla to make topping. • Take cake from oven and cool for about 10 minutes to let it firm up a bit, then sprinkle blueberries over it. Pour on topping and bake a further 10 minutes. • Cool cheesecake at least 3-4 hours. • May be refrigerated for a day or more before serving. • **Variation:** 15 oz. (425 mL) drained crushed pineapple may be substituted for the blueberries. Cheesecake may be topped with fresh blueberries, strawberries, pineapple or seasonal fruit just before serving. For a special dessert marinate cherries in Kirsch and use them as a garnish.

2	plain jelly rolls	2	
2 x 14 oz.	cans apricots, drained	2 x 398 mL	
¼ cup	brandy	50 mL	
¼ cup	sherry	50 mL	
	Bird's Custard Sauce		
¼ cup	slivered almonds	50 mL	
2-3	bananas, sliced	2-3	
½ cup	whipping cream	125 mL	

APRICOT TRIFLE

A family recipe used for special occasions.

Prepare jelly rolls. • Line large glass bowl with cooled jelly roll which has been sliced ⅓" (1 cm) thick. • Layer apricots over jelly roll. Pour brandy and sherry over the cake and apricots. Marinate overnight in a cool place. • The next day make a double recipe of Bird's Custard Sauce. • When cool, pour ¼ of the custard sauce over the jelly roll. Sprinkle with slivered almonds. Pour ¼ of custard sauce over almonds. Layer bananas over custard. • Pour the remaining custard over bananas. • Whip cream and cover entire dish of Trifle with cream. Garnish with additional apricots, dried apricots dipped in chocolate, or chocolate shavings. • Serves 10-12.

ORANGE MERINGUE TRIFLE

8" x 8"	day-old cake	20 x 20 cm
1 cup	orange juice	250 mL
6 tbsp.	sherry	90 mL
2	eggs, separated	2
⅛ tsp.	salt	0.5 mL
7 tbsp.	white sugar (divided)	105 mL
2 cups	hot milk	500 mL
1 tsp.	vanilla	5 mL

Cut cake into 1" (2.5 cm) cubes and place in 6 greased custard cups. Pour orange juice and sherry over the cake. • Combine egg yolks, salt and 3 tbsp. (45 mL) sugar. Gradually stir in hot milk and cook over boiling water for 5 minutes or until slightly thickened, stirring constantly. Add vanilla and cool quickly. • Pour custard over orange-soaked cake. • Make a meringue with the egg whites by adding 4 tbsp. (60 mL) sugar and beating until stiff. Pile meringue lightly on desserts and bake at 325°F (180°C) for 15 minutes. • Serve cold. • Serves 6.

CHOCOLATE ANGEL TRIFLE

1	angel food OR chiffon OR sponge cake	1
2	pkgs. red gelatin	2
2	pkgs. lemon pie filling	2
2	pkgs. chocolate wafers	2
2 x 19 oz.	cans fruit cocktail	2 x 540 mL
2 cups	whipping cream, whipped	500 mL
	cherries	
	chocolate	

Tear angel food cake into pieces and spread cake layer over bottom of a large glass bowl. Pour rum or sherry over cake. • Prepare 1 pkg. of gelatin. When slightly chilled, beat at high speed, pour over cake and chill until solid about 4 hours. • Crush 1 pkg. chocolate wafers and layer over gelatin. • Prepare 1 pkg. lemon pie filling. Beat egg white not used in filling until stiff. Fold into lemon filling. Pour over chocolate layer and let set, about 4 hours. • Drain 1 can of fruit cocktail and pour over the pie filling. • Start over with second pkg. of gelatin. Repeat chocolate wafer layer, lemon and fruit cocktail layers. • Spread whipped cream over second fruit cocktail layer. • Garnish with cherries, chocolate shavings, etc. • **Variation:** The chocolate pound cake , page 209, may be used as a base for this and rum OR Frangelico liqueur used instead of sherry.

Hint: Chilled egg whites will whip better than those at room temperature. A pinch of salt will help.

1	lady fingers sponge cake raspberry jam	1	# *ENGLISH TRIFLE*
6-8	coconut macaroons	6-8	
1 cup	sherry	250 mL	
2 cups	milk	500 mL	## *CUSTARD*
6	egg yolks	6	
½ cup	sugar grated rind of ½ a lemon	125 mL	
1 tsp.	salt	5 mL	*Truly delicious —*
2 oz.	brandy	60 mL	*rave reviews are guaranteed.*
1 tsp.	vanilla	5 mL	
½ tsp.	lemon extract	2 mL	## *TOPPING*
3 tbsp.	brandy	45 mL	
2 cups	whipping cream sugar to taste maraschino cherries (optional) slivered almonds (optional)	500 mL	

Line sides of large glass bowl with lady fingers, flat side towards bowl. Cover bottom of bowl with a 1″ (2.5 cm) layer of sponge cake. • Spread sponge cake with a generous layer of raspberry jam. Add a layer of macaroons, using about 6 macaroons, fill holes with broken macaroons. • Pour sherry over macaroon and cake layers. (You may do this one day ahead.) • To make custard, pour milk into saucepan and scald. • Combine lightly beaten egg yolks with sugar, lemon rind and salt in the top of a double boiler, slowly add scalded milk, stirring constantly. Place top of double boiler over simmering water. Cook on high heat, stirring constantly, until mixture thickens and coats spoon. Let cool. • Add brandy and vanilla and beat well. Pour custard over sponge cake and macaroons. • To make topping, combine lemon extract, brandy, whipping cream and sugar. Whip until stiff. • Spread whipped cream over the custard and swirl in a decorative pattern. • Garnish with cherries and almonds, if you wish. • This dessert is very simple to make, although it may look complicated. Just proceed 1 step at a time.

SHERRY ALMOND CHIFFON DESSERT

1 tbsp.	gelatin	15 mL
¼ cup	cold water	50 mL
1½ cups	milk	375 mL
⅓ cup	sugar	75 mL
½ tsp.	salt	2 mL
3	eggs, separated	3
¼ cup	sugar	50 mL
½ cup	whipping cream, whipped	125 mL
3 tbsp.	sherry	45 mL
½ tsp.	almond extract	2 mL
¼ cup	toasted blanched almonds	50 mL

Soften gelatin in cold water. • Mix milk, ⅓ cup (75 mL) sugar and salt, thoroughly, in a double boiler and heat until milk is scalded. • Stir about 3 tbsp. (50 mL) of hot mixture into 3 slightly beaten egg yolks and blend into milk mixture in the double boiler. Cook over simmering water until custard coats a silver spoon. Blend in softened gelatin and stir until dissolved. Cool until mixture begins to gel. • Beat egg whites, gradually adding ¼ cup (50 mL) sugar. Fold beaten egg whites and whipped cream into custard, and add sherry and almond extract. Fold in toasted almonds. • Pour into a large serving bowl; chill until firm. • This dessert can be used as pie filling in a precooked pastry or crumb crust.

POTS DE CRÈME

1 cup	semisweet chocolate chips	250 mL
1¼ cups	light cream, scalded	300 mL
½ cup	brandy	125 mL

Put all ingredients into a blender and blend until smooth. • Pour into small dessert dishes or wine glasses; chill 3 hours until firm. • Serves 6. • Delicious and extremely easy to make. • An elegant finale to any meal.

MOUSSE AU CHOCOLAT

1 lb.	bitter-sweet Swiss chocolate	500 g
8	eggs, separated	8
4 cups	whipping cream, whipped	1 L
	grated chocolate	

Melt chocolate in double boiler and let cool. Stir in the egg yolks, a little at a time, while stirring vigorously. • Whip the egg whites until stiff and fold in. Fold in most of the whipped cream, leaving some for decoration. • Decorate with grated chocolate or chocolate shavings.

½ cup	sugar	125 mL
⅔ cup	water	150 mL
12 oz.	semisweet chocolate morsels	340 g
3 cups	whipped cream candied violets	750 mL

CHOCOLATE MOUSSE

In a small pan, combine sugar and water. Simmer for 3 minutes. • Put chocolate morsels in blender, add sugar mixture, blend until smooth. • Fold chocolate mixture into whipped cream; spoon into individual dessert dishes. • Top with candied violets if desired. • Refrigerate several hours or overnight.

---

2 cups	whipping cream	500 mL
4	egg yolks	4
½ cup	granulated sugar	125 mL
1 tbsp.	vanilla extract	15 mL

BURNT CRÈME

Chef Zimmerman
Westin Hotel, Calgary

Preheat oven to 350°F (180°C). • Heat cream over low heat, until bubbles form around edge of pan. • Beat egg yolks and sugar together until thick and yellow, about 3 minutes. Beating constantly, pour cream in a steady stream into egg yolks. Add vanilla and pour into custard cups. • Place cups in baking pan that has from ½-1″ (1.3-2.5 cm) of boiling water in the bottom. Bake for 45 minutes. • Remove cups from water and chill, about 2 hours. • Sprinkle each custard cup with granulated sugar. Place on top rack under broiler and cook until sugar is medium brown. • Refrigerate before serving. • Serves 6.

---

1 cup	sugar	250 mL
¼ cup	sifted flour	50 mL
2 tbsp.	vegetable oil	30 mL
dash	salt	dash
2 tsp.	lemon peel	10 mL
⅓ cup	lemon juice	75 mL
1½ cups	milk, scalded	375 mL
3	egg yolks, beaten	3
3	egg whites, stiffly beaten	3
	whipped cream	

LEMON CUPS

Combine sugar, flour, oil and salt. Add lemon peel and juice. • Stir milk into egg yolks and add to the first mixture. • Fold in egg whites. • Pour into 8 ungreased 5-oz. (140 g) custard cups, filling ⅔ full. • Set custard cups into a shallow pan, filling pan to 1″ (2.5 cm) with hot water. • Bake at 325°F (160°C) for 40 minutes. • Garnish with whipped cream. • Serve warm or chilled.

ZABAGLIONE

An Italian delight.

5	egg yolks	5
¼ cup	sugar	50 mL
½ cup	Marsala	125 mL
¼ cup	dry white wine	50 mL

Combine egg yolks and sugar in the top of a double boiler over simmering water. • Remove from heat and using a rotary beater, beat for a few minutes until well-combined. • Place mixture back over simmering water, gradually mix in ½ the Marsala and ½ the white wine. Beat well. • Gradually stir in the remaining Marsala and wine. Beat constantly for about 10 minutes, or until mixture is thick and creamy. If mixture adheres to pan, quickly remove from heat and beat vigorously with a wooden spoon, especially around the base. • Pour into individual dishes. • **Note:** In place of Marsala, any favorite liqueur may be used. • An excellent topping for fresh fruit, or a warm topping for ice cream.

BAKED PEARS WITH CARAMEL SAUCE AND CHOCOLATE

Great dessert for Hallowe'en dinner - the color is perfect.

2	pears (Bosc suggested) pears DO NOT have to be ripe (10)	2
¼ cup	Hungarian Pear Liqueur (1¼ cups [300 mL])	50 mL
2 tbsp.	unsalted butter softened (⅔ cup [150 mL])	30 mL
2 tbsp.	sugar (⅔ cup [150 mL])	30 mL
¼ cup	heavy cream (1¼ cups [300 mL])	50 mL
	lemon juice to taste	
1 oz.	semisweet chocolate, melted and cooled slightly (1 square)	30 g

Arrange peeled, cored pears, halved lengthwise, cut-side-down in a buttered shallowed baking dish, just large enough to hold the pears in 1 layer, and pour liqueur over them. Dot the pears with butter, sprinkle with sugar and bake them in a preheated 425°F (220°C) oven, basting occasionally, for thirty minutes or until the pears are tender and the sugar is caramelized. • Swirl the cream into the baking dish, and bake the pears 5 minutes more, then transfer to a plate with a slotted spoon. • Whisk the mixture in the baking dish until the sauce is smooth, whisk in the lemon juice, then cover the bottom of the dessert plates. • Make partial lengthwise slits in ½ of each pear, then fan the cuts slightly, and arrange the pears in the dessert dish on the sauce. • Using a cone, decorate the sauce with piped chocolate and then draw the back of a knife across the chocolate to create a pleasing design. • Serves 2 or 10, larger amounts given in brackets. • See photograph opposite.

Baked Pears with Caramel Sauce and Chocolate, page 176
Truffles, page 230

2 cups	water	500 mL
2 cups	fresh OR frozen strawberries *	500 mL
2 tbsp.	sugar	30 mL
dash	nutmeg	dash
dash	cinnamon	dash
3 tbsp.	corn OR potato starch	45 mL
3 tbsp.	cold water	45 mL
	whipped cream	

STRAWBERRY COMPOTE

Gluten-Free

Bring 2 cups water (500 mL) to a boil in a saucepan and add strawberries, sugar and spices. • Mix cornstarch and cold water to make a smooth paste. • When fruit has cooked about 10 minutes, slowly stir starch mixture into the boiling "soup". Cook 2 more minutes or until clear and thickened. • Pour into a wide-topped serving bowl. • Cool quickly. • Serve chilled, topped with fluffs of whipped cream. **Variations:** Replace strawberries with: * blueberries. Add a little lemon juice, omit nutmeg. * raspberries. Add 1 drop almond flavoring and omit nutmeg. * gooseberries. Add a cinnamon stick for the 10-minute cooking, then remove. Omit nutmeg. * rhubarb. Increase sugar.

¾ cup	flour	175 mL
½ cup	white sugar	125 mL
1 tsp.	baking powder	5 mL
1 tsp.	cinnamon	5 mL
¼ tsp.	salt	1 mL
½ cup	milk	125 mL
1½ cups	coarsely chopped peeled apples	375 mL

CARAMEL APPLE PUDDING

¾ cup	packed brown sugar	175 mL
¼ cup	butter OR margarine	50 mL
¾ cup	boiling water	175 mL

CARAMEL SAUCE

In a mixing bowl combine all ingredients, excluding the sauce ingredients. • Pour into a 1½-quart (1.5 L) casserole. • Mix sauce ingredients together until sugar and butter are melted. • Pour the sauce over the pudding mixture. • Bake for 40-50 minutes at 375°F (190°C). • Serves 4. • This is delicious served warm and topped with a scoop of vanilla ice cream.

Hint: Before adding melted chocolate to your soufflé or mousse recipe, stir ⅓ of the whipped cream or egg white mixture into the chocolate. This lightens the chocolate which rewards you by allowing your dessert to reach dizzying new heights.

APPLE PAN DOWDY

4 cups	sliced apples	1 L
1 cup	brown sugar	250 mL
1 tsp.	cinnamon (optional)	5 mL
1 tsp.	salt	5 mL
1¼ cups	flour	300 mL
1 tbsp.	lemon juice	15 mL
¾ cup	water	175 mL
1 tbsp.	butter OR margarine	15 mL
1 tsp.	vanilla	5 mL
2 tsp.	baking powder	10 mL
3 tbsp.	butter, margarine OR shortening	45 mL
½ cup	milk (approximately)	125 mL

Place apples in a 4-quart (4 L) casserole. • Combine, sugar, ½ tsp. (2 mL) salt, ¼ cup (50 mL) flour, lemon juice and water. Cook for 2 minutes. Remove from heat, add butter and vanilla and pour over apples. • Combine 1 cup (250 mL) flour, remaining salt and baking powder. Cut in shortening. Stir in milk, using a fork, until mixture is wet. • Drop by spoonfuls over syrup and apples. • Bake at 400°F (200°C) for 35 minutes.

GUNDA'S APPLE CRUNCH

Gluten-Free

5	large apples. peeled, cored and sliced	5
½ cup	unsweetened apple juice	125 mL
1-1½ cups	cornflake crumbs	250-375 mL
2-3 tbsp.	brown sugar	30-45 mL
1 tsp.	cinnamon	5 mL
¼ tsp.	nutmeg	1 mL
¼ cup	butter OR margarine	50 mL

Preheat oven to 350°F (180°C). • Arrange apple slices in 8″ pie plate; pour in apple juice. • In medium bowl, mix together cornflake crumbs, brown sugar, cinnamon and nutmeg. Stir in melted butter with a fork. • Spread cornflake mixture over apples; bake for 30 minutes, until apples are tender and crust is crisp and golden. • Serves 8. • **Variations:** For those who like a little change, use ¼ cup (50 mL) apple liqueur and ¼ cup (50 mL) apple juice. Weight and cholesterol watchers can substitute diet margarine in this recipe.

One trouble with the world is that so many people who stand up vigorously for their rights fall down miserably on their duties.

2½ cups	fresh OR frozen blueberries	625 mL	
⅓ cup	sugar	75 mL	
dash	salt	dash	
1 cup	water	250 mL	
1 tbsp.	lemon juice	15 mL	
1 cup	all-purpose flour	250 mL	
2 tbsp.	sugar	30 mL	
2 tbsp.	baking powder	30 mL	
¼ tsp.	salt	1 mL	
1 tbsp.	butter OR margarine	15 mL	
½ cup	milk	125 mL	

BLUEBERRY DUMPLINGS

Bring the first 4 ingredients to a boil in a 3-quart (3 L) saucepan. Cover and simmer for 5 minutes. Add the lemon juice. • Sift together dry ingredients, cut in the butter until mixture is like coarse meal, add milk all at once. Stir only until flour is dampened. • Drop tablespoonful (15 mL) of batter into the simmering sauce, making 6 dumplings, not letting them overlap. Cover tightly. Cook over low heat for 10 minutes. • Serve hot with cream or ice cream. • **Variations:** For delicious seasonal variations, try apples with a dash of cinnamon and nutmeg, or peaches, cherries, rhubarb or plums.

2 tbsp.	butter OR margarine	30 mL	
¼ cup	all-purpose flour	50 mL	
⅓ tsp.	salt	1.5 mL	
2	eggs	2	
2 tbsp.	sour cream	30 mL	
⅓ cup	milk	75 mL	
1 tbsp.	grated lemon peel	15 mL	
¼ cup	sugar	50 mL	
2½-3 cups	sliced fruit *	625-750 mL	
2 tbsp.	dark rum OR fruit-flavored liqueur whipping cream, whipped	30 mL	

OLD-AMERICANA FRUIT CLAFOUTI

Clafouti batter is light and pancake-like so it's not a cobbler!

Place butter in a 1-quart (1 L) soufflé dish. Set in oven as it preheats to 375°F (190°C). When butter is melted, spread evenly over dish. • In a large bowl, beat flour, salt, eggs, sour cream, milk and lemon peel. • In another large bowl, combine sugar, prepared fruit and rum or liqueur. • Pour batter into buttered dish. • Top with fruit mixture. • Bake, uncovered, 35-40 minutes or until batter is puffed and top is lightly browned. • Serve hot with cream. • Makes 6 servings. • * Use sliced pears, apples, bananas, or peaches, halved apricots, strawberries, blueberries, raspberries, pitted cherries or halved pitted plums.

NANA'S CREAMY RICE PUDDING

Fabulous!

1 cup	raisins	250 mL
1 cup	cooked rice	250 mL
3 cups	milk	750 mL
1 tbsp.	butter OR margarine	15 mL
3	eggs	3
½ cup	sugar	125 mL
1 tsp.	vanilla	5 mL
¼ tsp.	cinnamon OR nutmeg	1 mL

Place raisins and rice in lightly buttered deep 6-cup (1.5 L) baking dish. • Heat milk and butter to scald. Lightly beat together eggs, sugar and vanilla. Gradually stir in heated milk. • Pour over raisins and rice. Sprinkle with spice. Set dish into a shallow pan with 1"-1½" (2.5-4 cm) hot water surrounding it. Bake at 350°F (180°C) for 1 hour. • Custard may be stirred into baked rice or left as sauce on top. • Serves 6. • **Variation:** For a firmer-textured pudding use up to 2 cups (500 mL) cooked rice.

RICE AND RAISIN PUDDING

Light and fluffy!

½ cup	rice, washed	125 mL
¼ tsp.	salt	1 mL
3 cups	boiling water	750 mL
2	egg whites	2
½ cup	white sugar	125 mL
2	egg yolks	2
3 cups	milk	750 mL
2 tbsp.	butter	30 mL
1 tsp.	vanilla	5 mL
½ cup	raisins, washed	125 mL

Cook rice with salt in boiling water for 5 minutes. Drain through a sieve; pour hot water over rice to separate kernels. Put in an ovenproof bowl. • Beat egg whites and set aside. Beat together sugar and egg yolks. Add milk, butter and vanilla to sugar mixture; then add to rice. Stir in raisins. Fold in beaten egg whites. • Place bowl in a pan of hot water and bake at 350°F (180°C) for 1 hour.

Home Recipe for Plant Fertilizer

1 tsp.	epsom salts	5 mL
1 tsp.	salt peter	5 mL
1 tsp.	baking powder	5 mL
⅓ tsp.	ammonia	5 mL

1 tbsp.	shortening	15 mL	
1 cup	flour	250 mL	
1 tsp.	salt	5 mL	
½-1 cup	raisins	125-250 mL	
½ cup	sugar	125 mL	
1½ tsp.	baking powder	7 mL	
½ cup	milk	125 mL	
½ tsp.	vanilla	2 mL	

HALF-HOUR HASTY PUDDING

¾ cup	brown sugar	175 mL	
1½ cups	boiling water	375 mL	
2½ tsp.	butter OR margarine	12 mL	
1 tbsp.	vanilla OR ¼ tsp. (1 mL) nutmeg	15 mL	

SAUCE

Cream shortening and then stir in the next 7 ingredients in order given. • Pour into a greased casserole dish. • Combine sauce ingredients and pour sauce over the batter mixture. • Bake at 350°F (180°C) for 30 minutes.

---

2 cups	milk	500 mL	
2 tbsp.	sugar	30 mL	
1″	piece of vanilla bean OR 1 tsp. (5 mL) vanilla extract	2.5 cm	
6	eggs, separated	6	
	salt		
1 cup	confectioners' (icing) sugar	250 mL	
	strawberry sauce OR fresh strawberries for garnish		

OEUFS À LA NEIGE

Snow Eggs.

Chef Zimmerman
Westin Hotel, Calgary

In a shallow saucepan, combine milk with sugar and vanilla bean. (If vanilla extract is used, add after the milk has been scalded.) Bring the mixture to a boil, stirring well to dissolve the sugar. • Beat egg whites with a few grains of salt and gradually add confectioners' or fine granulated sugar, beating well after each addition until the whites are very stiff. • Shape the beaten egg white into small eggs with 2 dessert spoons dipped into the milk. Drop the eggs into the scalded milk. Poach them for about 3 minutes, turning each egg over 2-3 times as it poaches. • Remove the eggs from the milk with a perforated spoon and drain them on a dry cloth. • Strain the milk through a fine sieve. • Beat 6 egg yolks well and gradually add the warm milk. Return the custard to the heat, stirring constantly until it just begins to thicken. Remove the pan from the heat and chill the custard. • To serve, pour the custard into a glass bowl and float the meringue eggs on it. • Serve with strawberry sauce or with a bowl of sweetened crushed strawberries.

Let us be the first to give a friendly sign, to nod first, smile first, and if such a thing is necessary, forgive first.

STEAMED PERSIMMON PUDDING

1 cup	fresh persimmon purée (3 peeled)	250 mL
2 tsp.	baking soda	10 mL
½ cup	butter, softened	125 mL
1½ cups	sugar	375 mL
2	eggs	2
2 tbsp.	dark rum	30 mL
1 tbsp.	fresh lemon juice	15 mL
1 cup	all-purpose flour	250 mL
1 tsp.	cinnamon	5 mL
½ tsp.	salt	2 mL
⅔ cup	coarsely chopped, pecans	150 mL

SAUCE

1	egg	1
1 cup	icing (confectioners') sugar	250 mL
2 cups	whipping cream, whipped	500 mL
1 tsp.	vanilla	5 mL

Grease a 2-quart pudding mold or coffee can. • Combine persimmon purée and baking soda in a small bowl and blend well. • Cream butter with sugar in a large bowl until light and fluffy. Beat in eggs, rum and lemon juice. Mix in flour, cinnamon and salt. • Stir in persimmon purée and pecans. Spoon batter into the prepared mold. Snap lid on mold or cover tightly with wax paper and foil. • Set mold on rack in a very large saucepan or kettle, large enough for water and steam to circulate freely around the mold. Place pan over low heat. Add water to come halfway up the sides of the mold. Cover pan and steam pudding, maintaining water at a gentle simmer, for 2 hours or until a tester inserted in the center, comes out clean. • To make sauce, beat 1 egg with icing sugar. Fold gently into whipped cream. Add vanilla. • Serve with hot pudding. • **Note:** This pudding freezes well. It makes a lovely light Christmas pudding. Persimmons are usually available October to December.

Success: *To laugh often and love much, to win the respect of intelligent persons and earn the affection of children. To earn the approbation of honest critics and endure and to be loyal of false friends. To appreciate beauty. To find the best in others. To give oneself. To leave the world a bit better, whether by a healthy child, a garden patch, or a redeemed social condition. To have prayed and laughed with enthusiasm and sung with exaltation. to know even one life has breathed easier because you have lived. This is to have succeeded. (Anonymous).*

1	large apple	1	
1	banana	1	

¼ cup	all-purpose flour	50 mL
⅔ cup	cornstarch	150 mL
1	whole egg	1
¾ cup	water	175 mL

2 cups	oil for deep-frying	500 mL

SYRUP

1 tsp.	oil	5 mL
¾ cup	sugar	175 mL
1 tbsp.	sesame seed	15 mL

1	large bowl of ice water with ice cubes	1	

Lily and Nicky Chan
Lily Restaurant, Calgary

Peel apple and banana, cut into 1¼" (3 cm) cubes. • Put flour, cornstarch and egg into a big bowl. Mix with ¼ cup (50 mL) cold water. • Heat oil in wok over high heat until it reaches 425°F (220°C). Coat apple and banana cubes with batter. Deep-fry until golden brown. Drain well. • Put 1 tsp. (5 mL) oil in wok. Cook sugar over medium-high heat until golden brown. • Add sesame seeds, then fruit to syrup. Mix well, then put on a oiled serving platter. Immediately dunk each apple and banana into ice water, one by one, take out and serve.

---

15 oz.	frozen raspberries	425 mL
½ cup	boiling water	125 mL
1 tbsp.	gelatin (7 g env.)	15 mL
1 tbsp.	lemon juice	15 mL
1	egg white	1
½ tsp.	grated lemon rind	2 mL
1 cup	whipping cream, whipped	250 mL

RASPBERRY ROMA

Cut frozen fruit into 16 chunks. • Using an electric blender, blend boiling water and gelatin for 2-3 seconds. Add lemon juice, egg white and lemon rind, blend 2-3 seconds. Add fruit, 1 chunk at a time. Fold mixture into whipped cream. • Chill until firm. • Serves 6. • **Variations:** Substitute blackberries OR strawberries OR half strawberries and half peaches for the raspberries. Boiling fruit juice may be substituted for the boiling water.

"Children are the keys of Paradise." (R. H. Stoddard)

STRAWBERRIES ROMANOFF II

4 cups	fresh strawberries	1 L
2 tbsp.	sugar	30 mL
2 cups	strawberry ice cream	500 mL
½ cup	sour cream	125 mL
2 tbsp.	orange liqueur	30 mL

Sprinkle cleaned berries with sugar. Cover and chill. • Meanwhile, stir ice cream just to soften. Fold in sour cream and liqueur. Cover and freeze for 1 hour. • To serve, top each serving of berries with a dollop of ice cream mixture. • Makes 6-8 servings. • Strawberries Romanoff I is on page 159 of "Among Friends" Volume I.

FROZEN LEMON DESSERT

*Gluten-Free ***

4	egg yolks	4
¾ cup	sugar	175 mL
¼ cup	lemon juice	50 mL
2 tsp.	grated lemon rind	10 mL
⅛ tsp.	salt	0.5 mL
1 cup	whipping cream, whipped	250 mL
4	egg whites, stiffly beaten	4
½ cup	graham cracker OR cornflake crumbs *	125 mL

Beat egg yolks until thick and lemon colored, gradually beat in sugar. Add lemon juice, rind and salt. • Fold in whipped cream and then the beaten egg whites. Always fold in egg whites last. • Cover bottom of a 9" x 13" (4 L) pan with ¼ cup (50 mL) crumbs. Pour in sherbet mixture and cover with the remaining crumbs. • Store in freezer until ready to use. • * For gluten-free diets, substitute cornflake crumbs for graham cracker crumbs.

FREEZER DELIGHT

32	chocolate cookies with vanilla filling	32
¼ cup	soft butter OR margarine	50 mL
¼ cup	crème de menthe	50 mL
4 cups	vanilla ice cream	1 L
½ cup	roasted pecans	125 mL

Crush the cookies and blend with the butter. Put ⅔ of cookie mixture into the bottom of a 8" x 12" (3 L) pan. • Mix crème de menthe and ice cream together and blend well. Spoon the ice cream over the crushed cookies. Mix remaining cookies with nuts and sprinkle on top. • Store in freezer for at least 12 hours before serving. • This dessert remains delicious for 1 week in the freezer, after which time it may become syrupy. • Serves 12.

---

7 oz. pkg.	chocolate wafers	200 g
½ cup	melted butter	125 mL
6¼ oz.	frozen lemonade concentrate	178 mL
16 oz.	frozen whipped cream	500 mL
10 oz.	sweetened condensed milk	300 mL

FROZEN CHOCO/ LEMON DESSERT

Crush the wafers and mix with the melted butter. Pat crumbs, except for ½ cup (125 mL), into an 8" x 8" (2 L) pan • Combine milk, frozen cream and lemonade. Pour mixture over crust. • Sprinkle remaining crumbs on top and freeze. • Serve frozen.

1 cup	vanilla wafer crumbs	250 mL
2 tbsp.	sugar	30 mL
¼ cup	butter OR margarine	50 mL
4	large eggs	4
¾ cup	sugar	175 mL
1 oz.	square unsweetened chocolate, melted and cooled	30 g
1 tsp.	instant coffee	5 mL
½ cup	butter OR margarine	125 mL
½ tsp.	vanilla	2 mL

MOCHA CREAM DESSERT

FILLING

Mix crumbs, sugar and butter together and press into the bottom of an 8" x 8" (2 L) pan. Bake at 350°F (180°C) for 5 minutes; cool. • To make the Mocha Cream Filling, separate eggs, putting whites in a medium mixing bowl. Beat whites until foamy, gradually add ¼ cup (50 mL) sugar, so that the whites hold straight stiff peaks. Set aside. • Dissolve coffee in hot chocolate. • Beat butter and then gradually and thoroughly beat in remaining ½ cup (125 mL) sugar. Add egg yolks, then chocolate-coffee mixture and vanilla. Beat well. Fold in egg whites. • Spread over the crumb crust and refrigerate cake until serving or freeze immediately. • Makes 9 servings and keeps indefinitely if well covered . • **Note:** it is important to blend instant coffee into melted chocolate while coffee is hot.

Hint: Before the holiday baking sessions that require grated orange and lemon peel, select and wash oranges and lemons. Put in plastic bag in freezer. The frozen fruit grates well and the juice is fine when fruit is thawed.

MOM'S STRAWBERRY ICE CREAM

1 cup	sugar	250 mL
1 tbsp.	flour OR cornstarch *	15 mL
⅛ tsp.	salt	0.5 mL
1	egg, separated	1
1½ cups	milk	375 mL
2 tsp.	vanilla	10 mL
1½ cups	strawberries, fresh or frozen, unsweetened	375 mL

Gluten-Free

Mix first 3 ingredients in a saucepan. Add egg yolk and ¼ cup (50 mL) milk, blend well. Add remaining milk and cook over low heat until thick, stirring constantly. Cool. • Stir in vanilla and pour into freezing tray. Freeze until nearly firm, then turn into bowl and heat until creamy. Add egg white and beat until double in volume. • Fold in berries, put back in freezing tray or dish and freeze. •
* Use cornstarch for gluten-free diets.

MARASCHINO ICE CREAM

4 cups	milk	1 L
pinch	salt	pinch
2 cups	sugar	500 mL
1 tbsp.	vanilla	15 mL
4 cups	cream	1 L
4	oranges, juice of	4
1	lemon, grated rind of	1
8 oz.	maraschino cherries, finely chopped	250 mL

Combine milk, salt and sugar and bring just to a boil. Cool. • Add vanilla and then stir in the cream. • Put cream mixture in a 4-quart (4 L) ice cream freezer, freeze mixture partially, then add orange juice, lemon rind and the maraschino cherries. • Finish the freezing process.

BANANA ICE CREAM

12	bananas	12
8 cups	whipping cream	2 L
1½ cups	sugar	375 mL
2 tbsp.	vanilla	30 mL
½ tsp.	salt	2 mL
2 tbsp.	lemon juice	30 mL

Combine all ingredients. Freeze in an ice-cream freezer, using 2 portions of ice to 1 of rock salt, if you have an old-fashioned freezer. **Variation:** Add banana liqueur.

"Song brings of itself a cheerfulness that makes the heart of joy." (Euripides)

1¼ cups	fine gingersnap crumbs (about 25 cookies)	300 mL
¼ cup	sugar	50 mL
¼ cup	melted butter	50 mL
4 cups	vanilla ice cream, softened	1 L
1 cup	cooked pumpkin	250 mL
½ cup	firmly packed brown sugar	125 mL
½ tsp.	salt	2 mL
¼ tsp.	nutmeg	1 mL
1 tsp.	ground ginger	5 mL
1 tsp.	vanilla	5 mL
	whipped cream for garnish	
	pecans	

PUMPKIN ICE CREAM FREEZE

Combine gingersnap crumbs, sugar and butter. Reserve ½ cup (125 mL) of crumb mixture. Press remaining crumbs into a 9″ x 9″ (2.5 L) pan. Set aside. • Combine remaining ingredients except for the whipped cream and pecans. Stir just until combined. Pour over the crumb layer. • Sprinkle with reserved crumb mixture. • Freeze until firm (at least 4 hours). • Remove from freezer and let sit at room temperature for a few minutes. • Cut into squares. • Garnish with whipped cream and pecans. • Serves 8-10.

The Volunteer Reward:

Many will be shocked to find
When the Day of Judgement nears
That there's a special place in heaven
Set aside for Volunteers.

Furnished with big recliners,
Satin couches and footstools
Where there's no committee chairman
No group leaders or car pools,
No knitting booties or raising money,
No bazaar or bake sale,
There will be nothing to staple
Not one thing to fold or mail
Telephone lists will be outlawed,
But a finger-snap will bring
Cool drinks and gourmet dinners
And rare treats fit for a king

You ask, who'll serve these privileged few?

And work for all they're worth?
Why all those who reaped the benefits,
And not once volunteered on earth.

PIES

DOWN-UNDER APPLE PIE

9"	unbaked pastry shell	23 cm
6	tart apples	6
1 cup	sugar	250 mL
2 tbsp.	flour	30 mL
1 tsp.	cinnamon	5 mL
1 tsp.	grated lemon peel	5 mL
⅛ tsp.	cloves	0.5 mL
⅛ tsp.	salt	0.5 mL
½ cup	flour	125 mL
¼ cup	sugar	50 mL
⅛ tsp.	salt	0.5 mL
½ cup	grated Cheddar cheese	125 mL
¼ cup	melted butter	50 mL
	sour cream for topping	

Line pie plate with pastry and flute the edges. • Peel, quarter, core the apples and slice them thinly. • Mix together 1 cup (250 mL) sugar, 2 tbsp. (25 mL) flour, cinnamon, lemon peel, cloves and salt and toss lightly with the apple slices. • Arrange the apples, overlapping the slices, in the pastry-lined pan. • Combine the rest of the ingredients, except butter and sour cream. Mix in butter and sprinkle the topping over the apples. • Bake at 400°F (200°C) for 40 minutes or until the topping and crust are golden brown. • Let the pie cool on a wire rack and serve it warm, topping each slice with a generous spoonful of sour cream.

FRESH PEACH PIE

	pastry for a double-crust pie	
5	large peaches, sliced	5
1 tbsp.	flour	15 mL
1 cup	sugar	250 mL
pinch	salt	pinch
1	egg, beaten	1
2 tbsp.	butter	30 mL

Prepare pastry and line pie plate with pastry. • Arrange peaches in pie shell. • Combine flour, sugar, salt and egg. Pour over peaches. Turn into pastry shell. Dot with butter. Adjust top crust or make a lattice top. • Bake at 400°F (200°C) for 10 minutes. Reduce heat and bake at 350°F (180°C) for 30 minutes or until nicely browned. • See photograph, page 192A.

9"	unbaked pastry shell	23 cm	**PEACH**
2½-3 tbsp.	tapioca	37-45 mL	**CRUMB PIE**
¾ cup	sugar	175 mL	
¼ tsp.	salt	1 mL	
4 cups	sliced fresh peaches	1 L	
1-2 tbsp.	lemon juice	15-30 mL	
⅓ cup	packed brown sugar	75 mL	**CRUMB TOPPING**
¼ cup	flour	50 mL	
½ tsp.	cinnamon	2 mL	
2½ tbsp.	softened butter	37 mL	

Prepare pastry shell. Combine tapioca, sugar, salt, peaches and lemon juice. Pour filling into the prepared pie shell. ● To make the crumb topping, combine all ingredients with a fork until the crumbs are size of large peas. ● Sprinkle pie with crumb topping and bake at 425°F (220°C) for 45-50 minutes or until syrup boils with heavy bubbles that do not burst.

1¾ cups	flour	425 mL	**PEAR TART**
11 tbsp.	butter OR margarine	160 mL	
¼ cup	sugar	50 mL	
2	egg yolks	2	
¼ tsp.	water or more	1 mL	
4 drops	vanilla	4 drops	
6	pears	6	
1¼ cups	sugar	300 mL	**FILLING**
6 tbsp.	flour	90 mL	
3	eggs	3	
¾ cup	butter OR margarine	175 mL	

To make pâte sucre, combine flour, butter and sugar until it looks like coarse meal. Add egg yolks, water and vanilla, stir lightly with a fork and gather into a ball. Refrigerate dough for at least 3 hours. Roll dough out ⅛" (0.5 cm) thick and fit into a fluted 9" (23 cm) pan. ● Core and peel sufficient amount of pears to fit halves in singly on pastry. Slice halves, not quite through lengthwise in ⅛" (0.5 cm) slices. Open slices into a fan shape. Arrange halves, petal fashion, on pastry. ● Combine sugar and flour and mix in eggs. Melt butter until golden brown and mix in. Pour butter mixture over pears and bake 1 hour at 375°F (190°C). **Variations:** Substitute sliced peaches or 3 cups (750 mL) rhubarb, cut into 1" (2.5 cm) pieces, for pears.

No matter how busy people are, they are never too busy to stop and talk about how busy they are.

PLUM PIE À L'ALSACIENNE

9"	pastry for a single crust pie	23 cm
½ cup	graham cracker crumbs	125 mL
2 lbs.	ripe purple plums (about 12)	1 kg
½ cup	sugar	125 mL
⅛ tsp.	ground cinnamon	0.5 mL
2 tbsp.	sugar	30 mL
	whipped cream	
	slivered almonds	
	mint sprigs	

Prepare pie shell. • Sprinkle graham cracker crumbs on bottom of unbaked pastry shell. • Halve and pit plums. • Place plums snugly in shell, skin-side-down, in concentric circles. • Sprinkle ½ cup (125 mL) sugar evenly on top. • Bake at 450°F (230°C) for 10 minutes, then reduce heat to 350°F (180°C) for 35 minutes. • Remove from oven and combine cinnamon and sugar and sprinkle over baked pie. • Garnish with whipped cream, toasted slivered almonds and mint sprigs. • Serve warm.

RHUBARB CRUMBLE PIE

½ cup	melted butter	125 mL
½ cup	rolled oats	125 mL
½ cup	flour	125 mL
⅔ cup	brown sugar	150 mL
3 cups	raw rhubarb, cut up	750 mL
½ cup	sugar	125 mL
1½ tbsp.	flour	22 mL
	whipped cream for garnish	

Combine melted butter, rolled oats, ½ cup (125 mL) flour and brown sugar. Firmly pack into 9" (23 cm) pie plate, leaving ¾ cup (175 mL) for top. • Cover with rhubarb. Combine ½ cup (125 mL) sugar and 1½ tbsp. (22 mL) of flour and sprinkle over rhubarb. Place remaining ¾ cup (175 mL) oat mixture over top. • Bake at 350°F (180°C) for 45 minutes or until rhubarb is soft and tender. • Serve with whipped cream.

Hint: To make a lattice cover for your pie, weave lattice (strips of dough) on a circle of waxed paper, refrigerate or freeze, and then slide onto your pie. Trim and join to the bottom crust with a little cold water.

CRANBERRY-RAISIN PIE

	pastry for 9″ (23 cm) lattice-top pie	
3 cups	fresh cranberries	750 mL
1 cup	raisins	250 mL
1 cup	water	250 mL
½ cup	lemon juice	125 mL
¾ cup	brown sugar	175 mL
2 tbsp.	cornstarch	30 mL
½ tsp.	salt	2 mL
½ tsp.	cinnamon	2 mL
½ tsp.	nutmeg	2 mL

Prepare pastry. ● In a medium saucepan, combine cranberries, raisins, water and lemon juice. Cook and stir until the cranberries pop, approximately 8 minutes. ● Combine brown sugar, cornstarch, salt, cinnamon and nutmeg, add to hot cranberry mixture. Cook quickly, stirring constantly until mixture thickens and bubbles. Remove from heat. ● Pour mixture into pastry-lined pie plate. ● Top filling with strips arranged in lattice fashion, trim and crimp edges. ● Bake at 400°F (200°C) for 30-40 minutes. If edges brown too quickly, cover with foil during the last 10-15 minutes. ● Cool. ● Serves 6-8.

SOUR CREAM RAISIN PIE

9″	baked pastry pie shell	23 cm
¾ cup	sugar	175 mL
2 tbsp.	cornstarch OR 1 tbsp. (15 mL) flour	30 mL
1 tsp.	cinnamon	5 mL
½ tsp.	grated nutmeg	2 mL
¼ tsp.	cloves	1 mL
3	egg yolks, beaten	3
1 cup	sour cream	250 mL
1 cup	raisins	250 mL

MERINGUE TOPPING

¼ tsp.	salt	1 mL
¼ tsp.	vanilla	1 mL
3	egg whites	3
6 tbsp.	sugar	90 mL

Mix sugar, cornstarch and spices in a small saucepan. Blend in beaten egg yolks, then sour cream and raisins. Cook over low heat, stirring constantly, until thick. Cool and pour into the baked pastry shell. ● To make meringue, add salt and vanilla to egg whites; beat, adding sugar gradually until stiff and sugar is dissolved. ● Spread over pie, sealing to pastry edges. ● Bake at 350°F (180°C) for 12-15 minutes or until golden. ● Cool. ● **Variation:** This pie may also be prepared using an unbaked pie crust, filled with uncooked filling. Bake at 450°F (230°C) for 10 minutes; reduce heat to 350°F (180°C) for 30 minutes. Cool.

GREEN TOMATO RAISIN PIE

	Best-Ever Pie Crust, below	
5 cups	diced green tomatoes	1.25 L
1¼ cups	sugar *	300 mL
¼ cup	oil	50 mL
2 cups	raisins	500 mL
¼ cup	vinegar	50 mL
1 tsp.	salt	5 mL
1 tbsp.	cinnamon	15 mL
½ tsp.	nutmeg (optional)	2 mL
1 tsp.	cloves	5 mL

Combine all ingredients in a saucepan. • Boil slowly for 1-2 hours. Stir often. • Bottle and keep in refrigerator or freezer. • Use as required for pie or tart filling. • * ¼ cup (50 mL) of sugar may be replaced with ¼ cup of honey. **Variation:** Green Tomato Pie: Combine tomatoes, vinegar and honey. Cook over low heat until tomatoes are tender. • Cool to lukewarm. • Omit raisins and oil. • Combine sugar, salt, nutmeg, using only 1 tsp. (5 mL) cinnamon, and add ¼ cup (50 mL) of flour. • Stir into tomato mixture. • Pour into uncooked pastry shell. Add top crust. Slit to let out steam. • Sprinkle crust with sugar. • Bake at 400°F (200°C) for 45 minutes.

BEST-EVER PIE CRUST

½ lb.	lard	250 g
½ tsp.	salt	2 mL
2½ cups	flour	625 mL
¼ cup	cold water	50 mL
2 tbsp.	vinegar	30 mL

Cut together lard, salt and flour with pastry cutter. Add water and vinegar and lightly mix with a fork. • Squeeze into a ball and keep in refrigerator or freezer until ready to use. • Bake unfilled pie shells in a preheated 450°F (230°C) oven for 10-12 minutes.

FOOD FOR THOUGHT

"And he who gives a child a treat
Makes joyous bells ring in heaven's street
And he who gives a child a home
Builds palaces in Kingdom come." (John Mansfield)

Fresh Peach Pie, page 188
Peach Hummer, page 62

PUMPKIN CHIFFON PIE

9"	baked pastry pie shell	23 cm
1 tbsp.	gelatin (7 g pkg.)	15 mL
½ cup	cold water	125 mL
½-⅔ cup	brown sugar	125-150 mL
½ tsp.	salt	2 mL
½ tsp.	ginger	2 mL
½ tsp.	cinnamon	2 mL
½ tsp.	nutmeg	2 mL
1¼ cups	mashed cooked pumpkin	300 mL
3	egg yolks, beaten	3
½ cup	milk	125 mL
3	egg whites	3
¼ cup	sugar	50 mL
	whipped cream for garnish	

Soften gelatin in cold water. Let stand. • Combine brown sugar, salt, ginger, cinnamon, nutmeg, pumpkin, egg yolks and milk in a heavy saucepan or in the top of a double boiler. Cook slowly over medium heat until mixture boils. • Remove from heat and stir in gelatin, until thoroughly dissolved. • Place saucepan in a pan of cold water, until mixture mounds slightly. • Beat egg whites and sugar until stiff. Carefully fold into pumpkin mixture. • Pour into cooked pie crust. • Refrigerate until ready to serve. • Serve with sweetened whipped cream.

CHESS PIE

9"	baked pie shell	23 cm
4	egg yolks, beaten	4
1 cup	cream	250 mL
¾ cup	sugar	175 mL
1 tsp.	cinnamon	5 mL
½ tsp.	cloves	2 mL
4	egg whites	4
8 tbsp.	sugar	120 mL

Prepare pie shell. • Combine and cook egg yolks, cream, ¾ cup (175 mL) sugar, cinnamon and cloves until thick. Pour into pie shell. • Beat egg whites, with 8 tbsp. (120 mL) sugar until stiff, to make meringue. Mound meringue on top of pie, sealing all edges to prevent shrinkage, and bake at 350°F (180°C) for 10-15 minutes. **Variation:** This Nova Scotia recipe is called Jefferson Davis Pie in the southern U.S. where they add ½ cup (125 mL) each of chopped dates, raisins and pecans.

"I love these little people; and it is not a slight thing when they who are so fresh from God, love us." (Charles Dickens)

PUMPKIN-PECAN PIE

10"	deep, unbaked pie shell	25 cm
8 oz.	pkg. cream cheese softened	250 g
¾ cup	brown sugar	175 mL
1 tsp.	cinnamon	5 mL
1 tsp.	nutmeg	5 mL
½ tsp.	ginger	2 mL
¼ tsp.	cloves (optional)	1 mL
¼ tsp.	allspice (optional)	1 mL
½ tsp.	salt	2 mL
3	eggs	3
1 cup	canned pumpkin	250 mL
1 cup	milk	250 mL
1 tsp.	vanilla	5 mL
1 tbsp.	brown sugar	15 mL
1 tbsp.	butter OR margarine	15 mL
1 tbsp.	flour	15 mL
	whipped cream for garnish	
	pecan halves for garnish	

Prepare pie shell. • Beat together cream cheese, brown sugar, spices and salt. Add eggs, 1 at a time, beating well after each addition. • Stir in pumpkin, milk and vanilla. Pour into unbaked pie shell. • Filling is generous, so crimp crust edges high. Bake at 375°F (190°C) for 40 minutes. • Remove from oven. • Combine brown sugar, butter and flour to make topping. • Add topping to center of pie. • To serve add whipped cream to outer rim of pie. • Add pecans in a circular pattern.

SHOOFLY PIE

9"	unbaked pastry shell	23 cm
½ tsp.	soda	2 mL
¾ cup	boiling water	175 mL
¾ cup	dark molasses	175 mL
½ cup	brown sugar	125 mL
1½ cups	flour	375 mL
¼ cup	butter	50 mL

Prepare pastry shell. • Dissolve soda in hot water and molasses. • Combine sugar, flour and butter and rub into crumbs. • Pour ⅓ liquid mixture into pie shell, add ⅓ crumbs, continue, ending with crumb mixture on top. Bake at 375°F (190°C) for 35 minutes.

½ cup	butter OR margarine, softened	125 mL
1 cup	white sugar	250 mL
1	egg, beaten	1
2 tbsp.	milk	30 mL
½ tsp.	vanilla	2 mL
1¾ cups	flour	425 mL
2 tsp.	baking powder	10 mL
½ tsp.	salt	2 mL
12 oz.	cream cheese	340 g
½ cup	sugar	125 mL
½ tsp.	vanilla OR almond flavoring	2 mL
	seasonal fresh fruit for topping (pineapple, strawberries, oranges, kiwi, black or green grapes, peaches, raspberries, blueberries, etc.)	
2 tbsp.	cornstarch	30 mL
½ cup	sugar	125 mL
½ cup	fruit juice	125 mL
2 tbsp.	water	30 mL

FRUIT PIZZA

To make crust, cream butter, adding sugar gradually, then add well-beaten egg, milk and vanilla. • Mix flour, baking powder and salt together. • Add to first mixture and blend well. • Press on a greased pizza pan, using well-floured fingers. • Bake at 350°F (180°C) for 10-12 minutes, until golden. • Cool thoroughly. • To make filling, combine cream cheese, sugar and flavoring. • Using a spatula, spread the cream cheese mixture on the cooled cookie crust. • Arrange fruit on top in circles or spirals to make a decorative pattern. Any fruit will work but drain well. • To make glaze, combine cornstarch, sugar, fruit juice and water. Mix together, heat until thickened. • Cool slightly and then spread or drizzle over fruit. • This mixture may seem fairly thin when you put it on. • Chill for 2 hours before serving.

Cook: Do you want me to cut this pizza into 6 or 8 pieces? Man: You'd better make it 6 — I don't think I can eat 8 pieces.

STRAWBERRY OR PEACH TARTE

2 cups	flour	500 mL
1 tsp.	salt	5 mL
1 cup	shortening, ½ lb. (250 g)	250 mL
6-7 tsp.	cold water	30-35 mL
½ cup	finely chopped almonds	125 mL

FILLING

2 cups	whipping cream, whipped	500 mL
½ cup	sugar	125 mL
½ tsp.	almond extract	2 mL
4 cups	sliced strawberries OR peaches	1 L
14 oz.	can crushed pineapple, drained	398 mL
	strawberries, garnish	

Combine first 5 ingredients to prepare pastry dough. • Divide dough in half and roll each half to ¼" (1 cm) or less thickness in a large circle. Place flat on cookie sheets. • Prick with fork, bake in 400°F (200°C) until slightly brown. • To make the filling, stir together the whipped cream, sugar and almond extract. Reserve 1 cup (250 mL) for topping. • Fold in strawberries and pineapple. • Spread strawberry filling between the cooked pastry layers. • Top with reserved cream, and garnish with strawberries. • Serves 10.

RUM CREAM PIE

1¼ cups	crushed graham wafers	300 mL
¼ cup	melted butter	50 mL
¼ cup	white sugar	50 mL
6	egg yolks	6
1 cup	sugar	250 mL
1 tbsp.	gelatin (7 g pkg.)	15 mL
½ cup	cold water	125 mL
2 cups	whipping cream	500 mL
½ cup	dark rum	125 mL
	bitter-sweet chocolate	

To make a graham wafer crust, blend together first 3 ingredient and press into a deep pie plate. • Refrigerate until firm. • To make pie filling, beat egg yolks until light and fluffy, then beat in sugar. Set aside. • Soak gelatin in cold water, then bring to a boil. Remove from heat and pour gelatin over egg mixture, stirring vigorously. Set aside and cool. • Whip cream until stiff and then fold whipped cream into egg mixture. Gently stir in the dark rum. Cool filling for a short time and when it is starting to firm slightly, pour into shell. • If there is too much filling set it aside to use as pudding. • The cream mixture should just reach to ¼" (1 cm) of top of graham crust. • Sprinkle pie with shaved chocolate.

2 cups	whipping cream	500 mL
5	bunches of Lavender flowers *	5
9	egg yolks	9
½ cup	sugar	125 mL
1	sheet puff pastry	1

LAVENDER PIE

Bernard and Fernando
Versailles Dining Room,
Calgary

Place the cream and lavender in a saucepan and bring to a boil. Let cool. Strain out the herbs. • Place the yolks and sugar in a bowl. Beat with an electric mixer until they turn white. Add the lavender-flavored cream. • Roll the puff pastry out on a lightly floured surface, until large enough for an 8″ (20 cm) flan tin. Fit pastry into flan tin. Trim edges with rolling pin. Refrigerate for 10 minutes. • Fill pastry with the egg mixture and bake at 300°F (150°C) for about 20 minutes, until filling is set. • Serves 8. • * Available in French delicatessens.

---

5 cups	whipping cream, whipped	1.25 L
3-4 tbsp.	sugar	45-60 mL
¾ cup	Kahlúa	175 mL
¾ cup	milk	175 mL
1	large bag chocolate chip cookies	1
	chocolate for garnish	

KAHLÚA PIE

Whip cream, add sugar and refrigerate. • Mix Kahlúa and milk. • Dip each cookie into the Kahlúa mixture, for 3 seconds each. Crumble half the cookies in the bottom of a 9″ (23 cm) pie plate. • Pour half the whipped cream over cookies. • Sprinkle the rest of the crumbled cookies over whipped cream. • End with the remaining half of whipped cream. • Shave part of a chocolate square over the top layer of whipped cream. Chill. • Rich and delicious! For best effect, use a glass see-through pie plate. • Serves 8-10.

---

7 oz.	pkg. chocolate wafers	200 g
4 tbsp.	melted butter	60 mL
⅔ cup	milk	150 mL
24	large marshmallows	24
1 cup	whipping cream	250 mL
2 oz.	crème de menthe	60 mL

FROZEN GRASSHOPPER PIE

Crush wafers and stir in butter. • Line a 9″ (23 cm) pie plate with crumbs, reserving a small amount. Cool. • Melt marshmallows in milk. Blend well. Chill. • Whip cream until stiff and add crème de menthe. • Fold in the cooled marshmallow mixture. • Pour into crust; freeze overnight. • Serve cold.

CHOCOLATE BANANA PIE

2 cups	fine wafer crumbs	500 mL
⅓ cup	melted butter OR margarine	75 mL
½ cup	butter OR margarine	125 mL
1½ cups	icing sugar	375 mL
2	eggs	2
1 cup	whipping cream	250 mL
¼ cup	sugar	50 mL
2 tbsp.	cocoa	30 mL
1	ripe banana, mashed	1
1 cup	chopped pecans OR walnuts	250 mL

Mix crumbs and butter together and press into a 9″ (23 cm) deep pie plate, reserving 2 tbsp. (30 mL) for topping. • With mixer, beat butter and add icing sugar; when light add eggs, 1 at a time, beating well after each addition. Spread mixture on crumbs. • Whip cream until it holds peaks, then add sugar and cocoa. Fold in mashed ripe banana and chopped pecans or walnuts. • Spread on icing sugar mixture. • Sprinkle with remaining crumbs. • Chill 24 hours or freeze. • Serve cut in wedges. • Makes 9-12 servings.

MUD PIE

1¼ cups	crushed chocolate wafers	300 mL
4 tbsp.	melted butter OR margarine	60 mL
1 qt.	coffee ice cream, softened	1 L
3	squares semisweet shocolate	3
¼ cup	whipping cream	50 mL
2 tbsp.	butter OR margarine	30 mL
¼ cup	sugar	50 mL
1 tsp.	vanilla	5 mL
	whipping cream, whipped for garnish	
	cherries for garnish	

Combine crumbs and butter and press on the bottom and sides of a 9″ (23 cm) pie plate. Bake for 10 minutes at 375°F (190°C) or 2 minutes on HIGH in a microwave. • Cool completely. • Spread ice cream on crumbs. Put in freezer until firm. • On low heat, melt chocolate, cream, butter and sugar. Stir on heat until smooth and just reaches the boiling point. Remove from heat. Add vanilla and cool slightly. • Using a large spoon, pour and drip chocolate mixture over the ice cream until the whole surface is covered. • Freeze for 1½ hours. • You can top with whipped cream and a cherry if desired.

4	eggs, separated	4
⅛ tsp.	salt	0.5 mL
½ tsp.	cream of tartar	2 mL
1½ cups	sugar	375 mL
5 tbsp.	lemon juice	75 mL
2 tsp.	grated lemon peel	10 mL
1 cup	whipping cream, whipped	250 mL

LEMON ANGEL PIE

To make meringue shell, beat egg whites until frothy, add salt and cream of tartar; beat until stiff. Add 1 cup (250 mL) sugar gradually; continue to beat until mixture is glossy and very stiff. • Line bottom and sides of a well-greased 9″ (23 cm) pie plate with the meringue. • Bake in a very slow oven, 275°F (140°C) for 1 hour. • Cool. • To make filling, beat egg yolks until thick and light, add remaining ½ cup (125 mL) sugar, lemon juice and grated rind. Cook in top of a double boiler until very thick, stirring constantly. • Cool. • Spread half the whipped cream in the cooled meringue shell; add lemon filling, spreading evenly. Top with remaining whipped cream. • Chill in the refrigerator for 24 hours. Cut into wedges to serve. • Serves 6-8.

2	egg whites	2
1 tbsp.	cold water	15 mL
2 tbsp.	sugar	30 mL
1 tsp.	cornstarch	5 mL
½ tsp.	baking powder	2 mL

FLUFFY MERINGUE

Beat together the egg whites and water until mixture holds its shape. • Mix together sugar, cornstarch, and baking powder. • Stir into egg whites until well blended. • Spread over the pie and bake in 325°F (160°C) oven for 15 minutes. • This recipe will cover 2 small pies or 1 large. • This does not stick to the knife when cutting.

1 lb.	lard, at room temperature	500 g
1 cup	boiling water	250 mL
6 cups	sifted all-purpose flour	1.5 L
2 tsp.	baking powder	10 mL
2 tsp.	salt	10 mL

HOT WATER PIE CRUST

Foolproof.

Put lard into a large mixing bowl. Add boiling water and beat until creamy. Combine and gradually stir in sifted dry ingredients. • Divide dough and wrap in 4 parcels in plastic wrap and chill thoroughly. Each is enough for 1 double-crust pie. • This will keep for 2-3 weeks in the refrigerator and frozen for several months.

CAKES

RHUBARB CAKE

1½ cups	brown sugar	375 mL
1	egg	1
½ cup	butter OR margarine	125 mL
½ tsp.	salt	2 mL
1 tsp.	vanilla	5 mL
1 cup	sour milk *	250 mL
2 cups	chopped fresh rhubarb	500 mL
2 cups	flour	500 mL
1 tsp.	baking soda	5 mL
½ cup	white sugar	125 mL
1 tsp.	butter	5 mL
1 tsp.	cinnamon	5 mL

Cream together sugar, egg and butter. Add salt, vanilla and sour milk and beat well. Stir rhubarb, flour and baking soda into the creamed mixture. Mix well. Pour into a 8" x 12" (3 L) greased pan. ● Combine last 3 ingredients and sprinkle on mixture in pan. ● Bake at 350°F (180°C) for 35 minutes or until done. ● * To make sour milk put 1 tbsp. (15 mL) of vinegar OR lemon juice in 1 cup (250 mL) measure and fill with milk. **Variation:** Omit rhubarb and vanilla. Replace with 2 cups (500 mL) blueberries or saskatoons and 1 tsp. (5 mL) almond flavoring or lemon rind.

BRAZIL NUT TROPICAL CAKE

A very attractive cake for special holidays.

3 cups	Brazil nuts shelled	750 mL
1 lb.	pitted dates	500 g
1 cup	drained maraschino cherries	250 mL
¾ cup	flour	175 mL
¾ cup	sugar	175 mL
½ tsp.	baking powder	2 mL
½ tsp.	salt	2 mL
3	eggs	3
1 tsp.	vanilla	5 mL

Grease a 9½" x 5½" x 2½" (2 L) loaf pan. Line with greased wax paper. Heat oven to 300°F (150°C). ● Place fruit and nuts in large bowl. Sift flour, sugar, baking powder and salt over fruit mixture. Mix with hands until nuts and fruit are coated. ● Beat eggs, until foamy, add vanilla, stir into fruit mixture. Spread evenly in a prepared loaf pan. Bake for 1¾ hours. ● This cake is very attractive when sliced. Sprinkle cake with icing sugar, if you wish, or you may frost with Cream Cheese Icing or a Butter Orange Icing.

VEGETABLE CAKE

3	eggs, separated	3
1½ cups	sugar	375 mL
1 cup	shredded raw carrots	250 mL
1 cup	shredded raw beets (peeled)	250 mL
½ tsp.	salt	2 mL
1 cup	oil	250 mL
3 tbsp.	hot water	45 mL
1 tsp.	cinnamon	5 mL
2 cups	flour	500 mL
1 tsp.	vanilla	5 mL
2½ tsp.	baking powder	12 mL

CREAM CHEESE ICING

¼ cup	butter OR margarine	50 mL
4 oz.	cream cheese	125 g
1½ cups	icing sugar	375 mL
½ tsp.	vanilla	2 mL

Beat together egg yolks and sugar. Add the vegetables, salt, oil, hot water, cinnamon, flour and vanilla. Mix well. • Beat egg whites with the baking powder until stiff, then fold into the cake mixture. Pour into a greased 9″ x 13″ (4 L) pan. • Bake at 350°F (180°C) for 40 minutes. • Let cool. • To make the icing, melt butter and beat in the cheese. Add icing sugar and vanilla. • Spread on the cooled cake.

GOOD 'N' EASY CHRISTMAS CAKE

Gluten-Free

16 oz.	mixed candied fruit	450 g
13 oz.	seedless raisins	375 g
2 oz.	chopped nuts (optional)	55 g
1	pouch Good'n Easy Pastry Mix	1
½ cup	butter	125 mL
½ cup	brown sugar	125 mL
4	eggs	4
1 tsp.	allspice	5 mL
½ tsp.	salt	2 mL
2 tbsp.	rum	30 mL

Place oven rack in lower center of oven. Preheat oven to 300°F (150°C). • Lightly grease tube pan and line bottom and sides with 2 layers of waxed paper. Grease waxed paper. • Combine fruit, raisins and nuts, and sprinkle with 2 tbsp. (30 mL) of the pastry mix. Mix well. • In another bowl, cream together butter and sugar until light and fluffy. • Add eggs 1 at a time with a spoonful of mix and beat well. • Fold in remaining mix , allspice and salt. Stir in fruit and nuts. Add rum. Mix thoroughly. Pour into prepared tube pan. • Bake 2 hours or until skewer comes out clean. Remove from oven. • Let stand 1 hour. • Turn cake out on rack and peel off paper. • Let cake cool at least 12 hours before wrapping and storing in airtight container.

CHOCOLATE CHERRY FRUIT CAKE

The chocolate-lover's Christmas cake.

2 lbs.	halved red cherries	1 kg
2 lbs.	dark raisins	1 kg
1 lb.	slivered almonds	500 g
4 cups	all-purpose flour	1 L
6 oz.	unsweetened chocolate (6 squares)	170 g
1 lb.	butter, softened	500 g
3 cups	white sugar	750 mL
8	large eggs	8
2 tsp.	vanilla	10 mL
2 tsp.	baking powder	10 mL
1 tsp.	salt	5 mL
1 tsp.	ground cloves	5 mL
1 cup	cherry brandy	250 mL

This makes 1 set of round or square pans. • Line pans with 2 layers of greased brown paper. • Put fruit and almonds in large mixing bowl. Mix fruit well with 1 cup (250 mL) of the flour. • Break up chocolate and melt in paper-covered measuring cup in microwave. Stir. • Cream butter until fluffy, add sugar gradually, beating thoroughly. • Beat in eggs, 1 at a time. Add slightly cooled chocolate and vanilla. Add baking powder, salt and cloves. Add flour alternately with brandy. Add dough to fruit and mix with big spoon. May need a little more flour at this time. • Bake at 275°F (140°C) with a pan of water on bottom shelf of oven. • Halfway through baking, when cake is firm on top, cover loosely, with a piece of foil, to minimize drying. • Cook small cake about 2½ hours, medium 3 hours and large 3½ hours. Test with broom straw. • When done, cool in pans. Remove cakes, leaving 1 layer of brown paper on cake. Before covering, paint top of cake with more cherry brandy. • Wrap in plastic wrap and put in plastic bags with twist ties. • Store in cookie tin in cool place, repaint with brandy once a week for 3-4 weeks. • Freeze before cutting - cut when partially frozen. • Will keep indefinitely in freezer.

SIG'S BEATEN CAKE

4	egg yolks	4
⅓ cup	cold water	75 mL
1½ cups	sugar	375 mL
⅓ tsp.	vanilla	1.5 mL
⅓ tsp.	lemon juice	1.5 mL
1/6 tsp.	almond extract	0.6 mL
1½ cups	cake flour	375 mL
¼ tsp.	salt	1 mL
4	egg whites	4
½ tsp.	cream of tartar	2 mL

Beat yolks and water until 6 times original volume. Slowly beat in sugar. Add vanilla, lemon, almond extract. • Sift in flour and salt and stir. • Beat egg whites until stiff, with cream of tartar and fold into batter. • Bake in an ungreased angel food pan for 1 hour at 325°F (160°C). • Invert to cool.

3	eggs	3
1 cup	white sugar	250 mL
1 cup	light molasses	250 mL
1 tsp.	EACH powdered cloves, ginger, cinnamon	5 mL
1 cup	vegetable oil	250 mL
2 cups	all-purpose flour	500 mL
2 tsp.	baking soda	10 mL
2 tbsp.	warm water	30 mL
1 cup	boiling water	250 mL

CROSS CREEK GINGERBREAD

Place eggs, sugar, molasses, cloves, ginger, cinnamon and oil in a mixing bowl and beat well. Sift in flour, and beat well. • Dissolve baking soda in the warm water. Stir into the beaten mixture. Then add boiling water and beat. • Pour into a 9″ x 13″ (4 L) greased pan and bake for 45-50 minutes at 350°F (180°C). • Batter will seem thin but bakes into the most delicate and delicious gingerbread ever. **Variation:** Orange Cake: substitute 1 cup (250 mL) white or golden syrup for the molasses. • Substitute 1 cup (250 mL) hot orange juice for the boiling water. • Omit the cloves and ginger; substitute cinnamon and nutmeg.

2	eggs, separated	2
1½ cups	unsweetened orange juice concentrate	375 mL
1 tsp.	vanilla	5 mL
2 tsp.	baking soda	5 mL
¾ tsp.	ground cloves	3 mL
¾ tsp.	cinnamon	3 mL
¾ tsp.	allspice	3 mL
¼ cup	oil	50 mL
2 cups	Ener-G potato mix	500 mL

POTATO MIX SPICE CAKE

Gluten-Free, without sugar.

Preheat oven to 350°F (280°C). • Separate the eggs. Beat the egg whites to dry peaks. Reserve. • Beat the egg yolks, juice, vanilla, baking soda, spices and oil together until frothy. Mix in potato mix. • Fold egg whites gently and thoroughly into batter. • Bake in 2 greased 8″ (20 cm) cake pans for 30 minutes or until done. • Let cool slightly before inverting cake out of pan onto wire rack to finish cooling. • For a sugar-free icing, whip ½ cup (125 mL) whipping cream and then fold in ¼ cup (50 mL) orange or apple juice concentrate. • Refrigerate 2 hours before applying.

One of the mysteries of life is how the boy who wasn't considered good enough to marry the daughter can be the father of the smartest grandchildren in the world.

BUTTER-SCOTCH SUNDAE CAKE

1 cup	soft butter	250 mL
2 cups	packed brown sugar	500 mL
4	eggs, separated	4
2⅔ cups	sifted cake flour	650 mL
1 tbsp.	baking powder	15 mL
1 tsp.	salt	5 mL
1 cup	milk	250 mL
1½ tsp.	vanilla	7 mL
	Butterscotch Filling	
2	bananas	2
	Boiled Icing	
	Butterscotch Glaze	

BUTTERSCOTCH FILLING

1 cup	brown sugar, packed	250 mL
3 tbsp.	flour	45 mL
pinch	salt	pinch
1 cup	milk	250 mL
2	egg yolks, lightly beaten	2
2 tbsp.	butter	30 mL
1 tsp.	vanilla	5 mL
½ cup	chopped walnuts	125 mL

BOILED ICING

½ cup	sugar	125 mL
2 tbsp.	water	30 mL
¼ cup	corn syrup	50 mL
2	egg whites	2
1 tsp.	vanilla	5 mL

BUTTERSCOTCH GLAZE

¼ cup	brown sugar, packed	50 mL
2 tbsp.	water	30 mL
3 tbsp.	butter	45 mL

Heat oven to 350°F (180°C). Grease generously and flour 3, 8″ or 9″ (1.2 or 1.5 L) round layer pans, at least 1½″ (4 cm) deep. • Cream butter until light and fluffy. Add sugar gradually, creaming well after each addition. Continue beating until fluffy. • Add egg yolks, 1 at a time, beating well after each addition. Sift flour, baking powder and salt together. Combine milk and vanilla. Add sifted dry ingredients to creamed mixture alternately with milk mixture, stirring until blended after each addition and beginning and ending with dry ingredients. • Beat egg whites until stiff but not dry and fold into first mixture. Pour into prepared pans. • Bake 25-30 minutes or until tops spring back when touched lightly in the centre. Cool in pans about 5 minutes then turn out on cake racks. Cool. • Put Butterscotch Filling between layers, topping each layer of filling with a layer of sliced bananas. • Ice sides and top of assembled cake with Boiled Icing and drizzle Butterscotch Glaze around edge of top, allowing it to run down sides.

BUTTERSCOTCH SUNDAE CAKE
(continued)

To make Butterscotch Filling, combine sugar, flour and salt in saucepan, stirring to blend well. Add milk gradually, stirring until smooth. Set over moderate heat and bring to a boil, stirring. Boil 1 minute. Stir at least half of the hot mixture gradually into egg yolks. Pour back into pan and return to heat. Bring to a boil, stirring constantly. Boil 1 minute. Remove from heat. Stir in butter, vanilla and nuts and cool. • To make Boiled Icing, combine sugar, water and corn syrup in small saucepan. Bring to boil and boil hard, without stirring, to 242°F (96°C) (syrup spins 6-8″ [15-20 cm] thread when dropped from the tines of a fork). • Beat egg whites until stiff. Pour hot syrup in a thin stream into egg whites, beating constantly. Continue beating until stiff peaks form. Blend in vanilla. • To make Butterscotch Glaze, combine all ingredients in small saucepan. Boil hard 1½ minutes without stirring. Cool slightly.

---

1 cup	chopped dates	250 mL	
1 cup	boiling water	250 mL	
1 tsp.	baking soda	5 mL	
½ cup	butter	125 mL	
1 cup	white sugar	250 mL	
1	egg, lightly beaten	1	
1 tsp.	baking powder	5 mL	
¼ tsp.	salt	1 mL	
1½ cups	flour	375 mL	
½ cup	chopped nuts	125 mL	

QUEEN ELIZABETH CAKE

5 tbsp.	brown sugar	75 mL
3 tbsp.	butter	45 mL
2 tbsp.	cream	30 mL
¾ cup	coconut	175 mL

BROILED TOPPING

Mix dates, water, and baking soda and set aside to cool. • Cream butter and sugar, then add the egg. • Mix and add the dry ingredients alternately with the date mixture. • Bake in a 9″ x 9″ (2.5 L) pan for 30-45 minutes at 350°F (180°C). • Combine brown sugar, butter, cream and coconut, boil for 3 minutes and spread on the cake while the cake is still warm. • Return to oven or place under broiler until topping is brown. **Variation:** For topping, combine ½ cup (125 mL) each of brown sugar, chocolate chips, chopped nuts and 2 tsp. (10 mL) of flour. Sprinkle topping on unbaked batter and bake as above. Do not broil.

God grant me the serenity to accept the things I cannot change.
Courage to change the things I can, wisdom to know the difference.

ELVIS PRESLEY CAKE

2 cups	brown sugar	500 mL
½ cup	butter OR margarine	125 mL
¼ cup	rolled oats	50 mL
1 cup	boiling water	250 mL
2	eggs	2
1 cup	flour	250 mL
1 tsp.	baking soda	5 mL
1 tsp.	cinnamon	5 mL
½ tsp.	allspice	2 mL
½ cup	chopped nuts	125 mL
½ cup	chopped dates	125 mL
pinch	salt	pinch

BROWN SUGAR ICING

½ cup	butter OR margarine	125 mL
1 cup	brown sugar	250 mL
1 tsp.	milk	5 mL
1 tsp.	vanilla	5 mL
	icing sugar	

Pour boiling water over the brown sugar, margarine, and rolled oats and let stand for 20 minutes. • Add the rest of the ingredients except for the icing. • Pour batter into a 9″ x 9″ (2.5 L) pan and bake for 40 minutes at 350°F (180°C). • To make the brown sugar icing, melt the margarine in a saucepan and add the sugar; let mixture boil for 2 minutes, stirring constantly. Add milk and while stirring bring to a boil again. Cool and add the vanilla. Stir in enough icing sugar to thicken.

DANDY OHIO CAKE

2 cups	sugar	500 mL
⅔ cup	butter (scant)	150 mL
3	eggs	3
1 cup	milk	250 mL
3 cups	flour	750 mL
3 tsp.	baking powder	15 mL
pinch	salt	pinch
3 tbsp.	molasses	45 mL
¼ tsp.	cloves	1 mL
½ tsp.	cinnamon	2 mL
1 cup	raisins	250 mL

Cream together sugar and butter, beat in eggs, 1 at a time. Stir in milk and 2½ cups (625 mL) flour, alternating in thirds. Into last ½ cup (125 mL) flour, stir in the baking powder and salt. Stir into batter. When mixed, put ⅔ of the mixture in 2, 9″ x 9″ (2.5 L) greased and waxed papered pans. • To the remaining third of the batter add remaining ingredients. Bake in third pan for 20 minutes at 350°F (180°C). The third layer may take longer. • Put cake together with the spice layer in middle. Frost with Boiled Icing, page 204 • Our traditional birthday cake.

4	medium oranges	4
½ cup	sugar	125 mL
½ cup	soft shortening	125 mL
1 cup	sugar	250 mL
2¼ cups	sifted flour	550 mL
¼ tsp.	soda	1 mL
2 tsp.	baking powder	10 mL
1 tsp.	salt	5 mL
1 tbsp.	grated orange rind	15 mL
2	egg whites	2

FRESH ORANGE CAKE

½ cup	butter	125 mL
2	egg yolks	2
⅛ tsp.	salt	0.5 mL
¼ cup	orange-sugar mixture	50 mL
1 tsp.	grated orange rind	5 mL
¼ tsp.	lemon rind (optional)	1 mL
3½ cups	icing sugar	875 mL

ORANGE CREAM ICING

Grate the rind from 2 of the oranges. • Peel 3 of the oranges, removing all white next to the pulp. Discard peelings. • Section these oranges, discarding membrane and seeds. Cut the sections into tiny pieces. Squeeze remaining orange and add juice to cut-up oranges. • Measure out 1¼ cups (300 mL) orange and juice and add ½ cup (125 mL) sugar, stirring until dissolved. Take out ¼ cup (50 mL) and save for icing. • Heat oven to 350°F (180°C). Grease and flour 2, 8″ (20 cm) round layer cake pans. • Cream shortening well. Add 1 cup (250 mL) sugar and cream well. Add dry ingredients alternately with orange-sugar mixture. Stir in grated orange rind. • Beat egg whites stiff but not dry and fold in. • Bake about 25 minutes. Cool. • To make icing, combine butter, egg yolks and salt; beat until fluffy. Stir in orange-sugar mixture, orange and lemon rind. Blend in enough icing sugar to make a good spreading consistency. • Put icing between cake layers and on top and sides of cake.

Recipe for A Happy Life

Take the following ingredients:

1 cup of positive thoughts
1 cup of kind deeds
1 cup of consideration for others
2 cups sacrifice
2 cups well-beaten faults
3 cups forgiveness

Mix thoroughly, add tears of joy, sorrow and sympathy. Flavor with love and kindly service. Fold in 4 heaping cups of prayer and faith. After pouring all this into your daily life, bake well with the heat of human kindness.

Serve with a smile any time, and it will satisfy the hunger of many souls.

Icing on the cake. Worry is the advance interest you pay on troubles that seldom come.

COCONUT LAYER CAKE

3	large eggs, room temperature, separated	3
1 cup	sifted sugar	250 mL
1 cup	sifted cake flour	250 mL
2 tbsp.	melted butter	30 mL

FILLING

1 tbsp.	gelatin melted (7 g pkg.)	15 mL
2 cups	whipping cream, whipped	500 mL
¼ cup	coconut syrup (4 tbsp. [60 mL])	50 mL
2 cups	stiff vanilla custard cream (homemade)	500 mL
3 oz.	shredded coconut flakes	85 g

Best if prepared 1 day in advance.

To make the cake, combine the egg yolks and sugar, whip in the top of a double boiler over simmering water, until thickened. Remove from heat; continue whipping until completely cold. Add butter and flour. Stir until blended.   •   Beat egg whites until stiff but not dry. Fold them lightly into the batter.   •   Pour the batter into a greased and floured 10″ (25 cm) tube pan and bake in a 400°F (200°C) oven for ½ hour.   •   When done, cut the cake in 3-4 layers and fill with the cream.   •   To make the filling, sprinkle gelatin over whipping cream, to soften, whip cream, beating in coconut syrup, until cream holds its shape. Fold whipped cream into custard. Spread custard on layers of cake, stacking them as you go. Cover top and sides of cake with custard also. Decorate top and sides of cake with coconut flakes.

BEST ORANGE SPONGE CAKE

6	eggs, separated	6
1½ cups	fine sugar	375 mL
¾ cup	orange juice	175 mL
1½ cups	flour	375 mL
1½ tsp.	baking powder	7 mL

Beat egg yolks with sugar, approximately 3 minutes. Add juice and beat another 2 minutes. Stir in flour and baking powder and beat 3 minutes.   •   Beat egg whites until stiff and fold into the rest of the batter.   •   Pour into an ungreased 9″ (23 cm) tube pan.   •   Bake at 325°F (160°C) for 45 minutes or until cake springs back when touched.

Hint: *When separating eggs for cakes or soufflés, separate the eggs when they are cold but let them stand covered, at room temperature, for at least 1 hour before using them.*

¾ lb.	butter OR margarine (1½ cups [375 mL])	365 g	
1 lb.	icing sugar	500 g	**CHERRY**
6	eggs	6	**POUND CAKE**
3 cups	flour	750 mL	
1	large jar maraschino cherries, drained	1	

Cream butter and sugar. Add eggs, 1 at a time, beating well between each addition. Add flour gradually, beating well. Add cherries. • Bake in a greased tube pan at 300°F (150°C) for 1½ hours. • No baking powder or flavoring is necessary.

1 cup	butter	250 mL	
2 cups	sugar	500 mL	**MEMORABLE**
4	eggs	4	**CHOCOLATE**
2 tsp.	vanilla	10 mL	**POUND CAKE**
4 oz.	German sweet chocolate bar (if possible), melted	115 g	
3 cups	flour, sifted	750 mL	
1 tsp.	salt	5 mL	
½ tsp.	baking soda	2 mL	
½ tsp.	cinnamon	2 mL	
¼ tsp.	nutmeg	1 mL	
1 cup	buttermilk	250 mL	

Cream together butter and sugar until light and fluffy. Add eggs, 1 at a time, beating well. Blend in vanilla. Add melted chocolate. • Sift together flour, baking soda, salt and spices. • Add to creamed mixture, alternately with buttermilk. Pour into buttered 10″ (25 cm) tube or loaf pan. Bake at 300°F (150°C) for 1 hour and 30-35 minutes. • Cool in pan for 10 minutes. Remove and cool thoroughly. • Serve, dusted with icing (confectioner's) sugar. • Serves 12-14.

1 cup	butter	250 mL	**EGGNOG**
2 cups	icing (confectioners') sugar	500 mL	**REFRIGERATOR**
5	egg yolks	5	**CAKE**
¼ cup	rye or brandy	50 mL	
1 cup	toasted slivered almonds	250 mL	
1	angel food cake	1	
1 cup	whipping cream, whipped	250 mL	

Cream butter and sugar together. Mix in egg yolks 1 at a time, blending well after each. Stir in rye and nuts. • Cut cake into 2 or 3 layers. • Spread with rye filling. • Ice with whipped cream.

MINCEMEAT ICE-CREAM CAKE

1	angel food cake	1
1 qt.	vanilla ice cream	1 L
1 cup	prepared mincemeat	250 mL
½ cup	slivered blanched almonds, toasted	125 mL
1 tsp.	grated orange peel	5 mL
1 cup	whipping cream, whipped	250 mL
	almonds	
	maraschino cherries	

Rub crumbs off the cake. Cut cake horizontally into 3 even layers. • Stir ice cream just to soften. Fold in mincemeat, almonds, and orange peel and spread between cake layers. • Freeze until firm. • Before serving, frost top and sides with whipped cream. • Decorate with almonds and maraschino cherries. • Makes 10 servings.

MILLIE'S ANGEL FOOD DREAM CAKE

1 tbsp.	gelatin	15 mL
2 tbsp.	cold water	30 mL
1 cup	almonds	250 mL
1 tsp.	butter OR margarine	5 mL
½ cup	hot water	125 mL
⅔ cup	white sugar	150 mL
3 oz.	unsweetened chocolate (3 squares)	85 g
4	eggs, separated	4
1 tsp.	vanilla	5 mL
	angel food cake, 1 large or 2 small	
2 cups	whipping cream, whipped	500 mL
	grated chocolate	

Soak gelatin in cold water. • Combine almonds and butter. Spread on cookie sheet, bake at 300°F (150°C) until golden and then crush fine. • In double boiler, combine hot water, sugar and chocolate. Stir until chocolate melts, add gelatin. Cook 5 minutes. • Beat egg yolks to blend, add chocolate mixture a little at a time, then return to stove and cook 2 minutes. • Cool to lukewarm (cold water in bottom of double boiler). • When cool, add vanilla. • Beat egg whites until stiff. Fold into chocolate. • Beat whipping cream, fold in and add ½ of the almonds. Oil a tube pan. • Slice Angel Food cake into 3 layers. Layer cake and cream mixture in pan. Refrigerate overnight. To serve turn out on plate, top with whipping cream, almonds and grated chocolate.

Don't buy a turkey that is missing a leg or a wing.
Buy the complete bird - it won the fight.

1	Angel Food cake	1	
6 oz.	pkg. chocolate chips	170 g	
1 tbsp.	sugar	15 mL	
dash	salt	dash	
1	egg yolk, beaten	1	
1	egg white, beaten	1	
¾ cup	whipping cream, whipped	175 mL	

CHOCOLATE-FILLED ANGEL FOOD

Bake and cool an Angel Food cake. Cut about a 1" (2.5 cm) slice off the top and then break out pieces from the centre of the remaining cake and retain these pieces. • Melt chocolate in double boiler or microwave. • Add sugar and salt. Stir in egg yolk. Cool. • Add beaten egg white. Combine with pieces removed from cake. Fill the cavity of the base of the cake and put on the top. • Ice with whipped cream. Let set, refrigerated, before serving.

---

2 cups	graham wafers	500 mL
2 cups	icing (confectioners') sugar	500 mL
½ cup	melted butter OR margarine	125 mL
½ cup	soft butter OR margarine	125 mL
2	eggs	2
1 tsp.	vanilla	5 mL
4	bananas	4
19 oz.	can crushed pineapple, drained	540 mL
1½ cups	whipping cream, whipped *	375 mL
	maraschino cherries	
	nuts	
	shaved chocolate	

BANANA SPLIT CAKE

Mix graham wafers and melted margarine and spread in a 9" x 13" (4 L) pan. Put in refrigerator. • Beat powdered sugar, butter, eggs and vanilla exactly 10 minutes. • Spread on top of crumbs. • Cut bananas lengthwise, lay on filling. • Drain pineapple and spread over bananas. • Spread whipped cream over all. • Garnish with cherries, nuts and shaved chocolate. • **Variation:** The crumb base may be substituted by a 2-layer sponge cake. • Split each cake layer and spread each with 3 tbsp. (45 mL) strawberry jam. Mash bananas with 1 tsp. (5 mL) lemon juice and combine with whipped cream, saving ⅓ cup (75 mL) of cream for garnish. • Spread banana cream mixture over jam on each cake layer. • Stack cake rounds and garnish with cream, cherries, nuts and chocolate.

CHOCOLATE CHIFFON CAKE

1¾ cups	flour	425 mL
1¾ cups	white sugar	425 mL
⅓ cup	cocoa	75 mL
1 tbsp.	baking powder	15 mL
1 tsp.	salt	5 mL
½ cup	oil	125 mL
7	egg yolks	7
1 cup	water	250 mL
2 tsp.	vanilla	10 mL
7	egg whites	7
½ tsp.	cream of tartar	2 mL

Sift together first 5 ingredients. • Make a well and add next 4 ingredients. Beat until smooth. • Beat egg whites with cream of tartar until stiff. • Fold into chocolate mixture. • Pour into a greased 10″ (25 cm) tube pan. • Bake at 325°F (160°C) for 65-70 minutes.

CHOCOLATE CREAM ROLL

4	eggs, separated	4
¾ cup	sugar	175 mL
1 tsp.	vanilla	5 mL
6 tbsp.	sifted cake flour	90 mL
6 tbsp.	cocoa	90 mL
½ tsp.	baking powder	2 mL
¼ tsp.	salt	1 mL
1-2 cups	whipping cream	250-500 mL

Beat the egg whites until stiff but not dry. Gradually beat in the sugar until mixture stands in peaks. • Beat the yolks until thick and lemon-colored. • Fold into the first mixture. Add the vanilla. Fold in the sifted dry ingredients. • Turn out into a 10″ x 15″ (25 x 38 cm) baking pan which has been lined with a double thickness of waxed paper. • Bake at 400°F (200°C) for 15 minutes. • Turn out onto a damp cloth. Remove paper at once and cut off crisp edges. • Spread with whipped cream and roll up like a jelly roll. • Wrap again in waxed paper and put in refrigerator until ready to serve. • Serves 8-10.

POTATO MIX CHOCOLATE CAKE

Gluten-Free

4	eggs, separated	4
1⅓ cups	granulated sugar	325 mL
¼ cup	oil	50 mL
2 tbsp.	powdered chocolate	30 mL
1 tsp.	vanilla	5 mL
1 cup	milk	250 mL
2½ cups	Ener-G potato mix	625 mL

Preheat oven to 350°F (180°C). • Beat egg whites until stiff. Reserve. • In large bowl, beat egg yolks. Add sugar and beat. Mix in oil, chocolate and vanilla. • Alternately, beat in milk and potato mix. Gently fold egg whites into batter. Pour into greased angel food cake pan. Bake for 45 minutes. • Turn pan upside down on wire rack and let cool for 2 hours before cutting.

---

3 tbsp.	cocoa	45 mL	
1 cup	boiling water	250 mL	
2 cups	sugar	500 mL	
½ cup	shortening	125 mL	
2	eggs, separated	2	
2 cups	flour	500 mL	
½ tsp.	salt	2 mL	
1 tsp.	baking soda	5 mL	
½ tsp.	cloves	2 mL	
½ cup	buttermilk	125 mL	

LUCKY CHOCOLATE CAKE

Dissolve cocoa in boiling water and let it cool. Cream sugar, shortening and egg yolks until smooth. • Sift together flour, salt, baking soda and cloves and add to creamed mixture alternately with buttermilk and cocoa. • Beat 2 egg whites until very light and fold into batter. • Quickly pour into 2, 9″ (23 cm) greased square layer pans or a 9″ x 13″ (4 L) pan and bake for 25 minutes at 350°F (180°C). **Variation:** Try substituting 2 cups (500 mL) of brown sugar for the white sugar.

1¾ cups	sifted flour	425 mL
1¼ cups	sugar	300 mL
1½ tsp.	baking powder	7 mL
1 tsp.	baking soda	5 mL
¾ tsp.	salt	3 mL
¼ cup	cocoa	50 mL
½ cup	soft shortening	125 mL
1 cup	mashed banana	250 mL
⅓ cup	buttermilk	75 mL
2	eggs	2
½ cup	finely chopped walnuts	125 mL

CHOCOLATE WALNUT BANANA CAKE

Sift flour, sugar, baking powder, baking soda, salt and cocoa together into a large mixing bowl. • Add shortening, banana and ½ the buttermilk. Beat 300 strokes by hand or 2 minutes with electric mixer. Add remaining buttermilk and the eggs. Beat 2 minutes more. Stir in walnuts. • Pour into 2, 8″ (20 cm) round layer pans, greased and lined with paper, or use a loaf pan. • Bake at 350°F (180°C) for 25-30 minutes.

The best household hint I know is to "train your husband and children" to share the load.

FRUITED DOUGHNUT BALLS

2 cups	sifted all-purpose flour	500 mL
½ tsp.	baking soda	2 mL
¼ tsp.	salt	1 mL
2	egg yolks, beaten	2
½ cup	sugar	125 mL
½ cup	sour milk	125 mL
2 tbsp.	orange juice	30 mL
½ cup	finely chopped pecans	125 mL
¼ cup	chopped raisins	50 mL
¼ cup	finely chopped dates	50 mL
1 tsp.	grated orange peel	5 mL
	sugar for garnish	

Sift together flour, baking soda and salt. • Combine egg yolks, sugar, sour milk and orange juice. Stir into the dry ingredients. • Add nuts, fruits, and peel. Stir to blend. • Drop by teaspoonfuls into deep hot fat, 350°F (180°C), and fry 4-5 minutes or until brown on all sides, turning once. • Drain on paper towel. • Roll in sugar. • Makes 2 dozen.

TEED'S CHOCOLATE MARSHMALLOW ICING

6	marshmallows	6
6 tbsp.	cream	90 mL
1 oz.	bitter chocolate (1 square)	30 g
3 tbsp.	butter	45 mL
pinch	salt	pinch
2¼ cups	icing sugar	550 mL

Place everything, except icing sugar, in pan and heat until melted. Remove from heat, beat in icing sugar. • **Variation:** Add 1 tsp. (5 mL) instant coffee for a Mocha Icing.

FLUFFY FLOUR FROSTING

4 tbsp.	flour	60 mL
1 cup	milk	250 mL
¾ cup	butter OR margarine (do NOT use soft type)	175 mL
1 cup	sugar	250 mL
1 tsp.	vanilla	3 mL

Mix flour and milk together, bring to a boil, stir until thickened and formed into a ball. Set aside to cool. • Beat butter, sugar and vanilla until peaks form. • Beat flour mixture for 2 minutes, add butter mixture and beat until peaks form. • Makes enough frosting for a 9" x 13" (4 L) cake or a 9" (23 cm) double layer cake.

SQUARES

1 cup	flour	250 mL	
½ cup	butter OR margarine	125 mL	
¼ cup	white sugar	50 mL	
¼ tsp.	salt	1 mL	
1 cup	sugar	250 mL	
2 tbsp.	flour	30 mL	
¼ tsp.	baking powder	1 mL	
2	eggs, beaten	2	
3 tbsp.	lemon juice	45 mL	
1 tsp.	grated lemon rind	5 mL	
	icing sugar		

LEMON BARS

Blend together first 4 ingredients. • Press into a 9" (23 cm) square pan. • Bake for 20 minutes at 350°F (180°C). • Let cool. • Make a custard by mixing together the rest of the ingredients. • Pour over the cooled bottom layer. • Bake for 25 minutes at 350°F (180°C). • When cool sprinkle with icing sugar. • **Variation:** Sprinkle ½ cup (125 mL) of shredded coconut over cooked, cooled base. Pour lemon egg mixture over coconut and bake as above.

1½ cups	flour	375 mL	
¼ tsp.	baking powder	1 mL	
½ cup	sugar	125 mL	
¾ cup	butter OR margarine	175 mL	
8 oz.	pkg. cream cheese	250 g	
1	egg	1	
10 oz.	sweetened condensed milk	284 mL	
½ tsp.	lemon extract	2 mL	
19 oz.	can blueberry pie filling	540 mL	

BLUEBERRY CHEESE BAR

Sift flour, baking powder and sugar together. Cut butter into the flour. • Pat into a greased pan 9" x 13" (4 L) and bake at 350°F (180°C) for 15 minutes. • Beat together the cream cheese, egg, condensed milk and lemon, then spread over first mixture. • Swirl blueberry filling over the cheese mixture with a knife. • Bake at 350°F (180°C) for 35 minutes. • **Variation:** Try cherry or peach or your favorite pie filling instead of blueberry.

APPLE CRUMBLE SQUARES

½ cup	butter OR margarine	125 mL
1 cup	flour	250 mL
½ cup	sugar	125 mL
1	lemon, juice and grated rind of *	1
3	juicy apples (MacIntosh are best)	3
¼ cup	sugar	50 mL
	cinnamon	
	icing (confectioners') sugar	

Mix butter, flour, and sugar together until crumbly. Add lemon rind. ● Line an 8" (20 cm) square dish with ½ of this mixture. ● To make filling, slice the apples and toss with sugar and cinnamon. Add lemon juice. * ● Spread apple mixture over the base. Top with the rest of the crumb mixture and bake at 350°F (180°C) for approximately 34 minutes. ● While warm, cut into small squares. ● Sprinkle generously with icing sugar. ● * Use less lemon juice if apples are tart.

RUSSIAN SHEET COOKIES

6 tbsp.	butter OR margarine	90 mL
½ cup	sugar	125 mL
1	egg, separated	1
1 tbsp.	light cream	15 mL
½ tsp.	vanilla	2 mL
1 cup	flour	250 mL
1 tsp.	baking powder	5 mL
½ cup	apricot preserves OR jam	125 mL
	orange liqueur	
⅓ cup	sugar	75 mL
½ tsp.	cinnamon	2 mL
⅓ cup	chopped pecans	75 mL

Cream butter and sugar. Add egg yolk, cream and vanilla. ● Sift flour with baking powder and add to creamed mixture. Mix well and chill for 1 hour. ● Pat onto a small buttered cookie sheet. ● Thin the apricot preserves or jam with orange liqueur. Spread apricot preserves over cookie batter. ● Beat egg white until soft peaks form. Gradually add sugar and cinnamon to whites, beating until stiff. ● Spread the egg white mixture over preserves and sprinkle with pecans. ● Bake at 350°F (180°C) for 10-12 minutes, turn pan once during baking. ● Cut into squares. ● These won't last long!! ● **Variation:** Combine ¼ cup (50 mL) butter, 1 cup (250 mL) sugar, 1 egg, 1 tsp. (5 mL) vanilla and 2 cups (500 mL) shredded coconut. Spread this mixture over the apricot preserves layer. Omit other toppings and bake at 325°F (160°C) for 25 minutes.

2 cups	sugar	500 mL
1½ cups	oil	375 mL
4	eggs, beaten	4
2 cups	flour	500 mL
2 tsp.	baking soda	10 mL
2 tsp.	cinnamon	10 mL
1 tsp.	salt	5 mL
3 cups	grated carrots	750 mL
2 cups	flaked coconut	500 mL
1 cup	chopped nuts	250 mL

CARROT BARS

Add sugar and oil to the eggs and beat well. Add flour and other dry ingredients, blend until smooth. Stir in carrots, coconut, and nuts. • Bake at 350°F (180°C) for 30-40 minutes in a large greased jelly-roll pan. • Frost with your favorite butter icing.

½ cup	butter OR margarine	125 mL
1 cup	brown sugar	250 mL
2	eggs, beaten	2
¾ cup	flour	175 mL
½ tsp.	baking powder	2 mL
¼ tsp.	salt	1 mL
1 tsp.	vanilla	5 mL
¾ cup	walnuts OR pecans	175 mL

BUTTER-SCOTCH SQUARES

Melt butter and brown sugar in a saucepan. • Add beaten eggs, then the dry ingredients and walnuts OR pecans. • Bake in a greased 8″ (20 cm) square pan for 20 minutes at 350°F (180°C). • Ice with Butterscotch Icing if desired, or try Brown Sugar Icing, page 206.

⅔ cup	melted butter	150 mL
3 tbsp.	cocoa	45 mL
1	egg	1
½ cup	sugar (white OR brown)	125 mL
32	crushed graham wafers	32
¾ cup	chopped nuts (optional)	175 mL
1 tsp.	vanilla	5 mL

CHOCOLATE SQUARES

Bring first 4 ingredients to a boil. • Add graham wafers, nuts and vanilla and mix well. • Pour into a 8″ (20 cm) cake pan and cool. • Ice with chocolate icing and top with crushed nuts or use Fudge Topping, page 218. **Variation:** Try with ½ cup (125 mL) EACH of chopped nuts and shredded coconut.

WALNUT-FUDGE BROWNIES

⅓ cup	butter OR margarine	75 mL
2 oz.	unsweetened chocolate (2 squares)	60 g
1 cup	sugar	250 mL
2	eggs, beaten	2
½ tsp.	vanilla	2 mL
¾ cup	flour	175 mL
¼ tsp.	salt	1 mL
½ cup	broken walnuts	125 mL

Melt butter and chocolate together and cool slightly. Add the remaining ingredients and mix well. • Pour into a greased 8″ (20 cm) square pan and bake at 375°F (180°C) for 25-30 minutes. • Remove from oven and cool a few minutes, then turn out on a cake rack. • Cool before slicing. • Makes 20 brownies. • Ice with Fudge Topping, below, if you like.

FUDGE TOPPING

1½ cups	icing (confectioners') sugar	375 mL
⅛ tsp.	salt	0.5 mL
2¼ tbsp.	cocoa	35 mL
2¼ tbsp.	very soft butter	35 mL
2¼ tbsp.	warm, strong coffee	35 mL
½ tsp.	vanilla	2 mL
¼ cup	broken walnuts	50 mL

Measure all ingredients except walnuts into a mixing bowl. Stir until well blended. • Spread over cooled brownies and top with nuts. • Use this topping for any squares or cakes, double if necessary.

BROWNIE MIX

1¼ cups	skim milk powder	300 mL
4 cups	sifted flour	1 L
4 tsp.	baking powder	20 mL
2 tsp.	baking soda	10 mL
2 tsp.	salt	10 mL
1¼ cups	cocoa	300 mL
4 cups	white sugar	1 L

THE BROWNIES

½ cup	chopped nuts	125 mL
2	eggs	2
3 tbsp.	water	45 mL
1 tsp.	vanilla	5 mL
½ cup	melted butter	125 mL

Combine the first 7 ingredients and store in a cool dry place in a covered container. • To make brownies, take 2½ cups (625 mL) of the mix and add to it the remaining ingredients. • Bake in a greased 9″ (23 cm) square pan at 350°F (180°C) for 35-40 minutes.

1½ cups	all-purpose flour	375 mL
½ cup	packed brown sugar	125 mL
¾ cup	butter OR margarine	175 mL
1½ cups	medium-grind coconut	375 mL
2 tbsp.	butter OR margarine	30 mL
2 tbsp.	milk	30 mL
1½ cups	icing (confectioners') sugar	375 mL
½ tsp.	peppermint flavoring	2 mL
6 tbsp.	butter OR margarine	90 mL
½ cup	instant chocolate drink powder	125 mL

CHOCOLATE PEPPERMINT SQUARES

To prepare bottom layer, crumble first 4 ingredients together and pat into an ungreased 9″ (23 cm) square pan. Bake at 350°F (180°C) for 20 minutes. Set aside to cool. • To make the filling, combine the butter, milk, icing sugar and peppermint in a bowl and beat well. Spread over the cooled bottom layer. • To make the top layer, melt butter in a small saucepan over low heat, add chocolate powder and stir. Remove from heat and cool slightly before pouring over the filling. Spread smooth to cover, allow to set. • Cut into squares. • Freezes well. • Keep chilled.

¾ cup	butter OR margarine	175 mL
1 tsp.	salt	5 mL
1 tsp.	vanilla	5 mL
½ cup	white sugar	125 mL
1½ cups	brown sugar	375 mL
2	eggs, separated	2
1 tbsp.	water	15 mL
2 cups	flour	500 mL
1 tsp.	baking powder	5 mL
½ tsp.	baking soda	2 mL
6 oz.	pkg. chocolate chips	175 g
½ cup	chopped nuts	125 mL

CHOCOLATE CHIP MERINGUE SQUARES

Combine butter, salt, vanilla, white sugar and ¾ cup (175 mL) brown sugar. Add egg yolks and water and blend well. • Sift flour, baking powder and baking soda. • Mix flour into the first mixture. • Pour into a 9″ x 13″ (4 L) greased baking pan. • Spread chips and nuts on top. • Beat egg whites until stiff, then beat in ¾ cup (175 mL) brown sugar. • Spread over chips and nuts. • Bake at 325°F (160°C) for ½ hour or until brown on top.

Hint: Try a little cream of tartar in your 7 Minute Frosting, it will not get dry and crack.

COOKIES

COCONUT MACAROONS

2	egg whites	2
dash	salt	dash
½ tsp.	vanilla	2 mL
⅔ cup	sugar	150 mL
1⅓ cups	flaked coconut	325 mL

Beat egg whites with the salt and vanilla until soft peaks form. Gradually add sugar, beating until stiff. Fold in coconut. • Drop by rounded teaspoons onto a greased cookie sheet. • Bake at 325°F (160°C) for about 15-20 minutes. • Watch carefully. • Makes about 1½ dozen.

FRUIT AND NUT MERINGUES

2	egg whites	2
¼ tsp.	salt	1 mL
½ cup	sugar	125 mL
½ tsp.	vanilla	2 mL
1 cup	chopped dates OR candied cherries	250 mL
1 cup	chopped pecans	250 mL

Beat egg whites and salt until stiff, not dry. Gradually beat in sugar until stiff peaks form. Add vanilla. Fold in fruit and nuts. • Drop by teaspoonsful (5 mL) on lightly greased cookie sheets. Bake on lightly greased cookie sheets. Bake at 250°F (120°C) until crisp, 25-30 minutes. Turn heat off and leave meringues in oven until cool. • Store in cool dry area.

NANA'S NORWEGIAN COOKIES

1 cup	sugar	250 mL
1 cup	shortening	250 mL
1 cup	butter	250 mL
1	egg	1
½ tsp.	vanilla	2 mL
½ tsp.	almond extract	2 mL
2 cups	flour	500 mL
½ tsp.	salt	2 mL
	sugar	

Cream sugar, shortening and butter. Add egg, vanilla, almond extract and mix well. Mix in flour and salt. Cover; refrigerate 1 hour. • Shape into balls on ungreased baking sheet, 1½″ (4 cm) apart. Press down with fork. Sprinkle with sugar before baking. Bake at 375°F (190°C) for 10 minutes.

1¼ cups	sugar	300 mL	
2-3	egg whites	2-3	*KRANSEKAGE*
2 lbs.	marzipan (pure almond paste)	1 kg	
	icing (confectioners') sugar		
	Confectioners' Icing, recipe follows		

Mix all ingredients together. Knead or use dough hook. • Roll into long sausage rolls, about 18" (46 cm) long and 2-3" (5-7 cm) in diameter. Roll in icing sugar. Cut roll into slices and put on baking sheet. • Cookies may be shaped by pinching roll into a peak with fingers, before slicing. • Decorate with Confectioners' Icing, using pastry bag and very narrow cone.

3½ cups	icing (confectioners') sugar	875 mL	*CONFECTIONERS' ICING*
2	egg whites	2	
1½ tbsp.	lemon juice OR vinegar	22 mL	

Sift icing sugar. • Beat egg whites until stiff. Gradually beat in sugar and lemon juice until icing has an elastic consistency. Add a little more lemon juice if needed. • Cover with a damp cloth until ready to use. • Pipe icing onto cookies with a pastry bag.

½ cup	butter	125 mL	*ALMOND FINGERS*
3 tbsp.	icing (confectioners') sugar	45 mL	
1 cup	flour	250 mL	
1 tsp.	cold water	5 mL	
1 tsp.	almond flavoring	5 mL	
½ tsp.	vanilla	2 mL	
1 cup	finely chopped almonds OR pecans	250 mL	
	granulated sugar		
	chocolate frosting		
	chocolate sprinkles		

Combine all ingredients, except granulated sugar, chocolate frosting and chocolate sprinkles. • Form into fingers and roll in granulated sugar. • Place on an ungreased baking sheet. • Bake at 350°F (180°C) for 10-12 minutes. • Frost both ends with chocolate frosting and dip in chocolate sprinkles or dip both ends of fingers in a parawax/chocolate mixture. • **Variation:** Cookies may also be shaped into small balls, flattened slightly and baked as above for 9-10 minutes

OSLO KRINGLE

4 oz.	butter OR margarine (½ cup [125 mL])	125 g
1 cup	water	250 mL
1 tsp.	almond extract	5 mL
1 cup	flour	250 mL
3	eggs	3

ICING

1 cup	icing (confectioners') sugar, sifted, more if needed	250 mL
2 tbsp.	warm milk	30 mL
½ tsp.	almond extract	2 mL
	cherries for garnish	
	nuts for garnish	

Place butter and water in a saucepan. Boil until butter melts. Stir in almond extract; add flour and cook until the mixture leaves the sides of the pan. Stir until absolutely smooth. • Remove from heat and add the eggs, 1 at a time, beating well after each addition. • Spoon mixture onto a cookie sheet, in 3 portions. Spread each with a spoon, across width of the cookie sheet making 3" (7 cm) wide strips, 3 strips. • Bake at 425°F (220°C) for 15 minutes, then reduce heat to 400°F (200°C) and bake for 15 minutes longer. • Cool. • To prepare the icing, mix all ingredients until smooth. Add more icing sugar if icing is too thin. Spread on strips. • Decorate with cherries and nuts if you wish. • Slice diagonally, about 1½" (4 cm) wide. • These are best eaten the same day they are made - that is not a hard chore. • Delicious! • Serves 12.

WALNUT-FILLED CRESCENTS

1 lb.	shortening	500 g
4 cups	flour	1 L
1 tsp.	salt	5 mL
1 tbsp.	dry yeast (7g pkg.)	15 mL
1 cup	lukewarm milk	250 mL
2	eggs, well-beaten	2
2 cups	ground walnuts	500 mL
½ cup	sugar	125 mL
2	egg whites	2
1 tsp.	lemon juice	5 mL

Cut shortening into flour and salt. • Combine yeast with milk and let stand for 10 minutes. • Add eggs to yeast and stir into flour mixture. Mix dough well. • Keep in a covered bowl in refrigerator overnight. • Next morning roll out dough on granulated sugar and cut into triangles. • To prepare filling, mix walnuts, sugar, egg whites and lemon juice until fairly smooth. • Place a small amount of filling on wide end of triangle, roll up and place on greased baking sheet. Shape into crescents. • Bake at 350°F (180°C) for 20-30 minutes or until golden brown. • **Variation:** Poppy seeds OR cinnamon OR apple filling OR coconut could be used in the filling mixture.

1¼ cups	brown sugar, packed	300 mL
6 cups	flour	1.5 L
½ tsp.	baking soda	2 mL
¼ tsp.	salt	1 mL
1 lb.	butter	500 g
1	egg	1
	sugar (optional)	

LAST-MINUTE SHORTBREAD

Mix and sift sugar, flour, baking soda and salt into large bowl. Work in butter until cornmeal consistency. Add unbeaten egg and blend. Knead until dough cracks. Roll out to ¼'' thick. ● Bake on ungreased cookie sheet at 300°F (150°C). ● Sprinkle sugar on shortbread if desired.

---

1 cup	butter OR margarine, softened	250 mL
8 oz.	pkg. cream cheese, softened	250 g
1 cup	sugar	250 mL
1 tsp.	vanilla	5 mL
2½ cups	flour	625 mL
¼ tsp.	salt	1 mL
½ cup	chopped pecans	125 mL

CREAM CHEESE COOKIES

Cream butter and cheese together. Add sugar and vanilla. Beat until fluffy. Gradually add the flour and salt. Stir in the pecans. ● Cover and refrigerate for 15 minutes. ● Shape into 4 rolls, wrap in foil and refrigerate overnight. ● Heat oven to 325°F (160°C). ● Slice rolls ¼'' (1 cm) thick. ● Bake cookies on a greased cookie sheet for approximately 15 minutes or until lightly browned.

---

1 cup	butter OR margarine	250 mL
1 cup	white sugar	250 mL
1	egg	1
1⅓ cups	flour	325 mL
½ tsp.	salt	2 mL
½ tsp.	baking soda	2 mL
1 tsp.	baking powder	5 mL
1½ cups	rolled oats	375 mL
¾ cup	coconut	175 mL
6 oz.	pkg. chocolate chips	175 g

OATMEAL CHIP COOKIES

Cream together butter and sugar; stir in the egg. ● Sift together flour, salt, baking soda and baking powder and add to the creamed mixture. ● Stir in oats, coconut and chips. Drop by spoonfuls on greased cookie sheets. ● Bake at 350°F (180°C) for 15-20 minutes, depending on the size of the cookie. ● When doubling this recipe, use 1 cup (250 mL) brown sugar and 1 cup (250 mL) white sugar.

DATE-FILLED COOKIES

1½ cups	flour, plus 1 tbsp.	390 mL
1 tsp.	baking soda	5 mL
2 tsp.	baking powder	10 mL
½ tsp.	salt	2 mL
1½ cups	oatmeal	375 mL
¾ cup	soft butter	175 mL
1 cup	brown sugar	250 mL
1	egg	1
4 tbsp.	milk	60 mL
1 tsp.	vanilla	5 mL

FILLING

1 cup	white sugar	250 mL
1 cup	water	250 mL
2 cups	chopped dates (1 lb. [500g])	500 mL
½ tsp.	vanilla	2 mL

Sift together flour, baking soda, baking powder and salt. • Add oatmeal and set aside. • Cream the butter, add the brown sugar and the egg. Mix well. • Stir in the dry ingredients and the milk and vanilla. • Chill the dough in the refrigerator. • Roll out very thinly and cut into small cookies with a 2″ (5 cm) diameter cutter. • Bake on lightly greased cookie sheets at 325°F (170°C) for ½ hour. • To prepare the filling, boil sugar, water and dates until soft. Cool and add the vanilla. • Spread the cooled filling between 2 cookies. • Makes 60 date-filled cookies.

CHOCOLATE CRISPIES

1 oz.	square semisweet chocolate	30 g
1 oz.	square unsweetened chocolate	30 g
½ cup	soft butter OR margarine	125 mL
1 cup	white sugar	250 mL
2	eggs	2
½ tsp.	vanilla	2 mL
½ cup	all-purpose flour	125 mL
⅛ tsp.	salt	0.5 mL
½ cup	unsweetened coconut OR chopped walnuts	125 mL

Melt chocolate squares, add to the soft butter and mix well. Stir in the sugar. Add eggs, 1 at a time, beating well after each addition. Add vanilla, flour and salt, mixing well. • Spread mixture on a greased cookie sheet. Sprinkle with coconut or nuts. • Bake at 400°F (200°C) for about 11-12 minutes. • While warm cut into bars. • Makes approximately 3 dozen cookies. • **Note:** A shorter time gives a chewier cookie; for a crispier cookie bake a little longer.

¾ cup	butter OR margarine	175 mL
¾ cup	sugar	175 mL
½ cup	lightly packed brown sugar	125 mL
1	egg	1
1 cup	whole-wheat flour	250 mL
1 cup	rolled oats	250 mL
¾ cup	coconut	175 mL
¼ cup	wheat germ	50 mL
1 tsp.	baking powder	5 mL
1 tsp.	baking soda	5 mL
1½ cups	raisins	375 mL

COCONUT-OATMEAL COOKIES

Cream butter, sugars and egg thoroughly. Add remaining ingredients, except for the raisins. Stir in raisins. • Drop by spoonfuls onto lightly greased baking sheets. • Flatten slightly with floured fork. • Bake at 350°F (180°C) for 12-15 minutes. • Makes about 4 dozen cookies.

⅔ cup	sugar	150 mL
3 tbsp.	flour	45 mL
1 cup	well-drained crushed pineapple	250 mL
3 tbsp.	lemon juice	45 mL
2 tbsp.	butter	30 mL
½ cup	pineapple juice	125 mL
⅔ cup	butter OR shortening	150 mL
1 cup	sugar	250 mL
2	eggs, beaten	2
1 tsp.	vanilla	5 mL
2½ cups	flour	625 mL
¼ tsp.	baking soda	1 mL
¼ tsp.	salt	1 mL
2 tbsp.	thick sour OR sweet cream	30 mL

PINEAPPLE FILLED COOKIES

COOKIE

Prepare filling ahead of time to allow it to cool. To make the filling, blend sugar and flour together then add the remaining ingredients. Cook slowly, stirring constantly until thick. Remove from heat and cool. • To make cookies, cream butter, then add sugar gradually, beating constantly. Beat in the eggs and the vanilla. • Sift flour, baking soda and salt together and add to butter and eggs. • Roll dough and cut into rounds with a 2″ (5 cm) cutter. • Place 1 tsp. (5 mL) of filling on each round. • Fold over like a turnover, press edges gently together using a fork. • Place on lightly greased cookie sheets. • Bake at 425°F (220°C) for 15 minutes or until done. **Variations:** Jam, apples, raisins or mincemeat may be substituted for the pineapple filling.

MOLASSES COOKIES

1 cup	sugar	250 mL
1 cup	shortening	250 mL
1 cup	molasses	250 mL
1	egg	1
1 tbsp.	baking soda	15 mL
½ cup	boiling water	125 mL
1 tsp.	salt	5 mL
1 tsp.	cinnamon	5 mL
2 tsp.	ginger	10 mL
2 tsp.	ground cloves	10 mL
4-5 cups	flour	1-1.25 L

Cream together sugar and shortening until light, then blend in the molasses and the egg. • Dissolve baking soda in boiling water, add then add to the sugar mixture. • Mix dry ingredients together. • Gradually add the dry ingredients to the sugar mixture, mixing well to make a soft dough. • Roll out ¼" (1 cm) thick, cut into rounds or fancy shapes, place on greased baking sheets and bake at 375°F (190°C) for 8-10 minutes. • Makes 6-7 dozen.

SPECULAAS

1 lb.	butter OR margarine	500 g
1¼ cups	brown sugar	300 mL
1¼ cups	white sugar	300 mL
2	eggs	2
6 cups	flour	1.5 L
2½ tsp.	cinnamon	12 mL
1½ tsp.	ground cloves	7 mL
1½ tsp.	allspice	7 mL
1 tsp.	baking powder	5 mL

Cream together butter and the sugars. Stir in the eggs. Combine remaining ingredients; stir into egg mixture. • Roll out the dough and use cookie cutters to make different shapes. Place on greased cookie sheeets. Bake at 300°F (150°C) for 10-15 minutes. • This recipe is great for gingerbread houses or gingerbread men.

Thank heaven for the little things.
The happiness that friendship brings.
A smile, a hug, a gentle touch.
The cheery word that says so much.
The dancing flowers, the warming sun.
The starry sky when day is done.
All these give me a heart that sings.
Thank heaven for the little things.

1 cup	crunchy peanut butter	250 mL
1 cup	white sugar	250 mL
1	egg	1

PEANUT COOKIES

Gluten-Free

In a small bowl, blend together all ingredients. • Shape into 1″ (2.5 cm) balls. Place balls on greased cookie sheets and flatten with a fork. • Bake at 350°F (180°C) for 10-12 minutes. • Cool cookies before removing them from cookie sheets. • Makes 2½-3 dozen cookies. • And "NO, we didn't forget any ingredients." • **Variation:** Try ½ white and ½ brown sugar or all brown sugar.

¾ cup	crunchy peanut butter*	175 mL
¾ cup	mashed potato	175 mL
¾ cup	white sugar	175 mL
1	egg	1
½ cup	rice flour	125 mL
¼ cup	cornstarch	50 mL
2 tsp.	cream of tartar	10 mL
1 tsp.	baking soda	5 mL
1 tsp.	vanilla	5 mL
¼ cup	coarsely chopped OR halved peanuts (optional)	50 mL

CRUNCHY PEANUT BUTTER COOKIES

Gluten-Free

In a bowl, cream together peanut butter and potato. Beat in sugar until fluffy. Beat in egg. • Combine rice flour, cornstarch, cream of tartar and baking soda. Add to peanut butter mixture and mix well. Stir in vanilla. • Refrigerate for 25 minutes or until batter firms up (batter should be soft but not sticky). • Form batter into balls; place 2½″ (6 cm) apart on nonstick baking sheet. Using a fork dipped into rice flour, flatten cookies to about ¼″ (5 mm) thickness. • Sprinkle with peanuts. • Bake in 375°F (190°C) oven for about 15-20 minutes or until golden brown. • Makes 3 dozen cookies. • * You may also use smooth peanut butter if you prefer.

Swallowing angry words is a lot easier than eating them.

NANA'S PEANUT BUTTER COOKIES

¾ cup	peanut butter	175 mL
½ cup	butter OR margarine	125 mL
½ cup	brown sugar	125 mL
½ cup	white sugar	125 mL
1	egg	1
¼ tsp.	baking soda	1 mL
1¼ cups	flour	300 mL
1 tsp.	vanilla	5 mL

Mix all ingredients together in order given. • Roll into small balls. • Place on an ungreased cookie sheet and flatten balls with a fork • Bake at 350°F (180°C) for 10-12 minutes.

GOLDEN FANCIES

1 cup	butter OR margarine	250 mL
½ cup	brown sugar	125 mL
1	egg	1
½ cup	syrup	125 mL
¼ cup	hot water	50 mL
2 tsp.	baking soda	10 mL
3 cups	flour	750 mL
	jam, any flavor	

Mix ingredients in order given, except for jam; add a little more flour if necessary. • Roll out and cut in 2½" (6 cm) squares. • Place 1 tsp. (5 mL) of jam in the center of each square and fold, 1 corner to another, pinching points together. • Bake at 400°F (200°C) until cookies are golden brown. Watch carefully - these cookies burn easily.

Fourteen Commandments for Living

1. If you open it, close it.
2. If you turn it on, turn it off.
3. If you unlock it, lock it.
4. If you break it, admit it.
5. If you can't fix it, call in someone who can.
6. If you borrow it, return it.
7. If you value it, take care of it.
8. If you make a mess, clean it up.
9. If you move it, put it back.
10. If it belongs to someone else and you want to use it, get permission.
11. If you don't know how to operate it, leave it alone.
12. If it's none of your business, don't ask questions.
13. If it ain't broke, don't fix it.
14. If it will brighten someone's day, say it.

CANDY

SCHOKOLADE-WURST

Chocolate Sausage.

3⅓ cups	almonds with peels	875 mL
3½ cups	sugar	875 mL
3½ cups	melted chocolate	875 mL
1¾ cups	mixed peel	425 mL
1	egg	1
8	cloves	8
	a touch of cinnamon	
	sugar for coating	

Grind the almonds. • Mix all the ingredients together, shape into 1 big or 2 small rolls. Roll these in sugar and wrap in waxed paper. • Let dry in warm room. • I put these and the Teufelspillen, below, on a clean board, covered with a cloth, on top of the kitchen cupboards for about 1 week. • Cut before serving into slices, as needed.

TEUFEL-SPILLEN

Devil's Pills.

Truly delicious!

4½ cups	chocolate, melted	1.125 L
4½ cups	sugar	1.125 L
4½ cups	ground almonds	1.125 L
½	egg	½
a drop	of almond essence	a drop
	sugar for coating	
	rum and water, mixed, to taste	
1-2	egg yolks	1-2
	icing (confectioners') sugar	

Combine chocolate, sugar, almonds, ½ egg, almond essence, just enough rum and water to give desired consistency. • Form into little balls, roll them in sugar and press a hole in the middle with your thumb. • Make a paste of 1 or 2 egg yolks and icing sugar, paste has to be rather stiff. Fill holes with paste. • Let dry at room temperature for about 1 week.

Hint: When melting chocolate, try greasing the pot first, it speeds the transfer of chocolate from pot to bowl.

CHOCOLATE GRAND MARNIER BONBONS

2 cups	whipping cream	500 mL
2 lbs.	chocolate	1 kg
7 oz.	unsalted butter (⅞ cup [200 mL])	200 g
¼ cup	Grand Marnier	50 mL
4	egg yolks	4
1	egg	1
	small foil cups	

In double boiler, melt chocolate. • When completely melted, remove from heat, add butter and stir until the butter is melted. Add, a little at a time, cold whipping cream, stirring constantly. When well mixed, add Grand Marnier, and continue stirring. • Add the whole egg, mix in well, then add yolks one by one. • Make sure it is a well-homogenized paste. • If too soft, cool in refrigerator, stirring occasionally until right consistency. • Put chocolate mixture in pastry bag with star tip and fill foil cups. • Store in tins and refrigerate.

PRALINE CREAM TRUFFLES

22 oz.	couverture (chocolate melted and cooled)	625 g
1 lb.	unsalted cultured butter	500 g
8 oz.	praline, page 231	
1 cup	whipped cream	250 mL

Melt chocolate in double boiler, once melted completely set aside, stirring occasionally, to cool. • Beat softened butter in electric mixer until smooth. • Add praline, then add melted, cooled chocolate, beating all the time. Work fast and carefully so that the chocolate does not harden. Beat in the whipping cream. • Put the mixture in pastry bag with a ½" (1.3 cm) tip and, on baking sheet covered with waxed paper, pipe approximately 1" (2.5 cm) sticks. Pipe close together but not touching. Put in deep-freeze. • When frozen, dip in tempered chocolate with fork. Scoop out chocolate drop and roll in a cocoa and sugar mixture, which you make by sifting together, 3 times, equal amounts of icing sugar and Dutch unsweetened cocoa. When well set, pick them out of cocoa mixture and carefully put aside to finish setting. Store in a tin and refrigerate. • See photograph page 176A.

The clock of life is wound but once,
And no one has the power,
To tell just when the hands will stop,
At late or early hour.
Now is the only time you own,
Live, love, toil with a will,
Place no fault in tomorrow, for
The clock may then be still.

1 cup	sugar	250 mL	
1¼ cups	hazelnuts, skinned OR ½ blanched almonds and ½ skinned hazelnuts	300 mL	

PRALINE

Oil a baking sheet and set aside. • Place sugar in heavy-bottomed skillet and cook over medium heat, stirring constantly, until sugar is melted and caramel-colored, about 5-7 minutes. Stir in the nuts, blend until evenly coated. • Spoon onto prepared baking sheet and cool completely. • Pulverize in food processor, a little at a time, until very finely powdered. Keep in a jar.

2 cups	finely ground skinned hazelnuts	500 mL
2 cups	icing (confectioners') sugar	500 mL
1 cup	unsalted cultured butter, softened	250 mL
¼ cup	Frangelico liqueur toasted, whole, skinned hazelnuts tempered chocolate, recipe follows	50 mL

NOISSETTE ENROBÉE

Chocolate-Covered Hazelnut Centers.

Mix the finely ground skinned hazelnuts with icing sugar. • With an electric mixer, beat butter and nut and sugar mixture. Beat until well blended. Add ¼ cup (50 mL), or a little more, Frangelico liqueur and mix well, until you have a well-blended soft dough. Take a teaspoonful (5 mL) of that mixture and work it around a whole, toasted, skinned hazelnut. Put coated hazelnuts on a tray lined with waxed paper, so that they don't touch each other and let set in freezer. • Once set, dip them in well-tempered chocolate.

TEMPERED CHOCOLATE:

Melt chocolate completely, in the top of a double boiler, over just-boiling water. Cool chocolate in the refrigerator. To dip fruit, truffles, etc. in tempered chocolate, reheat chocolate in double boiler, over very low heat.

There is a destiny that makes us brothers. None go their way alone. All that we send into the lives of others. Comes back into our own.

PENUCHE

A family favorite.

2 cups	dark brown sugar	500 mL
1 cup	white sugar	250 mL
1 cup	milk	250 mL
¼ cup	cream	50 mL
2 tbsp.	butter	30 mL
1 tsp.	vanilla	5 mL
½ cup	walnuts	125 mL

Boil sugars, milk, cream and butter together, over low heat, until mixture forms a soft ball, 238°F (115°C), in cold water. Stir frequently. Remove from heat and do not stir for 20 minutes. Add vanilla and beat until creamy. Add nuts. Pour into buttered pan and cut in squares.

PRALINES

1¾ cup	sugar	425 mL
1 cup	boiling water	250 mL
⅛ tsp.	salt	0.5 mL
1 tbsp.	butter	15 mL
½ tsp.	vanilla	2 mL
1 cup	pecan halves	250 mL
¼ tsp.	rum, if desired	1 mL

Stir ½ cup (125 mL) sugar, in medium-sized saucepan, over medium heat, until it forms pale yellow-colored syrup. • Add water. Remove from heat and stir until smooth. Stir in salt, butter and 1¼ cups sugar and boil hard to soft-ball stage, 238°F (115°C). Remove from heat and let stand 5 minutes. • Add vanilla, pecans, and rum, if using, to syrup and stir until creamy, 3-5 minutes. • Drop from spoon onto waxed paper.

MAPLE SEAFOAM

1 cup	brown sugar	250 mL
1½ cups	maple sugar	375 mL
⅔ cup	water	150 mL
⅛ tsp.	salt	0.5 mL
2	egg whites, beaten	2
½ cup	nuts	125 mL
½ tsp.	vanilla	125 mL

Mix sugar, water and salt. Boil to hard-ball stage, 254°F (120°C). • Pour into beaten egg whites and beat until stiff. • Add rest of ingredients. Drop from spoon on waxed paper. Chill until firm.

Think of it - you can walk a mile and yet only move 2 feet.

2 cups	white sugar	500 mL	
¼ cup	honey	50 mL	
¼ cup	butter	50 mL	
½ cup	cream	125 mL	

HONEY CANDY

Mix together all ingredients and place on heat until mixture starts to boil. DO NOT stir until after it reaches a rolling boil. Test until drops of mixture in cold water form small balls. • Let cool, for just a few minutes. Beat until creamy and pour into lightly buttered 8" (2 L) square dish. Cool and cut into squares. • This is a recipe that our family has made for over 80 year. It is easy to make and delicious.

1-1½ lbs.	fondant	500-750 g
	peppermint essence OR oil	
	tempered chocolate (optional), see page 231	

PEPPERMINT FONDANT PATTIES

There are various ways of making these but none so simple. Place fondant, just as it comes from the box from your pastry or candy shop, in a heavy saucepan. DO NOT add water, but add just enough peppermint essence (flavoring) or oil of peppermint to your own taste. Start with a little at a time, to reach your own preference. • Place sheets of greaseproof paper on large baking sheets. Gently warm up the fondant, stirring all the time, until it acquires the thickness of thick or double cream. DO NOT allow the fondant to overheat, but remove from heat at the thick cream stage. • If you wish, divide the fondant into 3 parts. Add a little green, pink or any desired coloring. • Spoon some fondant into a pastry bag with a ¼" (1 cm) tip. Seal in fondant by twisting open end of pastry bag. Pipe onto prepared sheets, so that each mint spreads out to about 1" (2.5 cm) diameter, try to make thickness between ⅛-¼" (3 mm-1 cm). • After about 15 minutes, turn patties over for the underside to dry. They will come away from greaseproof paper quite readily. • These peppermint patties are delicious. You will be proud to serve them. I often put a dab of tempered chocolate in the middle of the white patties, but you play around with your own ideas, they are bound to be winners!

As years go by: Dear Lord, keep me from getting too talkative and thinking I must say something on every occasion. Release me from craving to straighten out everybody's affairs. Teach me the glorious lesson that occasionally it is possible that I may be mistaken. Make me thoughtful, not moody; helpful, not bossy. Give me the ability to see good things in unexpected places and talents in unexpected people, and give me, Oh Lord, the grace to tell them so.

AFTER-DINNER MINTS

1	egg	1
1 tsp.	peppermint extract	5 mL
1 tsp.	water	5 mL
	icing sugar	

Beat the egg white until stiff. Beat in peppermint and water. Add enough icing sugar to be able to roll in ropes. • Cut in ½″ (1.3 cm) lengths and harden.

CREAM FUDGE

2 cups	white sugar	500 mL
4 tbsp.	syrup	60 mL
⅔ cup	milk	150 mL
4 tbsp.	butter	60 mL
1 tsp.	vanilla	5 mL

Boil sugar, syrup and milk until it forms a soft ball in cold water. Add butter and boil a few minutes longer. • Add flavoring and beat until thick and foamy. • Put in a buttered 8″ (20 cm) square dish.

SMITH COLLEGE FUDGE

1 cup	brown sugar	250 mL
¼ cup	butter	50 mL
½ cup	cream	125 mL
1 cup	white sugar	250 mL
¼ cup	molasses	50 mL
2 oz.	chocolate (2 squares)	60 g
½ tsp.	vanilla	2 mL

Blend all ingredients in saucepan. Bring to a boil. Remove from heat. Stir until fudge syrup is thick and forms a thread. • Pour into 8″ x 8″ (1 L) pan. Let cool to set, cut into squares.

We would rather have one man or women working with us than 3 merely working for us. (Community Supporters)

⅔ cup	canned milk	150 mL
1⅓ cups	sugar	400 mL
½ tsp.	salt	2 mL
1½ cups	marshmallows (½ pkg.)	375 mL
1½ cups	chocolate chips	375 mL
1 tsp.	vanilla	5 mL
½ cup	chopped nuts	125 mL

AUNT SADIE'S FUDGE

Mix milk, sugar and salt over low heat. Bring to a boil. Boil 5 minutes. Remove from heat and add other ingredients. Stir until marshmallows melt. Pour into buttered 9" (23 cm) pan. Cut when cool. **Variation:** Butterscotch chips may be substituted for chocolate chips.

½ cup	chopped walnuts	125 mL
1⅓ cups	lightly packed brown sugar	325 mL
1 cup	butter OR margarine	250 mL
3 oz.	semisweet chocolate, grated * (3 squares)	90 g
	walnut pieces for garnish	

FREDERICTON WALNUT TOFFEE

Thoroughly butter a 9" (23 cm) square pan. • Spread walnut pieces in the pan. • In a heavy frying pan, mix together brown sugar and butter. Boil over medium heat, stirring constantly, for 12 minutes. • Pour toffee mixture quickly over nuts. • Sprinkle grated chocolate on top. When chocolate melts spread until smooth. • Sprinkle with chopped nuts. • Chill and break into pieces. • * OR 1 chocolate bar broken into pieces.

Recipe for a Happy Day

Take a dash of cold water,
A little leaven of prayer,
A little bit of sunshine gold,
Dissolved in morning air.

Add to your meal some merriment,
Add thought for kith and kin,
And then as a prime ingredient,
Plenty of work thrown in.

Flavor it with the essence of love,
And a little dash of play:
Let the dear old book, and a glance above,
Complete a well spent day.

DUKE'S MOTHER'S PULL TAFFY

1 cup	brown sugar	250 mL
1 cup	corn syrup	250 mL
2 tbsp.	butter	30 mL
1 tbsp.	lemon juice	15 mL

Cook all ingredients, without stirring, until syrup is brittle in cold water test. • Pour into buttered pan until cool enough to take out of pan. • Butter hands and start pulling until taffy reaches the creamy consistency you desire. • Pull Taffy is fun to make. My brother and I made this when we were very young. To this day the memory is so vivid and full of fun, I laugh over and over about our antics pulling the taffy back and forth.

PEANUT BRITTLE

Microwave.

1½ cups	peanuts	375 mL
1 cup	sugar	250 mL
½ cup	corn syrup	125 mL
1 tsp.	vanilla	5 mL
1 tsp.	butter	5 mL
1 tsp.	baking soda	5 mL

Combine peanuts, sugar and corn syrup. Microwave on HIGH for 4 minutes. • Remove and stir; microwave again for 3 minutes. • Remove and add vanilla and butter. Stir. Microwave for 2 minutes. • Remove and add baking soda. Stir and spread on lightly oiled cookie sheet. • Let set and then break into pieces.

Grandmother's Washday "Receet"

1. *bild fire in back yard to heet kettle of rain water.*
2. *set tub so smoke won't blow in eyes if wind is pert.*
3. *shave one hole cake lie soap in bilin wter.*
4. *sort things, make 3 piles. 1 pile white. 1 pile cullored. 1 pile work britches and rags.*
5. *stur flour in cold water to smooth, then thin down with bilin water.*
6. *rub dirty spots on board. scrub hard then bile. rub cullord but don't bile. just rench and starch.*
7. *take white things out of kettle with broomstick handle, then rench; blew and starch.*
8. *spred tee towels on grass, hang old rags on fence.*
9. *pore rench water on flower bed.*
10. *scrub porch with hot soapy water.*
11. *turn tubs upside down.*
12. *go put on cleen dress - smooth hair with side combs - brew cup of tea - set and rest and rock a spell.*

AND COUNT BLESSINGS.

We suggest you hang a copy over your automatic washing machine and when things look bleak, read it again.

CHILDREN

POPPYCOCK

1 cup	pecan halves	250 mL
1 cup	almonds OR mixed nuts	250 mL
8 cups	popcorn	2 L
1⅓ cups	white sugar	325 mL
1 cup	butter	250 mL
½ tsp.	cream of tartar	2 mL
½ cup	white corn syrup	125 mL
½ tsp.	baking soda	2 mL
½ tsp.	vanilla	2 mL

Combine nuts and popcorn in a large buttered bowl. • To make the sauce, boil sugar, butter, cream of tartar and syrup together until the hard-ball stage, about 250°F (120°C), a few drops of syrup dropped into cold water forms a very firm though still slightly pliable ball. Remove from heat and stir in baking soda and vanilla. • Pour over the popcorn mixture. • Put on cookie sheet and place in the refrigerator until set. Break into pieces.

POPCORN BALLS

24 cups	popped corn	6 L
4 tbsp.	butter	60 mL
1 cup	brown sugar	250 mL
½ cup	corn syrup	125 mL
7 oz.	can sweetened condensed milk	189 mL
½ tsp.	vanilla	2 mL

Put the popped corn into a large bowl and set aside. • Mix next 3 ingredients together in a pot. Bring to a boil and stir in milk and vanilla. Simmer until the soft-ball stage (mixture will form a soft ball when dropped into cold water) about 10 minutes. • Pour mixture over popcorn and mix well. • Form into balls and enjoy!

CRUNCHY WHEELS AND CHOCKS

8 oz.	Ritz bits	250 g
4 cups	Rice Chex cereal	1 L
1	pkg. dry Ranch-style dressing mix (not buttermilk)	1
⅔ cup	warm cooking oil	150 mL
2 tbsp.	dillweed	30 mL

Place crackers, cereal, dry salad dressing mix and dillweed in a leak-proof plastic bag. Shake gently until spices are evenly distributed. • Pour warm oil in bag and shake gently. • Store in refrigerator, turning now and again to mix flavors.

GRANOLA

6 cups	slow-cooking (large-flake) rolled oats	1.5 L
2 cups	quick-cooking rolled oats	500 mL
1 cup	brown sugar	250 mL
2 cups	wheat germ	500 mL
1½ cups	unsweetened coconut	375 mL
½ cup	sesame seeds	125 mL
¾ tsp.	salt	3 mL
½ cup	slivered OR chopped almonds	125 mL
½ cup	hulled sunflower seeds	125 mL
2 cups	natural bran	500 mL
¾ cup	water	175 mL
¾ cup	vegetable oil	175 mL
1½ tsp.	vanilla	7 mL

In a large bowl combine all ingredients except the water, oil and vanilla. • Combine these 3 ingredients and stir, mix into cereal mixture. • Spread in a shallow pan. • Bake for 1 hour at 275-300°F (140-150°C). Stir every 20 minutes. • Let cool before storing. • **Variation:** Substitute oat bran for natural bran.

GRANOLA BARS

1 cup	corn syrup	250 mL
2 tbsp.	cocoa	30 mL
2 cups	rice cereal	500 mL
½ cup	rolled oats	125 mL
½ cup	bran buds	125 mL
½ cup	flaked coconut	125 mL
½ cup	raisins	125 mL
½ cup	nuts	125 mL
½ cup	cornflakes	125 mL
1 tsp.	marmalade	5 mL
1 tsp.	vanilla	5 mL
1 tbsp.	peanut butter coconut.	15 mL

Boil corn syrup and cocoa for a few minutes in a large pot, until syrupy. • Add remaining ingredients, except coconut, to hot syrup. • Sprinkle coconut on the bottom of a buttered pan (size depends on thickness of bars you like) and press the granola mixture on top. • Slice when cool.

---

*It's a good idea to keep your words gentle and sweet -
you might have to eat them someday.*

CHOCOLATE DROPS

2 tbsp.	butter OR margarine	30 mL
6 oz.	chocolate chips	175 g
10 oz.	can sweetened condensed milk	284 mL
1 cup	flour	250 mL
1 tsp.	vanilla	5 mL
¼ cup	nuts (optional)	50 mL

Combine butter and chocolate chips. Heat over low heat until melted. Stir in remaining ingredients. • Drop by spoonfuls onto a baking sheet. • Bake for 10 minutes at 325°F (160°C).

BAKED CHOCOLATE CLUSTERS

2 cups	sugar	500 mL
½ cup	butter OR margarine	125 mL
½ cup	milk	125 mL
½ cup	cocoa	125 mL
1 tsp.	vanilla	5 mL
½ tsp.	salt	2 mL
3 cups	oatmeal	750 mL
1 cup	coconut	250 mL

Boil first 4 ingredients for 5 minutes. Do not overcook. • Remove from heat and add the rest of the ingredients. • Immediately drop by spoonfuls on wax paper and let harden. • **Note:** You must work quickly.

LAYER BAR COOKIES

Very rich and delicious.

½ cup	butter OR margarine	125 mL
1 cup	graham wafer crumbs	250 mL
12 oz.	semisweet chocolate pieces	350 g
1⅓ cups	flaked coconut	325 mL
½ cup	chopped walnuts	125 mL
10 oz.	can sweetened condensed milk	284 mL

Preheat oven to 350°F (180°C). • Melt butter in a 9" x 13" (4 L) pan. • Sprinkle crumbs evenly over butter. • Layer with chocolate, coconut and nuts. • Gently pour condensed milk over all. • Bake for 30 minutes. • Cool and cut into bars. **Variation:** Try a 6 oz. (175 g) pkg. EACH of butterscotch and chocolate chips instead of all chocolate pieces.

Laughter is a tranquilizer with no side effects.

4-6	slices sponge OR angel food cake OR Shortcake Rounds, below	4-6	*CHERRY SHORTCAKES*
½ tsp.	almond extract	2 mL	
19 oz.	can cherry pie filling	540 mL	
4-6 tbsp.	sour cream brown sugar	60-90 mL	

Place cake slices on dessert plates. • Stir almond extract into pie filling. • Spoon about ⅓ cup (75 mL) pie filling on each cake slice. Top each with 1 tbsp. (15 mL) sour cream and sprinkle with brown sugar. Makes 4-6 servings. • **Variation:** Instead of the sour cream you may substitute whipped topping, cottage cheese, yogurt, or softened cream cheese.

2½ cups	buttermilk biscuit mix	575 mL	*SHORTCAKE ROUNDS*
3 tbsp.	sugar	45 mL	
3 tbsp.	butter OR margarine, melted	45 mL	
½ cup	milk	125 mL	

Combine all ingredients with a fork to make a soft dough. • Spoon dough into 6 portions on ungreased baking sheets. • With floured fingers, flatten and shape each portion into a round, ½" (1.3 cm) thick. • Bake at 400°F (200°C) for 10 minutes or until golden brown. • Makes 6 shortcakes.

1	egg	1	*ICE-CREAM SANDWICHES*
½ cup	soft butter OR margarine	125 mL	
1 tsp.	vanilla	5 mL	
19 oz.	pkg. devil's food OR yellow cake mix	520 g	
2 quarts	ice cream	2 L	

Beat egg, butter and vanilla and about ½ of dry cake mix until smooth. Stir in the remaining mix. • Divide dough into 4 parts. • Roll each to 6" x 10" (15 x 25 cm) rectangle. • Cut into 8 rectangles 2½" x 3" (6 x 7 cm). • Place on ungreased baking sheets. • Bake 6-8 minutes at 375°F (190°C); the centers will be slightly puffed. • Prick surfaces of cookies with a fork. • Cool and remove from sheet. • Cut ice cream into rectangles about ¾" (2 cm) thick. Make sandwiches. • Wrap in foil or plastic. • Freeze at least 24 hours. • Makes 16.

A great man's path is strewn with the things he has learned to do without.

ICE-CREAM TREASURE BAR

2 cups	rice cereal, slightly crushed	500 mL
½ cup	chopped, toasted almonds	125 mL
½ cup	flaked coconut	125 mL
½ cup	brown sugar	125 mL
⅓ cup	melted butter	75 mL
1 quart	vanilla ice cream	1 L
½ cup	fruit salad topping	125 mL

Mix the first 5 ingredients. Press all but 1 cup (250 mL) into a 9″ x 13″ (4 L) pan. • Chill. • Stir vanilla ice cream just to soften. Add fruit salad topping and quickly swirl through ice cream. • Spoon over crust and top with remaining crumb topping. • Cover with foil and freeze until needed. • **Variation:** Use strawberry sundae topping instead of fruit salad topping and top with sliced fresh strawberries when serving.

PRALINE SUNDAES
*Gluten-Free ***

½ cup	butter OR margarine	125 mL
⅔ cup	packed brown sugar	150 mL
4 cups	cereal *	1 L
2 cups	vanilla ice cream	500 mL

Melt butter in a large saucepan. Blend in brown sugar. Cook until thick and smooth, about 6 minutes, stirring constantly. • Stir in cereal. Cook and stir a few minutes over low heat until cereal is coated. • Spread in a thin layer on ungreased baking sheet. Cool. • Divide ice cream among 4 dessert dishes. • Crumble the Praline Crunch cereal mix, sprinkle 2-3 tbsp. (30-45 mL) over each dish of ice cream. • Store remaining crunch in an airtight container. • Makes 4 servings. • *Any of the following: crispy corn puff cereal, cornflakes, toasted oat cereal, whole-wheat flake cereal. ** For gluten-free diets use corn or rice cereals.

POPSICLES

3 oz.	pkg. Jell-o *	85 g
2 cups	boiling water	500 mL
¼ oz.	pkg. Kool-Aid or Freshie *	6 g
½ cup	sugar	125 mL
2 cups	cold water	500 mL

Dissolve Jell-o in boiling water. Add Kool-Aid and sugar and stir well. Add cold water. • Pour into holders and freeze. • * Choose the same flavors, or flavors that blend well.

The middle of the road is where the white line is, and that's the worst place to drive.

7 cups	pineapple juice	1.75 L	
4 cups	orange sherbet	1 L	*PUNCH*
4 cups	vanilla ice cream	1 L	
3 cups	ginger ale	75 mL	

In a large mixing bowl, combine pineapple juice, orange sherbet and vanilla ice cream. Blend well with mixer. ● When ready to serve add ginger ale. ● This is a thick, tasty, rich punch. ● Serves 12 easily.

1 cup	pancake mix	250 mL	
½ cup	butter	125 mL	*CHEESE*
½ cup	Cheez Whiz	125 mL	*BALLS*

Mix all ingredients together and roll into balls, use approximately 1 tbsp. (15 mL) of dough. Chill thoroughly. ● Place balls on cookie sheet and bake at 375°F (190°C) for 10 minutes.

½ lb.	sliced boiled ham	250 g	
½ lb.	sharp Cheddar cheese	250 g	*HOT HAM*
⅓ cup	chopped green onions	75 mL	*AND CHEESE*
2	hard-boiled eggs, diced	2	*ROLLS*
½ cup	thinly sliced pimiento-stuffed olives	125 mL	
3 tbsp.	mayonnaise	45 mL	
½ cup	chili sauce	125 mL	
12	frankfurter rolls	12	

Combine all ingredients, except the rolls. Mix well and spread in split rolls. ● Wrap each roll in foil, tuck in ends securely. ● Heat in hot, 400°F (200°C), oven, until heated through and cheese is melted, approximately 20-30 minutes. Serves 4-12 children, depending on their ages.

The Seven Ages of Man

20 *is when you want to wake up romantic.*
30 *is when you want to wake up married.*
40 *is when you want to wake up successful.*
50 *is when you want to wake up rich.*
60 *is when you want to wake up contented.*
70 *is when you want to wake up healthy.*
80 *is when you want to wake up.*

PIZZA BUNS

¼ cup	oil	50 mL
1	medium onion, chopped	1
1	green pepper, chopped	1
4	celery stalks, chopped	4
½ lb.	Cheddar cheese, grated	250 g
½ lb.	mozzarella cheese, grated	250 g
6 oz.	salad olives, chopped	170 mL
¼ tsp.	garlic powder OR 1 garlic clove, minced	1 mL
1 tsp.	oregano	5 mL
14 oz.	can tomato sauce hamburger buns	398 mL

In hot oil, sauté chopped onion, green pepper and celery for 15-20 minutes until tender, but not brown. Cool. ● To the grated cheeses add chopped olives, garlic, oregano and tomato sauce. ● Add cooked vegetable mixture and stir to mix thoroughly. ● Spread on split hamburger buns and broil until bubbly. ● Store sauce mixture in covered container in the refrigerator. Keeps well for 2 weeks.

HAMBURGER MUFFINS

1¼ lbs.	hamburger	625 mL
10 oz.	can cream of mushroom soup	284 mL
1	egg	1
	chopped onion, to taste	
1 tbsp.	Worcestershire sauce	15 mL
¾ cup	grated yellow cheese	175 mL
	salt and pepper, to taste	
1	loaf white bread	1

Mix together all ingredients, except bread. ● Cut the crusts off very fresh bread slices. ● Butter 1 side only; with buttered side down, line muffin tins with bread slices, making sure you don't break the bread at the bottom. ● Fill each muffin cup with a good tablespoon (15-20 mL) of the hamburger filling. ● Bake at 350°F (180°C) for 30 minutes. ● This makes 2 dozen muffins. ● They can be frozen, then reheated, or can be served cold. ● Good with salad or potatoes.

A kid's idea of a balanced diet is a hamburger in each hand.

RECIPE INDEX

DONOR INDEX

249

Share AMONG FRIENDS with a friend

Order AMONG FRIENDS, Volume I or Volume II, at $15.95 per book, plus $1.50 per book for postage and handling:

Among Friends, Volume I ____ x $15.95 = $ _____
Among Friends, Volume II ____ x $15.95 = $ _____
Handling Charge _____ x $ 1.50 = $ _____
Total enclosed _____ $ _____

Visa # _____ Signature _____ Expiry Date _____
U.S. or International orders payable in U.S. funds. / Price subject to change

NAME: _____

STREET: _____

CITY: _____ PROV./STATE: _____

COUNTRY: _____ POSTAL CODE/ZIP: _____

A Great Gift Idea
Please make check, visa or money order payable to: AMONG FRIENDS
P.O. Box 6127, Station "A"
Calgary, Alberta, Canada T2P 1X5

For volume orders please call:
Among Friends Publishing Ltd.
Beulah Nelson — (403) 243-3693
Verneil Martin — (403) 243-3750
Gerry Watkins — (403) 244-4562
Warehouse (Lucille Steinhauer) — (403) 253-2266

Share AMONG FRIENDS with a friend

Order AMONG FRIENDS, Volume I or Volume II, at $15.95 per book, plus $1.50 per book for postage and handling:

Among Friends, Volume I ____ x $15.95 = $ _____
Among Friends, Volume II ____ x $15.95 = $ _____
Handling Charge _____ x $ 1.50 = $ _____
Total enclosed _____ $ _____

Visa # _____ Signature _____ Expiry Date _____
U.S. or International orders payable in U.S. funds. / Price subject to change

NAME: _____

STREET: _____

CITY: _____ PROV./STATE: _____

COUNTRY: _____ POSTAL CODE/ZIP: _____

A Great Gift Idea
Please make check, visa or money order payable to: AMONG FRIENDS
P.O. Box 6127, Station "A"
Calgary, Alberta, Canada T2P 1X5

For volume orders please call:
Among Friends Publishing Ltd.
Beulah Nelson — (403) 243-3693
Verneil Martin — (403) 243-3750
Gerry Watkins — (403) 244-4562
Warehouse (Lucille Steinhauer) — (403) 253-2266